T0301714

Recent Trends in Financial Engineering

Towards More Sustainable Social Impact

Recent Trends in Financial Engineering

Towards More Sustainable Social Impact

Editors

Constantin Zopounidis
Technical University of Crete, Greece

Carine Girard-Guerraud
Audencia Business School, France

Karima Bouaiss
University of Lille, France

World Scientific

NEW JERSEY • LONDON • SINGAPORE • BEIJING • SHANGHAI • HONG KONG • TAIPEI • CHENNAI • TOKYO

Published by

World Scientific Publishing Co. Pte. Ltd.
5 Toh Tuck Link, Singapore 596224
USA office: 27 Warren Street, Suite 401-402, Hackensack, NJ 07601
UK office: 57 Shelton Street, Covent Garden, London WC2H 9HE

Library of Congress Cataloging-in-Publication Data
Names: Zopounidis, Constantin, editor. | Girard-Guerraud, Carine, editor. | Bouaiss, Karima, editor.
Title: Recent trends in financial engineering : towards more sustainable social impact / editors, Constantin Zopounidis, Technical University of Crete, Greece, Carine Girard-Guerraud, Audencia Business School, France, Karima Bouaiss, University of Lille, France.
Description: Hackensack, NJ : World Scientific, [2023] | Includes bibliographical references and index.
Identifiers: LCCN 2022025478 | ISBN 9789811257919 (hardcover) | ISBN 9789811260483 (ebook) | ISBN 9789811260490 (ebook other)
Subjects: LCSH: Financial engineering. | Finance--Technological innovations. | Industrial management--Technological innovations.
Classification: LCC HG176.7 .R434 2023 | DDC 658.15--dc23/eng/20220701
LC record available at https://lccn.loc.gov/2022025478

British Library Cataloguing-in-Publication Data
A catalogue record for this book is available from the British Library.

Copyright © 2023 by World Scientific Publishing Co. Pte. Ltd.

All rights reserved. This book, or parts thereof, may not be reproduced in any form or by any means, electronic or mechanical, including photocopying, recording or any information storage and retrieval system now known or to be invented, without written permission from the publisher.

For photocopying of material in this volume, please pay a copying fee through the Copyright Clearance Center, Inc., 222 Rosewood Drive, Danvers, MA 01923, USA. In this case permission to photocopy is not required from the publisher.

For any available supplementary material, please visit
https://www.worldscientific.com/worldscibooks/10.1142/12892#t=suppl

Desk Editors: Aanand Jayaraman/Lum Pui Yee

Typeset by Stallion Press
Email: enquiries@stallionpress.com

Printed in Singapore

© 2023 World Scientific Publishing Company
https://doi.org/10.1142/9789811260483_fmatter

Preface

Widely used in the context of setting up corporate equity transactions, financial engineering also refers to the use of techniques useful for additional equity transactions (cash management and risk hedging) and portfolio management. Since the financial crisis of 2008 and, more recently, the COVID-19 pandemic crisis, these techniques have evolved. Several innovations in finance, both technological (crowdfunding and machine learning) and products (green bonds, impact investing, environmental social governance (ESG), and Exchange Traded Funds), complement traditional techniques for greater speed, mutualization, and sustainable societal impact.

The first part of this book is dedicated to the presentation of these financial innovations. The second part presents innovative products that integrate ESG issues. The last part of this book is a reflection on several ways to address societal challenges through these technological, environmental, and societal innovations by several financial actors.

The first part entitled "Financial Engineering and Innovation" focuses on how technological innovations are used in financial engineering (FE). In this part, FE is analyzed as a process of model creation with the help of approaches specific to data envelopment analysis such as (Chapter 1) "benefit of the doubt", (Chapter 2) Fintech such as crowdfunding platforms, and (Chapter 3) machine learning. FE is a process of using statistics, financial mathematics, econometrics, computer science, software technologies, and Fintech tools, such as artificial intelligence, to refine data analysis.

In Chapter 1, Eleni Androulidaki, Michalis Doumpos, and Constantin Zopounidis show how a method can solve the problem of incomplete data capture to guide innovation policies in European Union countries. The contribution of their work is to highlight that economic development is local and can only be facilitated by the development of relevant innovations.

In Chapter 2, Véronique Bessière and Eric Stéphany observe that a funding trajectory can consist of a succession of crowdfunding campaigns carried out by the two leading platforms: Kickstarter and Indiegogo. Their case study shows that this means of financing makes it possible to raise funds quickly thanks to a set of automated and inexpensive procedures. Their work also reveals that a succession of fundraising calls via websites offers the advantage of exercising new, more cognitive levers to optimize time to market while facilitating financial leverage through the complementary contribution of more traditional financial resources by venture capitalists.

In Chapter 3, Mathieu Mercadier focuses on capital structure and how one of its financial risks can be managed by a debt default hedging instrument, the credit default swap (CDS). Again, the objective of this empirical study including the COVID-19 pandemic period is to evaluate the reliability of a risk management method in order to improve its accuracy, using machine learning, which has become more widespread in the financial sector.

The second part of the book highlights "Issues in Financial Engineering" by focusing more specifically on environmental and social issues, especially the consequences of climate change. Two chapters focus on two specific products: the first is the green bond (Chapter 4) and the second concerns the social impact bond (Chapter 5). The last chapter looks at the impact of these issues on the financial performance of issuers (Chapter 6).

In Chapter 4, Yves Rannou, Pascal Barneto, and Mohamed Amine Boutabba study the interaction between the green bond and carbon markets in Europe. By comparing the dynamics of their prices and their volatility between 2014 and 2019, the authors identify a complementarity between these two markets, as the issuance of a green bond can be used to hedge against the risk linked to the price of carbon.

In Chapter 5, Vincenzo Buffa and Benjamin Le Pendeven focus on social impact bonds (SIBs) which emerged around 2010. This new product is a set of multi-stakeholder arrangements where private investors invest according to social considerations and are reimbursed by a public agency if and only if predefined social outcomes are achieved. The interest of their study is to present the diversity of impact investing approaches and schemes implemented around the world.

In Chapter 6, Marianna Eskantar, Michalis Doumpos, Angeliki Liadaki, and Constantin Zopounidis examine the impacts of ESG issues on the financial performance of firms. As Greece is still an immature country on these issues, the authors seek to identify differences in financial performance between companies that take these issues into account and those that do not. Using an operational multi-criteria UTADIS method, the authors identify significant differences between these firms in terms of working capital ratio, return on assets, and debt capacity.

Faced with the 17 Sustainable Development Goals (SDG) from the 2030 Agenda for Sustainable Development adopted by UN member states and the emergence of new systemic risks related to the climate emergency and cybersecurity, financial institutions (credit institutions, insurance companies, asset managers, and pension institutions) must integrate these issues into their business models. The scientific, political, and managerial debates now consider the conditions for implementing the integration of the SDG goals as well as these risks cited earlier, measuring their impact and the performance of the tools, products, and processes to be used. In the last part of this book, several "Reflections about Financial Engineering" are conducted to shed light on the new trends in FE. Contrary to the previous two parts, the chapters in part three are based on semi-structured interviews with FE professionals in order to identify past, present, and future transformations of shareholder activism (Chapter 7); an integrated analysis of sharing-related theories to identify the ethical conditions of these transformations through a more virtuous dialog enabled by digital tools (Chapter 8); and an analysis of the historical meaning of impact in finance and accounting so that reporting becomes a performative tool (Chapter 9).

In Chapter 7, Carine Girard-Guerraud, Jennifer Goodman, and Céline Louche discuss new trends in the investment policies of institutional investors. These are driven by the growing and immediate demand from their clients to demonstrate their positive impacts on the planet. To this end, their voting policies are increasingly oriented toward ESG issues. This convergence of financial and social activism requires specific skills. These are provided by members of their investor networks, non-governmental organizations, and the use of innovative techniques such as ETFs, voting platforms, and data analysis methods.

In Chapter 8, Sandrine Frémeaux and Carine Girard-Guerraud examine the ethical conditions for incorporating societal issues into finance. Based on theories related to sharing, the authors identify two conditions:

mutualization and democratization. They then analyze whether these two conditions are met by crowdfunding platforms in France. Their exploratory work reveals that the long-term stability of collaborative spaces facilitating dialog between several actors is not satisfied.

Finally, in Chapter 9, Delphine Gibassier focuses on the financialization of society and more specifically on the need to institute a common reporting language among financial and organizational actors. As analyzed in the previous chapters (see Chapters 5–7), ESG approaches that aim to mitigate risks are no longer sufficient for investors who are looking for a positive and measurable impact (see Chapter 7). The key seems to be impact reporting, a steering tool which measures not only the product (as analyzed in Chapter 5) but also the investment's performance. In this last chapter, Delphine Gibassier reviews how the concept of impact investment is constructed and then analyzes its implementation in practice, ending with a presentation about a multi-dimensional framework for impact reporting.

To conclude, all these new trends and reflections tend to integrate the new technologies presented in the first part of our work. Moreover, they can, under certain ethical conditions presented in Chapter 8, encourage dialog between investors and society while promoting economic development (Chapter 1) and social and ecological transformation.

© 2023 World Scientific Publishing Company
https://doi.org/10.1142/9789811260483_fmatter

About the Editors

Constantin Zopounidis is Professor of Financial Engineering and Operations Research, at Technical University of Crete (Greece), Distinguished Research Professor in Audencia Business School (France), and Senior Academician of both the Royal Academy of Doctors and the Royal Academy of Economics and Financial Sciences of Spain. He is also elected President since early 2012, of the Financial Engineering and Banking Society (FEBS).

He is Editor in the book series on Multiple Criteria Decision Making and Cooperative Management (Springer). He is also elected President since early 2012, of the Financial Engineering and Banking Society (FEBS).

In recognition of his scientific work, he has received several awards from international research societies. Recently, in 2012 he was the recipient of the Long-lasting Research Contribution Award in the field of Financial Engineering & Decision Making by ESCP Europe. In 2013 he received the Edgeworth-Pareto prestigious Award from the International Society of Multicriteria Decision Making and in 2015 he received the Award for Outstanding Contribution to Research in Management Science and Decision Making by Audencia Business School. In 2018, the Aristotle University of Thessaloniki awarded him the title of Honorary Doctor.

He has edited and authored 100 books in international publishers and more than 500 research papers in scientific journals, edited volumes, conference proceedings and encyclopedias in the areas of finance, accounting, operations research, and management science.

Carine Girard-Guerraud is professor at Audencia Business School, Nantes. She is research head of finance department. She teaches financial engineering, corporate governance and fintech on undergraduate, graduate and executive courses. Her research interests include shareholder activism and engagement; financial innovation (in particular, equity crowdfunding); and corporate governance. She is currently coordinating research projects on the financing of spin-offs and deeptech start-ups and on corporate purpose and ownership structure.

Karima Bouaiss is a Full Professor of Finance in LEA and IAE at the University of Lille. She teaches banking finance (Basel regulations; financial analysis of bank accounts; economic and financial environment, etc.), corporate finance (general policy and strategy; corporate governance; financial analysis; investment choices; financial engineering, etc.) and epistemology.

Her research areas are banking regulation and risks, financing of companies (Crowdfunding and Private equity) and governance of large international groups. Her research work is published in ranked journals.

Involved in the dialogue between the academic and professional worlds, Karima Bouaiss is a French Foreign Trade advisor to the Prefect of the region and to the French Ministers of Bercy and the Quai d'Orsay. She is a member of the Paris office in charge of studies and thematic groups.

© 2023 World Scientific Publishing Company
https://doi.org/10.1142/9789811260483_fmatter

Acknowledgments

The authors wish to express their gratitude to Professor Emeritus Stephen Gates for his rigorous review of the book.

© 2023 World Scientific Publishing Company
https://doi.org/10.1142/9789811260483_fmatter

Contents

Part 1

Financial Engineering and Innovation

© 2023 World Scientific Publishing Company
https://doi.org/10.1142/9789811260483_0001

Chapter 1

Evaluation of Innovation in EU Member States: A Multi-Dimensional Approach

Eleni Androulidaki[*], Michalis Doumpos[†], and Constantin Zopounidis[†,‡]

[*]*Mediterranean Agronomic Institute of Chania, Alsyllio Agrokepio, Chania, Greece*

[†]*Technical University of Crete, School of Production Engineering and Management, University Campus, Chania, Greece*

[‡]*Audencia Business School, Nantes, France*

Abstract

In recent years, the study of innovation systems has received significant attention. Within this framework, the European Innovation Scoreboard (EIS) was introduced in 2000 in order to provide indicators for monitoring the EU's progress in high-tech innovation as well as its relation to the progress of its major global competitors. In this study, we employ an alternative evaluation methodology based on the "Benefit of the Doubt" (BoD) variant of data envelopment analysis (DEA). In contrast to the unweighted construction in composite indicators in the EIS, the BoD weighting model takes into account the importance each dimension has for each country, offering significantly different results and, in some cases, favoring some of the lower-EIS performance groups. The question is whether the observed divergences are simply a matter of choice of a mathematical formula or if they serve political and financial expediencies. Also, the role innovation could play in the global scene in the future is one more suggestion for further research.

Keywords: Innovation; high-tech; indicators; Europe; data envelopment analysis

1. Introduction

Economists used to believe that development differences across countries could be sufficiently explained by a certain factor called "accumulated capital per worker" (Fagerberg & Srholec, 2008). However, from the 1960s onwards, the idea that prevailed was that development differences among countries are mainly caused by technological differences and that countries that did not develop appropriate technological capabilities were expected to lag behind. This way of thinking, combined with the elimination of an important issue of the past which was the lack of appropriate data that could be used for the innovation evaluation, provided researchers with new investigative opportunities on the subject (Fagerberg & Srholec, 2008) and led to significant studies of innovation systems (Carayannis, Grigoroudis, & Goletsis, 2016). It became standard practice to combine several indicators in order to form composite assessments and create scoreboards for the countries, regions, or sectors under consideration.

According to the existing literature, the assessment of the level of innovation of various socio-economic objects in general and in EU countries in particular is based on a number of factors such as knowledge, technological improvement, research and development (R&D), quality of allocation and use of private and public resources during innovative business processes, trade openness, foreign direct investments (FDI), and innovation support policies (Shane, 1992; Doloreux & Parto, 2005; Zabala-Iturriagagoitia *et al.*, 2007; Fagerberg & Srholec, 2008; Sharma & Thomas, 2008; van Hemert & Nijkamp, 2010; Asheim, Smith, & Oughton, 2011; Efrat, 2014; Bossle *et al.*, 2016; Carayannis, Grigoroudis, & Goletsis, 2016; Janger *et al.*, 2017; Carayannis, Goletsis, & Grigoroudis, 2018; Szopik-Depczyńska *et al.*, 2020; Tziogkidis *et al.*, 2020).

Within this framework, the European Innovation Scoreboard (EIS) was introduced upon the request of the Lisbon European Council in 2000 aiming to focus on high-tech innovation and monitor the EU's progress in becoming the most competitive and dynamic knowledge-based economy in the world. The EIS has undergone major changes since its 2000 pilot report (van Hemert & Nijkamp, 2010). However, measuring innovation efficiency through the EIS comes with certain limitations, such as assuming a simple weighted average approach, with equal weights for all indicators, without considering the special features of each country.

In this study, in an attempt to address the problem of the incomplete capturing of divergence among studied nations and choice of the optimal weights in the construction of composite indicators, we employ an alternative methodology based on the "Benefit of the Doubt" (BoD, Cherchye *et al.*, 2007) variant of data envelopment analysis (DEA). DEA is among the most popular methods for measuring the input–output efficiency of innovation systems. According to Cai (2011), in the DEA approach, each country/region is considered an independent decision-making unit (DMU). DEA measures the relative efficiency through which several DMUs transform multiple inputs to multiple outputs in similar contexts. BoD is based on linear programming, and its name comes from the fact that the information needed for the choice of the appropriate weighting system, for every single indicator, comes from the data itself and the weights are chosen in order to maximize the performance of each particular case separately (Grupp & Schubert, 2010). Thus, the better the DMU performs in a particular dimension, the more important this dimension is considered by the method for this DMU and the higher its weight is going to be.

The rest of the paper is organized into three more sections. An overview of the EIS and the literature review, regarding other surveys about the innovation of nations/regions, are presented in Section 2. Section 3 elaborates on the empirical analysis of the employed method and the results. Finally, Section 4 concludes the chapter and discusses some future research directions.

2. Literature Review

2.1. *An outline of the EIS*

Currently, the EIS follows the methodology of its 2017 edition, which is based on four main types of indicators, 10 innovation dimensions, and 27 different indicators. The overall performance of each country's innovation system for each year is summarized in a composite indicator which is called the "Summary Innovation Index" (SII) and is an unweighted average of the rescaled scores for all indicators. Performance scores relative to the EU for a full eight-year period (2012–2019) are also calculated and compared to the performance of the EU in 2012 and 2019. Finally, corresponding to the need for better understanding the performance differences on the innovation indicators used earlier, a set of contextual indicators, split into four main categories, was introduced in 2017, revised in 2018, and used ever since.

The procedure summarized earlier results in the classification of the countries in the following four performance groups[1]: (i) innovation leaders (the countries with a relative performance in 2019 above 125% of the EU average in 2019), (ii) strong innovators (the countries with a relative performance in 2019 between 95% and 125% of the EU average in 2019), (iii) moderate innovators (the countries with a relative performance in 2019 between 50% and 95% of the EU average in 2019), and (iv) modest innovators (the countries with a relative performance in 2019 below 50% of the EU average in 2019).

Apart from the EU countries, the annual EIS also includes a comparative assessment of the research and innovation performance of Iceland, Israel, Montenegro, North Macedonia, Norway, Serbia, Switzerland, Turkey, Ukraine, and the United Kingdom and on a more limited number of globally available indicators, Australia, Brazil, Canada, China, India, Japan, the Russian Federation, South Africa, South Korea, and the United States (European Innovation Scoreboard 2020; European Innovation Scoreboard 2020 Methodology Report).

The EIS is a useful tool that helps policymakers evaluate countries' relative strengths and weaknesses in research and innovation and prioritize which areas to boost in each case when it comes to innovation. Also, as Grupp and Schubert (2010) and van Hemert *et al.* (2010) state, its simplified approach of aggregating large amounts of information for each country in one single number is "eye-catching" and "easy-to-understand," thus, draws the attention of a wide range of people. On the other hand, measuring innovation efficiency through the EIS comes with certain limitation, such as the ones described in the following:

[1] The EIS 2020 report is the first edition published since the withdrawal of the United Kingdom from the EU and the thresholds between performance groups have been raised compared to the thresholds used in previous EIS reports in order to compensate for the effect of UK leaving the EU.

- As we mentioned earlier, in the EIS, the overall performance of each country's innovation system for each year is summarized through an unweighted average of all the simple indicators. The first problem with that is that the numbers for the simple indicators are taken for granted with little discussion on their validity, leaving room for manipulation by selection (Pavitt, 1988). Additionally, as van Hemert and Nijkamp (2010) and Grupp and Schubert (2010) state, arbitrarily using an unweighted mean value for the aggregation, without further checking its robustness with respect to weight changes, has been blamed for producing invalid results. Finally, even if weights are determined through optimization models, the issue that still remains is "compensability," which means that low values in one indicator could be offset by high values in another without affecting the final country score (Cherchye, Moesen, & Puyenbroeck, 2004).
- Furthermore, the diversity of the national and regional innovation systems (NIS and RIS) of member countries is not adequately captured leading to limited and distorted results (Tziogkidis *et al.*, 2020). It is unrealistic for the countries to strive for high results on all assessed innovation areas simultaneously (Szopik-Depczyńska *et al.*, 2020). Strategies for improving a country's well-being should be implemented according to each nation's/region's needs to be sustainable (van Hermet & Nijkamp, 2010).
- Handling cross-country differences is also hindered by the lack of data in some cases (Grupp & Schubert, 2010). Also, according to van Hermet and Nijkamp (2010), on an analytical level, comparability issues easily arise among the EU members due to differences in their methodologies or sampling methods or national contexts, e.g., lack of agreement on what constitutes tertiary education or, according to Papaioannou, Rush, and Bessant (2006), a lack of agreement on what public policy should be.
- Another issue is that the EIS encourages the creation of "European added value" programs which must be justified through cross-border cooperation although national governments often support public initiatives that are strictly related to their own economy. This creates a huge incoordination and the actual impact on countries is limited (van Hermet & Nijkamp, 2010). Finally, although the EIS recognizes the growing role of services' innovation, current statistics are still biased toward measuring technological innovation (van Hermet & Nijkamp, 2010).

2.2. *Overview of the literature*

In this section, six indicative evaluation studies regarding regional/ national innovation are cited in chronological order.

2.2.1. *Zabala-Iturriagagoitia et al. (2007)*

In their study, Zabala-Iturriagagoitia *et al.* (2007) confirm that although investing resources in innovation is important, their efficient exploitation is equally and even more important. They assert that regions which can afford fewer resources but are devoted to innovation achieve outstanding levels of efficiency in contrast to what the EIS predicts; on the other hand, innovation systems considered robust often don't reach the efficiency levels they were expected to. A main reason for the latter is that the higher a region's technological level is, the greater is its need for coordination. Thus, in the cases of technologically advanced regions where the extra required coordination efforts aren't made, lower-efficiency levels are achieved in comparison to other regions with similar investments.

The European regions' efficiency ranking for the study is constructed using data from the EIS, covering 161 European regions for 2002 and 187 regions for 2003. DEA methodology, containing efficiency measures of RIS performance in terms of technical efficiency, is used and the initial results are compared with those obtained using the Revealed Regional Summary Innovation Index (RRSII).

2.2.2. *Castellacci and Natera (2013)*

Although research over time has focused on the comparison of countries, not much attention has so far been given to the analysis of the evolution dynamics of different NISs when it comes to innovation evaluation systems. This omission (which is also reflected in the EIS ranking process) motivated Castellacci and Natera (2013) to introduce a set of indicators measuring national innovative capabilities and absorptive capacities for 87 countries in the period 1980–2007; they adopt a time-series perspective to investigate relationships and coevolution patterns among them. They make use of Panel Cointegration Analysis and of the idea that the two concepts of "innovative capability" and "absorptive capacity" are interlinked and their coevolution affects the growth of income per capita, representing a key mechanism that impacts the growth of NIS in the long run. Of course, the results of their interaction differ across country groups and specific patterns of NIS.

2.2.3. *Carayannis et al. (2016)*

The main aim of this study is to present an alternative assessment and classification for national and regional innovation efficiencies, identify potential gaps in the whole national or regional innovation process, and provide policy implications. It is based on applying DEA on a set of 23 European countries and their 185 corresponding regions and stressing the multiple stages that innovation processes should have when it comes to knowledge. The proposed framework is based on a hierarchical approach modeled as a multi-objective linear program (MOLP) for better consideration of the objectives and the constraints of the different stages and hierarchies of the innovation process at national and regional levels. Through this procedure and by combining their efficiencies, the studied objects are separated into four groups (knowledge creation leaders/laggers and knowledge innovation leaders/laggers) and accompanied by proposals for improving policies for each case.

The meta-analysis of the study focuses on whether environmental factors affect the estimated national and regional innovation efficiencies. For this reason, the "Quadruple Innovation Helix" (QIH) is used (Carayannis & Campbell, 2009). Its main assumption is that its four helices (university, industry, government, and civil society) are interrelated at the technological, institutional, behavioral, and cultural levels to generate a NIS.

Afterwards, for the national innovation systems and the set of the 16 indicators of the previous QIH to be examined for potential linkages between them and for country profiles to be developed, a multi-criteria decision aid (MCDA) approach (based on an ordinal regression model UTASTAR) is applied.

The major findings of this study imply the existence of inequalities in terms of innovation efficiency that impact countries' overall national efficiencies. In some cases, significant differences between the KPP and KCP efficiencies are observed both at the national and regional levels. Furthermore, this study reveals that indicators like university R&D expenditures, share of government sector on total employment, business networking, and university–industry collaboration play a significant role in national innovation efficiency. These findings provide a strong motivation for reconsidering traditional innovation theory and practice. The proposed approach provides a set of tools for a holistic view of the innovation efficiency measurement problem and for policy support and is only constrained by the availability of data in some cases.

2.2.4. *Janger et al. (2017)*

In 2013, the European Commission presented a new indicator, called the EU 2020 Innovation Indicator, which intended to capture innovation outputs, outcomes, and complement input indicators. The EU 2020 Innovation Indicator consists of four components: (1) patent applications (PCT), (2) economic significance of knowledge-intensive sectors (KIA), (3) trade performance of knowledge-intensive goods and services (COMP), and (4) employment in fast-growing firms in innovative sectors (DYN).

Aiming to evaluate the usefulness of the indicator, Janger *et al.* (2017) develop a conceptual framework that distinguishes two types of innovation outcomes at the sectoral level:

(1) *Structural change toward knowledge-intensive sectors*: The differential growth of value added from a firm's transition away from industries with lower levels of knowledge intensity to industries with higher knowledge intensity. By such a change, the share of output in knowledge-intensive industries in an economy's total output will increase changing the sector's composition of activities.
(2) *Structural upgrading*: The transition of a firm to more knowledge-intensive activities within a sector/industry without necessarily changing the composition of its economic activities or competitive advantages but changing its intra-sectoral composition of activities. Such upgrading may not necessarily be reflected in differential value-added growth at the firm level but in things like increasing the quality of goods and services, holding market shares, and prices constant.

According to Janger *et al.* (2017), by having three out of the four of its components (KIA, COMP, and DYN) focus on structural change as an innovation outcome, the EU 2020 Innovation Indicator adequately reflects the processes of structural change, but it does not appropriately address structural upgrading. It overrates countries specialized in knowledge-intensive sectors and underrates countries specialized in less knowledge-intensive sectors.

To support the above allegation, the authors suggest two structural-upgrading indicators: "Export Quality" (the share of low-, medium-, and high-quality exports of an industry: manufacturing only) and "Sector Adjusted R&D Intensity" (measuring the R&D intensity of countries by correcting for the industrial structure of both manufacturing and services). As a linear average of those, they build the "SU Indicator" and compare it with the EU 2020 Innovation indicator using the measurements of 2012 for all the 28 EU countries (including the UK). This comparison confirms that several countries that belong in knowledge-intensive sectors, without necessarily being at the highest level in their category, perform worse with the SU indicator. On the other hand, countries that focus on less knowledge-intensive sectors but are at a higher position on the "ladder" are among the "winning" countries with the SU Indicator.

Afterwards, they construct a modified EU 2020 Innovation Indicator as an arithmetic average of the four indicators used in the EU 2020 indicator and the two indicators of the SU indicator and compare it with the EU 2020 Innovation Indicator. The aim of this comparison is to evaluate the impact of the fact that the modified indicator contains more "upgrading" components than the EU 2020 Innovation Indicator but still less than the "change" components. Once more, the EU 2020 Innovation Indicator is found to penalize countries located close to the highest level in less knowledge-intensive sectors and benefit countries with large financial sectors or international value chains in knowledge-intensive sectors, even if they are at the lowest part of their chain.

2.2.5. *Szopik-Depczyńska et al.* (*2020*)

The study of Szopik-Depczyńska *et al.* (2020) has as its main aim is to investigate which resources and mechanisms trigger economic growth processes that enhance innovation and to identify groups of regions that are similar in light of specific indicators. For these purposes, the results of the Regional Innovation Scoreboard are used for 202 regions across 22 EU countries in 2017. Szopik-Depczyńska *et al.* (2020) also use a framework of 18 indicators, divided into five groups, as follows:

(a) Framework conditions: Human resources and attractive research systems (four indicators).
(b) Investments: Finance and support and firm investments (three indicators).

(c) Innovation activities: Innovators and linkages (five indicators).
(d) Intellectual activities: Intellectual assets (three indicators).
(e) Impacts: Employment impacts and sales impacts (three indicators).

The multi-criteria taxonomy method is used to study the disparities between the European regions in the field of innovations and the results show that the regions considered as the best, according to the Regional Innovation Scoreboard, are in some cases similar to the regions which have slightly worse achievement. The internal structure of region innovativeness also proves to be much more varied and those variations are also much less affected by location than traditionally thought. The study also classifies regions in different typological groups from the Regional Innovation Scoreboard 2017 study, as it combines groups of countries similar in terms of a larger number of indicators and not only due to their achieved average level similarity. Thus, the authors conclude that the traditional RIS methodology does not produce accurate results.

2.2.6. *Tziogkidis et al. (2020)*

The most comprehensive, in terms of country coverage, among the composite indicators that policymakers use to measure countries' innovation performance is the Global Innovation Index (GII). Applying multi-directional efficiency analysis on data from the 2016 GII, which assesses the innovation performance of 128 countries through the aggregation of 82 indicators, Tziogkidis *et al.* (2020) propose a two-step approach for the evaluation of countries' innovation efficiency. An issue that is addressed in this study is that of "compensability" which we have already mentioned in Section 1. GII is not free from this issue although DEA is used in its robustness exercise.

In the first step of their framework, Tziogkidis *et al.* (2020) measure innovation efficiency using the multi-directional efficiency analysis (MEA) (which is non-parametric, directional, and builds on the framework of DEA). MEA is well suited for dealing with the "compensability" issue and for capturing the diversity of NIS since it imposes a different directional vector for each country and allows each country to optimize each input–output dimension separately. Therefore, it offers individual efficiency scores for each innovation input and output. These scores can be used to examine possible asymmetries in the use of innovation resources across countries and to comprehend the differences that exist in national priorities.

To calculate MEA scores, in the first step, the variables used are *Input variables* (Institutions, Human Capital and Research, Infrastructure, Market Sophistication, and Business Sophistication) and *Output variables* (Knowledge and Technology Outputs and Creative Outputs). The second step of the framework assesses countries' sensitivities in innovation outputs caused by changes in innovation inputs by applying a multi-variate regression approach: local PLS regression. The logarithms of innovation outputs are regressed on the logarithms of innovation inputs while conditioning for each country's nearest neighbors (peer countries). The peers for each country are determined through three economic variables, which comprise "economic proximity." These are R&D expenditure, FDI net inflows (% GDP), and trade openness (as the ratio of the sum of a country's imports and exports to its GDP). This way, the notion of economic proximity in innovation policy evaluation extends beyond geographical or income boundaries. Finally, as a robustness check a multi-layer perceptron (MLP) is used, which is a non-linear, feed-forward neural network treated as a performance benchmark to evaluate whether PLS approximates the underlying data model adequately.

The results indicate that high-income countries in Europe are more innovation efficient on average than their counterparts elsewhere, while low-income countries seem to prioritize knowledge and technology outputs over creative ones. In contrast, the diversity in the estimated sensitivities cannot be associated with income or geography. They find, though, that countries are on average more responsive to investments in "Human Capital and Research", whereas "Knowledge and Technology" pillars are associated with the lowest sensitivities. "Business Sophistication" seems to be the innovation input that influences innovation outputs the least; they do not observe any patterns in the relationship between innovation inputs and sensitivities. However, the above conclusions do not apply universally. The direction that a country should follow can be different with respect to each (input) efficiency–(output) sensitivity combination. Three policy directions that can be followed are suggested, offering a platform for better-informed decision-making.

3. Empirical Analysis

In this chapter, to address the shortcomings of the naïve aggregation approach used in the EIS and the difficulty to specify *a priori* any generally acceptable weights for indicators used, we follow the example of

Cherchye *et al.* (2004) and use the BoD approach. In the general context of the analysis, we assume that n countries are evaluated on m indicators with y_{ij} denoting the value of the indicator i ($i = 1, \ldots, m$) for country j ($j = 1, \ldots, n$). The aim of an evaluation approach is to aggregate the elementary indicators into a single-valued composite indicator (CI_j) for each country defined as the weighted average of the original set of indicators.

3.1. *Data and indicators*

The analysis presented in the paper utilizes information from the EIS rankings from 2013 to 2020 for the current 27 EU countries plus Norway, Switzerland, Turkey, and the UK. The rest of the countries evaluated by the EIS are excluded due to lack of data, reduced economic strength, or limited interaction with the EU member states. The data are distinguished between the four main categories of indicators, 10 innovation dimensions, and 27 different indicators of the EIS 2020, which are summarized in Figure 1.

The first group of indicators (framework conditions) aims to show the supply of advanced skills in a country's community and considers a wide variety of educational fields. The second group of indicators (investments) covers expenditures on research and development, a key element for the quality and structure of innovation and economic growth. The third group (innovation activities) focuses on SMEs, on the improvement of products or production processes through in-house innovation, and on the flow of knowledge between public R&D institutions and enterprises, as well as between private companies. An important sign of innovation activity is also the number of patent applications, trademarks, and designs in relation to the regional GDP. The fourth group (impacts) concerns employment, export of mid- and hi-tech products, and the revenue of SMEs from the sale of new-to-market and new-to-firm innovations. This group of indicators reflects the country's international technological competitiveness because mid- and hi-tech products are the key factors of economic growth, productivity, and prosperity.

3.2. *Methodology*

The main steps of the BoD approach are the following:

(1) *Normalization*: The normalization of the data ensures that all indicators are measured on a common scale, which facilitates the interpretability of

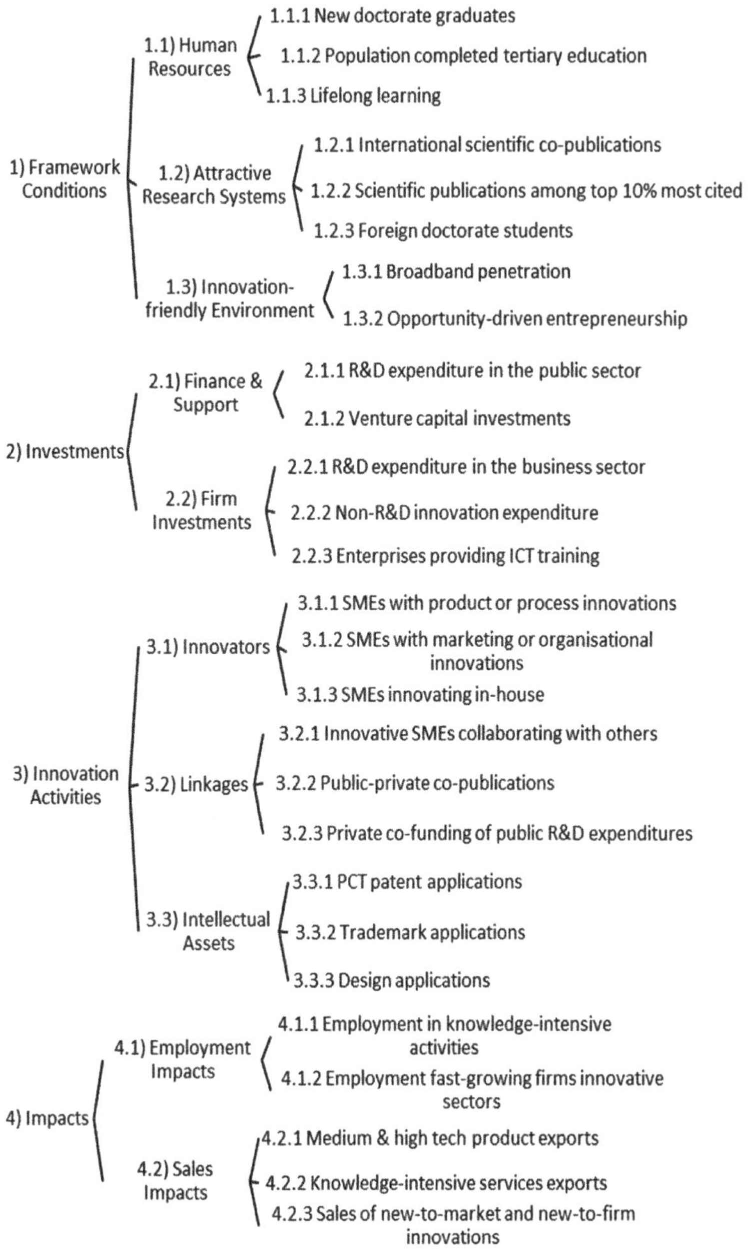

Figure 1. EIS indicator categories.

the composite indicator. For indicators in maximization form (i.e., indicators for which higher values indicate higher performance), the normalization is performed as follows:

$$y_{ij}^{'} = \frac{y_{ij}}{y_i^{\max}} \tag{1}$$

where y_{ij} denotes the data for country j on indicator i, $y_i^{\max}$ is the maximum value of indicator i, and $y_{ij}^{'}$ is the normalized performance of country j on indicator i, in relation to the best performing country. For indicators in minimization form (i.e., indicators for which higher values indicate lower performance), the normalization is performed as follows:

$$y_{ij}^{'} = \frac{y_i^{min}}{y_{ij}} \tag{2}$$

where $y_i^{\min}$ is the minimum value of indicator i. In both cases, the values of the normalized indicators vary between 0 and 1, with a lower value always corresponding to a worst and 1 corresponding to the best performance in the sample.

(2) *Aggregation*: After normalization comes the construction of a composite index CI_j for each country, which is defined as the ratio of the country's actual performance over its benchmark performance:

$$CI_j = \frac{\sum_{i=1}^{m} y_{ij}^{'} w_i}{\sum_{i=1}^{m} y_i^{*} w_i} \tag{3}$$

where w_i is the weight of indicator i and y_i^{*} is the normalized benchmark performance for indicator i. In this study, the benchmark performance for each indicator is derived from the data of the sample (endogenously); more specifically, we select as the benchmark the country k that maximizes the overall performance value under its optimal weights. Hence,

$$\sum_{i=1}^{m} y_{ij}^{'} w_i \leq \max_{y_k} \sum_{i=1}^{m} y_{ik}^{'} w_i = 1 \tag{4}$$

and CI_j can be rewritten as

$$CI_j = \max_{w_i} \frac{\sum_{i=1}^{m} y_{ij}^{n} w_i}{\max_{y_k} \sum_{1=1}^{m} y_{ik}^{n} w_i} = \max_{w_i} \sum_{i=1}^{m} y_{ij}^{n} w_i \tag{5}$$

(3) *Weights*: As far as the weights are concerned, first, we consider the restriction of non-negativity so that the CIs are non-decreasing functions whose values range from 0 to 1, with higher values representing better performances. Subsequently, to prevent the assignment of zero weight to any of the sub-indices, we set a lower L_i and an upper-bound U_i, $i = 1, \ldots, m$, such that $0 < L_i \leq U_i \leq 1$ and

$$L_i \sum_{i=1}^{m} y'_{ij} w_i \leq y'_{ij} w_i \leq U_i \sum_{i=1}^{m} y'_{ij} w_i \tag{6}$$

The above inequalities are also known as "Pie-share constraints" as they ensure that none of the indicators will be excluded during the evaluation of each country.

The implementation of the above BoD approach was implemented in the R programming language with the "Compind" package. As the analysis was based on a panel dataset of all the studied countries for the years 2012–2019, the results provide insights on each country's progress over time. The BoD analysis was performed in three stages: first for the 10 dimensions of Figure 1 (1.1 Human resources, …, 4.2 Sales impacts) and subsequently for the four main types of indicators (Framework conditions, …, Impacts). Finally, the overall performance of each country for the years 2012–2019 was derived. The results also include the weights that the method assigned to the 27 indicators, the 10 dimensions, and the four main types over time.

3.3. *Results*

Countries are expected to have differences between them when it comes to their engagement in innovation due to their different stages of socio-economic development. The question is whether those differences are adequately captured by the EIS ranking system offering the countries a fair treatment by policymakers and supporting institutions. As the BoD weighted model is considered to produce a less biased classification, more harmonized with the countries' strengths and weaknesses, we support the idea that it is crucial for the EIS reliability evaluation that BoD and EIS results are relatively consistent.

3.3.1. *EIS vs. BoD: Differences in overall performance results*

In Figure 2, based on the EIS rankings 2012–2019, we present in percentage form information about the following:

- the overall performance of the countries in 2019 (from left to right: six thick, dark gray columns for Innovation Leaders, nine thick, light gray columns for Strong innovators, 14 thin, dark gray columns for Moderate innovators, two thin, light gray columns for Modest innovators, and finally, one white column for the EU as a whole including the UK),
- the percentage change in the performance of each country (and the EU) between 2012 and 2019 (black columns), and
- the average performance of each country (and the EU) for the time period of 2012–2019 (white dots).

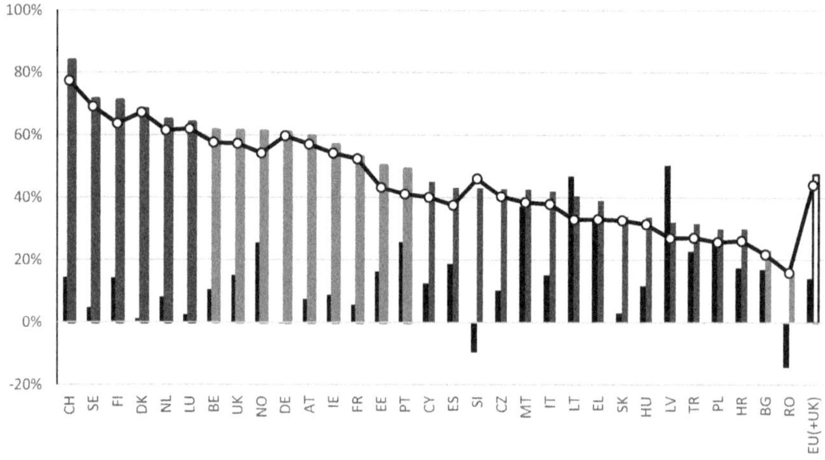

Figure 2. EIS overall 2019 performance (gray/white columns), % change between 2012 and 2019 (black columns), and overall performance mean value for the years 2012–2019 (white dots).

Almost all the average performances for the time period 2012–2019 are lower than their corresponding 2019 performance scores except Slovenia (Moderate innovator) whose average performance is greater than its 2019 score and higher than the average performance of Estonia and Portugal (Strong innovators).

Compared to their performance in 2012, Romania, Slovenia, and Germany are the only countries whose performance has declined: −14.45%, −9.63%, and −0.37%, respectively. The remaining countries have improved their performance from 1.13% (Denmark, from Innovation leaders) to 50.25% (Latvia, from Moderate innovators). At this point, we should stress that although some countries, like Latvia, still belong to lower-innovation groups than traditional innovators, like Denmark, they have significantly improved their overall performance according to the EIS data, since 2012.

Figure 3 presents similar results, this time based on the BoD evaluations. It is evident that there are obvious differences between the BoD and EIS ranking systems. More specifically, in the BoD 2019 performance chart, countries that belong to different EIS innovation groups are mixed with each other. Twelve countries (LU, IE, DE, NO, AT, CZ, MT, SK,

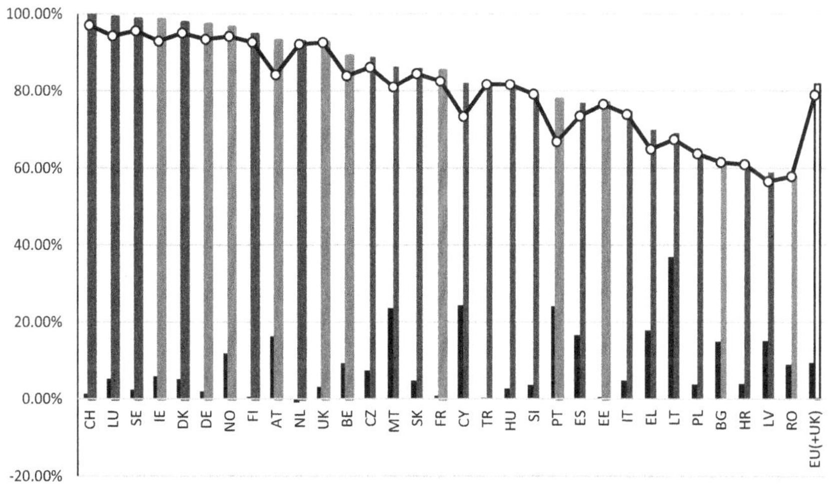

Figure 3. BoD overall 2019 performance (gray/white columns), % change between 2012 and 2019 (black columns), and overall performance mean value for the years 2012–2019 (white dots).

TR, HU, PL, and BE) show performance upgrading compared to the EIS, three remain stable (CH, HR, and RO), and 16 (SE, DK, FI, NL, UK, BE, FR, CY, SI, PT, ES, EE, IT, EL, LT, and LV) show lower performance. The greatest upgrading (nine positions) is that of Turkey which means that Turkey is the most underrated country in the EIS 2020 and the worst decline corresponds to Estonia (nine positions) which means that Estonia is the most overrated country in the EIS 2020.

Generally, regarding the 2019 evaluation results, the BoD ranking system

- upgrades 16% of the Innovation Leaders, 40% of the Strong innovators, 40% of the Moderate innovators, 50% of the Modest innovators, and 39% of all the countries;
- downgrades 68% of the Innovation Leaders, 60% of the Strong innovators, 53% of the Moderate innovators, 0% of the Modest innovators, and 51% of all the countries;
- leaves unaffected 16% of the Innovation Leaders, 0% of the Strong innovators, 7% of the Moderate innovators, 50% of the Modest innovators, and 10% of all the countries; and
- favors the lower-EIS performance groups.

Finally, the 2019 BoD performance scores are higher than their corresponding average performances for the 2012–2019 period except the cases of Poland, Bulgaria, and Croatia in which their 2019 performance is slightly lower than their historical average. As for the overall performance change between 2012 and 2019, all the countries except the Netherlands (−0.85%) show improvement variations from 0.26% (Turkey) to 36.82% (Lithuania).

3.3.2. *The variability of indicators and their impact on the evaluation results*

In Table 1, we can see the changes in the values of the 27 indicators, between 2012 and 2019, for each of the four innovation groups. What the four groups have in common, according to the table, is that their greatest improvement concerns indicator 1.3.1 (Broadband penetration). Innovation leaders and moderate innovators both show their greatest decrease since 2012 in 3.2.3 (Private co-funding of public R&D expenditures), Strong innovators in 3.3.3 (Design applications), and Modest innovators in 3.1.2 (SMEs with marketing or organizational innovations).

Table 1. Changes between 2012 and 2019 (in %).

	(1) Framework Conditions							
	1.1.1	**1.1.2**	**1.1.3**	**1.2.1**	**1.2.2**	**1.2.3**	**1.3.1**	**1.3.2**
Innovation Leaders	20.41	6.97	3.22	46.58	−3.46	17.11	139.22	36.10
Strong Innovators	2.45	7.26	10.18	50.07	−1.09	15.63	111.72	10.42
Moderate Innovators	17.35	13.68	8.91	70.01	29.00	128.91	1401.60	73.72
Modest Innovators	−18.70	2.32	5.67	39.13	50.94	52.25	98.30	5.37

	(2) Investments				
	2.1.1	**2.1.2**	**2.2.1**	**2.2.2**	**2.2.3**
Innovation Leaders	−3.03	63.39	3.44	23.66	25.49
Strong Innovators	−0.69	34.41	1.30	51.14	11.43
Moderate Innovators	−9.64	239.85	45.82	15.39	16.31
Modest Innovators	−21.01	71.48	51.92	−32.50	−4.29

	(3) Innovation Activities								
	3.1.1	**3.1.2**	**3.1.3**	**3.2.1**	**3.2.2**	**3.2.3**	**3.3.1**	**3.3.2**	**3.3.3**
Innovation Leaders	13.20	−0.48	−6.00	10.72	19.35	−14.43	−12.83	9.62	−11.22
Strong Innovators	34.87	9.75	30.71	37.57	15.59	5.96	8.24	18.50	−10.15
Moderate Innovators	25.20	−5.73	25.46	28.02	51.73	−14.87	−4.93	40.22	46.15
Modest Innovators	4.84	−35.12	−20.49	50.10	67.39	−18.93	−18.86	7.24	75.59

	(4) Impacts				
	4.1.1	**4.1.2**	**4.2.1**	**4.2.2**	**4.2.3**
Innovation Leaders	4.26	13.53	12.80	2.23	−7.64

(*Continued*)

Table 1. (*Continued*)

	(4) Impacts				
	4.1.1	**4.1.2**	**4.2.1**	**4.2.2**	**4.2.3**
Strong Innovators	7.17	12.08	8.24	0.28	22.40
Moderate Innovators	5.41	25.37	13.62	8.93	12.78
Modest Innovators	18.53	43.00	26.72	21.09	35.14

Based on the annual changes of the 27 indicators since 2012, the progress over time for the four groups according to the EIS results is presented in Table 2, while Table 3 presents the same information based on the BoD results. The two most extreme cases of divergence between the two tables concern the annual progress of moderate innovators regarding investments (EIS shows a 24.17% increase since 2012, while BoD shows a 48.67% decrease) and innovation activities (EIS shows a 5.54% increase since 2012, while BoD shows a 49.56% decrease). In both cases, BoD indicates that the annual change of the moderate innovators had been overestimated by the EIS. On the other hand, the cases with the greatest consistency between the two tables are those of innovation leaders regarding innovation activities (EIS and BoD show a 2.21% and 2.10% decrease, respectively, since 2012) and modest innovators regarding impacts (EIS and BoD show a 19.03% and 18.80% increase, respectively, since 2012).

4. Conclusions and Suggestions for Future Research

As expected, differences were observed between the EIS and the BoD evaluations. The BoD ranking system upgraded 39% of the countries, downgraded 51%, and left unaffected 10%, favoring in many cases the lower-EIS performance groups. The most underrated country in the EIS 2020 ranking was, according to the BoD, Turkey and the most overrated was Estonia. As for the overall performance change between 2012 and 2019, more countries showed an increase with BoD but the range of increases and decreases was more limited than in the EIS. Finally, the

Table 2. EIS changes over time (in %).

	(1) Framework Conditions							
	2012	**2013**	**2014**	**2015**	**2016**	**2017**	**2018**	**2019**
Innovation Leaders	67.25	67.84	69.72	70.84	72.82	77.47	79.80	82.05
Strong Innovators	45.67	46.31	46.95	46.88	48.06	50.57	52.67	54.48
Moderate Innovators	23.59	23.72	23.81	24.90	26.46	29.28	31.77	34.95
Modest Innovators	13.81	13.60	13.21	14.41	14.00	16.43	16.82	17.80
	(2) Investments							
Innovation Leaders	62.74	61.79	59.57	60.29	61.87	63.38	65.96	69.37
Strong Innovators	51.01	50.03	52.10	52.95	55.81	55.32	57.74	58.93
Moderate Innovators	31.12	32.23	32.90	34.46	34.79	33.85	35.80	38.64
Modest Innovators	19.00	15.17	14.88	11.37	13.96	13.98	12.40	14.36
	(3) Innovation Activities							
Innovation Leaders	69.73	70.35	67.71	67.16	67.82	67.04	68.07	68.19
Strong Innovators	55.17	55.22	52.30	52.36	54.52	54.90	59.96	59.14
Moderate Innovators	33.62	34.19	33.54	33.69	33.72	33.93	36.00	35.48
Modest Innovators	18.62	21.34	20.00	20.02	17.49	16.98	17.10	16.84
	(4) Impacts							
Innovation Leaders	57.87	57.77	57.65	58.48	57.00	56.32	57.03	60.50
Strong Innovators	49.58	49.49	50.00	52.10	52.93	52.22	52.97	54.03

(*Continued*)

Table 2. (*Continued*)

(4) Impacts								
Moderate Innovators	40.43	41.37	41.33	42.11	40.63	41.45	44.61	45.88
Modest Innovators	29.35	29.78	24.45	26.54	30.68	31.76	35.09	34.93
Overall Performance								
Innovation Leaders	65.54	65.74	65.02	65.43	66.22	67.23	68.74	70.49
Strong Innovators	49.96	51.03	50.77	51.22	52.97	53.53	56.42	57.03
Moderate Innovators	31.89	32.49	32.42	33.24	33.35	34.11	36.51	37.76
Modest Innovators	19.23	19.61	17.85	17.94	18.26	18.89	19.03	19.54

countries' BoD performance scores in 2019 were (for most of the countries) higher than their corresponding historical average for the time period of 2012–2019.

The changes in the values of the 27 indicators, between 2012 and 2019, showed that for all the four innovation dimensions, the greatest improvement concerns indicator 1.3.1 (broadband penetration). Moreover, the results revealed two extreme cases of divergence between BoD and EIR concerning the group of moderate innovators and the categories of investments and innovation activities. In both cases, the results revealed that the annual progress of the moderate innovators had been overestimated by the EIS. The cases in which we observed the greatest convergence between the two methods were those of innovation leaders and modest innovators in the fields of innovation activities and impacts, respectively.

Future research could be concerned with how EIS and similar tools can be more effectively integrated into the global political scene and affect decisions on the reinforcement of economic development (especially SMEs' support), the elimination of corruption and social inequalities, and the improvement in quality of life. Especially in an era when all these concepts are in crisis due to the COVID-19 pandemic and the changes it has caused on a global scale, nations should take more seriously the notion of reciprocity and utilize evaluation tools more substantially than

Table 3. BoD changes over time (in %).

	2012	2013	2014	2015	2016	2017	2018	2019
(1) Framework Conditions								
Innovation Leaders	91.12	91.86	91.60	92.59	93.63	93.53	95.24	97.11
Strong Innovators	70.13	70.83	70.96	72.11	73.50	73.32	75.11	76.04
Moderate Innovators	45.35	45.77	46.54	48.60	50.76	51.28	52.88	54.34
Modest Innovators	31.63	34.56	33.31	32.84	33.17	34.61	36.21	37.04
(2) Investments								
Innovation Leaders	91.42	90.24	84.86	86.53	90.30	91.19	88.56	87.35
Strong Innovators	74.08	74.16	75.82	77.76	79.47	78.15	79.29	81.73
Moderate Innovators	55.07	54.96	52.95	55.49	54.96	59.53	60.96	28.26
Modest Innovators	31.21	29.54	30.50	28.70	21.59	23.13	24.51	28.26
(3) Innovation Activities								
Innovation Leaders	91.02	90.72	90.17	88.08	90.56	89.24	89.18	89.11
Strong Innovators	71.15	72.53	76.11	76.08	83.52	82.71	83.10	83.01
Moderate Innovators	45.85	47.09	47.28	46.94	50.41	50.07	49.79	23.12
Modest Innovators	25.28	27.26	31.14	30.49	26.00	23.18	23.17	23.12
(4) Impacts								
Innovation Leaders	80.68	80.69	81.09	83.95	83.75	83.77	85.12	86.17
Strong Innovators	77.57	78.07	79.90	80.78	81.60	81.12	80.60	81.28
Moderate Innovators	70.96	71.83	70.71	71.03	75.22	75.20	75.35	70.02
Modest Innovators	58.94	60.13	62.26	65.50	69.43	69.11	69.89	70.02
Overall Performance								
Innovation Leaders	94.97	95.28	93.78	93.43	95.47	94.97	96.21	97.13
Strong Innovators	83.33	83.86	86.64	86.94	89.01	88.47	89.07	89.66
Moderate Innovators	68.26	69.46	70.40	71.25	74.47	74.67	75.25	75.66
Modest Innovators	53.12	54.15	54.94	57.46	57.63	57.22	58.32	59.46

before to help those in need and to find out why they have been lagging behind. Finally, as the health sector is the one that has currently been in great jeopardy, spreading anxiety all over the world about the future, another topic for further research could concern the ways innovation could be secularized and used as a tool in the fight for the predictability of unpredictable circumstances.

References

Asheim, B. T., Smith, H. L., and Oughton, C. (2011). Regional innovation systems: Theory, empirics and policy. *Regional Studies*, 45(7): 875–891.

Bossle, M. B., de Barcellos, M. D., Vieira, L. M., and Sauvée, L. (2016). The drivers for adoption of eco-innovation. *Journal of Cleaner Production*, 113: 861–872.

Cai, Y. (2011). Factors affecting the efficiency of the BRICSs' national innovation systems: A comparative study based on DEA and panel data analysis. Economics Discussion Papers 2011-52, Kiel Institute for the World Economy.

Carayannis, E. G. and Campbell, D. F. J. (2009). 'Mode 3' and 'Quadruple Helix': Toward a 21st century fractal innovation ecosystem. *International Journal of Technology Management*, 46(3/4): 201–234.

Carayannis, E. G., Grigoroudis, E., and Goletsis, Y. (2016). A multilevel and multistage efficiency evaluation of innovation systems: A multiobjective DEA approach. *Expert Systems with Applications*, 62: 63–80.

Carayannis, E. G., Goletsis, Y., and Grigoroudis, E. (2018). Composite innovation metrics: MCDA and the Quadruple Innovation Helix framework. *Technological Forecasting and Social Change*, 131: 4–17.

Castellacci, F. and Natera, J. M. (2013). The dynamics of national innovation systems: A panel cointegration analysis of the coevolution between innovative capability and absorptive capacity. *Research Policy*, 42(3): 579–594.

Cherchye, L., Moesen, W., and Puyenbroeck, T. (2004). Legitimately diverse, yet comparable: On synthesizing social inclusion performance in the EU. *Journal of Common Market Studies*, 42(5): 919–955.

Cherchye, L., Moesen, W., Rogge, N., and Puyenbroeck, T. (2007). An introduction to 'benefit of the doubt' composite indicators. *Social Indicators Research*, 82(1): 111–145.

Doloreux, D. and Parto, S. (2005). Regional innovation systems: Current discourse and unresolved issues. *Technology in Society*, 27(2): 133–153.

Efrat, K. (2014). The direct and indirect impact of culture on innovation. *Technovation*, 34(1): 12–20.

European Innovation Scoreboard 2020. (2020, June 23). Retrieved from European Commission: https://bit.ly/2VGawDx (last accessed August 9, 2021).

Fagerberg, J. and Srholec, M. (2008). National innovation systems, capabilities and economic development. *Research Policy*, 37(9): 1417–1435.

Grupp, H. and Schubert, T. (2010). Review and new evidence on composite innovation indicators for evaluating national performance. *Research Policy*, 39(1): 67–78.

Janger, J., Schubert, T., Andries, P., Rammer, C., and Hoskens, M. (2017). The EU 2020 innovation indicator: A step forward in measuring innovation outputs and outcomes? *Research Policy*, 46(1): 30–42.

Papaioannou, T., Rush, H., and Bessant, J. (2006). Benchmarking as a policy-making tool: From the private to the public sector. *Science and Public Policy*, 33: 91–102.

Pavitt, K. (1988). Uses and abuses of patent statistics. In van Raan, A. F. J. (Ed.), *Handbook of Quantitative Studies of Science and Technology*, Amsterdam, North-Holland, pp. 509–536.

Scoreboard, R. I. (2019). Methodology Report. Available at: https://bit.ly/3jDyAyP (last accessed: August 9, 2021).

Shane, S. A. (1992). Why do some societies invent more than others? *Journal of Business Venturing*, 7(1): 29–46.

Sharma, S. and Thomas, V. (2008). Inter-country R&D efficiency analysis: An application of data envelopment analysis. *Scientometrics*, 76(3): 483–501.

Szopik-Depczyńska, K., Cheba, K., Bąk, I., Kędzierska-Szczepaniak, A., Szczepaniak, K., and Ioppolo, G. (2020). Innovation level and local development of EU regions. A new assessment approach. *Land Use Policy*, 99: 104837.

Tziogkidis, P., Philippas, D., Leontitsis, A., and Sickles, R. C. (2020). A data envelopment analysis and local partial least squares approach for identifying the optimal innovation policy direction. *European Journal of Operational Research*, 285(3): 1011–1024.

van Hemert, P. and Nijkamp, P. (2010). Knowledge investments, business R&D and innovativeness of countries: A qualitative meta-analytic comparison. *Technological Forecasting and Social Change*, 77(3): 369–384.

Zabala-Iturriagagoitia, J. M., Voigt, P., Gutiérrez-Gracia, A., and Jiménez-Sáez, F. (2007). Regional innovation systems: How to assess performance. *Regional Studies*, 41(5): 661–672.

© 2023 World Scientific Publishing Company
https://doi.org/10.1142/9789811260483_0002

Chapter 2

Reward-Based Crowdfunding: A Key Component in Development and Funding Strategies

Véronique Bessière and Eric Stéphany

University of Montpellier, Montpellier, France

Abstract

This chapter aims to better understand how a young company can use its funding trajectory as the basis for its development trajectory. Financial players provide capital and also meet other business needs, such as the need for knowledge, legitimacy, credibility, and visibility at local, national, and international levels. These needs evolve over time, and each financial partner's interactions with the company help create a specific trajectory (Bessière *et al.*, 2020) that will allow the company to develop.

Keywords: Reward crowdfunding; equity crowdfunding; funding trajectory; entrepreneurial finance

1. Introduction

The funding difficulties faced by young companies are well known and have been documented by academic researchers (Hall & Lerner, 2010) and business players alike. However, the seed capital landscape has changed significantly in the last 15 years (Wallmeroth, Wirtz, & Groh, 2017;

Block *et al.*, 2018) with the arrival of various forms of crowdfunding (CF), the structuring of business angels (BAs) into networks, and the intervention of early-stage venture capital (VC) (Bessière, Stéphany, & Wirtz, 2020). CF in particular offers several funding methods that can contribute to a young company's development throughout the different phases of its venture. Bruton *et al.* (2015) state that CF is helping to transform the financing of start-ups and that the expanding choices in financing new ventures are changing the nature of entrepreneurship.

Two forms of CF are particularly well suited to seed capital: reward-based CF (RBCF) and equity CF (ECF). RBCF involves reward-based donations. Sponsors interested in a project can support it by making a donation. The reward can be symbolic (such as an entry in a donor book) or tangible (a gift or pre-purchase of the product being created, as in the famous case of the Pebble watch on Kickstarter in 2012). This CF model is applied by platforms such as Kickstarter and Indiegogo. ECF is very different; a company's fundraising takes the form of a capital increase and the contributors become shareholders. These new financing players coexist with the traditional players (BAs and VC) and overlap in the financing of start-ups, reflecting the emergence of a new financing cycle.

Seed capital is an entrepreneurial firm's first real financing operation. "Seed capital may be defined as the external equity financing provided 'before there is a real product or company organized' (NVCA 2004)" (Dimov & Murray, 2008, p. 128). The funds obtained are generally earmarked for project design, finding a product–market fit, and the company's initial business activities. This phase is characterized by a high degree of uncertainty about the project and about its ability to become a gazelle or, ideally, a unicorn.

During the seed phase, the founder seeks to validate the transition from an idea to an economically viable project. This phase is characterized by the need for financing, necessary for developing the prototype or the minimum viable product (MVP), but also and above all by knowledge needs relating to the market, potential customers, and commercial development possibilities for the product. RBCF is, therefore, used by entrepreneurs not only to raise the initial funds to develop a project but also to seek feedback on how consumers perceive the project, to develop its visibility and reputation, and to exchange ideas with enthusiasts or early adopters. Sponsors in an RBCF campaign are driven by multiple motivations: the reward, the pleasure of novelty, the feeling of being part of a community, or the desire to support an entrepreneur (Ordanini *et al.*,

2011). Their participation is the result of an affective process (Davis *et al.*, 2017), enabling the entrepreneur to collaborate with a host of enthusiasts who are happy to discuss the product, its use, its technology, and its design, including its color, size, and price. In this respect, RBCF could be compared to a marketing tool. This feedback from the crowd is also found in ECF (Bessière & Stéphany, 2016; Bessière *et al.*, 2020).

This chapter aids in understanding better how a young company can use its funding trajectory as the basis for its development trajectory. Financial players not only provide capital but also meet other business needs, including the need for knowledge, legitimacy, credibility, and visibility at local, national, and international levels. These needs evolve over time, and each financial partner's interactions with the company help to create a specific trajectory (Bessière *et al.*, 2019) that will allow the company to develop. This trajectory-based approach is new. It emphasizes the multiple configurations and reconfigurations that mark the young company within the seed capital ecosystem (Gurău & Dana, 2020). These configurations are co-constructed with the different financial partners as the company develops and its needs evolve. An essential attribute of success is the entrepreneur's ability to exploit the opportunities of the seed funding ecosystem and to rely on the right partner at the right time in an evolving system. We will use a case study of the company Catspad to examine the cognitive contributions of the interactions between the crowd and the entrepreneurs in two successive RBCF campaigns.

2. A Case Study of Reward-Based Crowdfunding

The case studied is particularly interesting because it mobilized two RBCF platforms that integrate different fundraising formats. The success of these two campaigns demonstrated the existence of a potential market (via the pre-purchases made) and provided a set of cognitive resources through exchanges with the crowd.

We employ a case study methodology based on a set of interviews with the managing entrepreneurs of the start-up under study. This methodological approach is justified by the exploratory and emerging nature of the work on funding trajectories. It helps us to understand how the interactions between the various funding actors built a trajectory conducive to the success of the project's business model. The funding trajectory is presented chronologically with, for each stage, the objectives sought, the actors involved, and the level of funds raised.

Catspad's entrepreneurial adventure began in 2015. The team was initially composed of two entrepreneurs with different profiles (one technological and one financial). The project was technological, innovative, and easy to understand. Catspad is a designer smart food and water dispenser for cats. It ensures that appropriate food and water are distributed to the cat for up to one month according to a sensor placed on the cat's collar. The cat's owner can use a smartphone app to remotely monitor the cat's food and water consumption.

The project was initially supported by a business school incubation structure. The first funds obtained (in love, money, and through grants) were used to fund feasibility and prototyping studies with the aim of filing a patent. From its very first month of existence, the start-up won numerous awards. As soon as they had created the company, the two entrepreneurs hired a community manager and pursued a social network-based communication strategy.

2016 was a pivotal year for the project. It joined a regional technological incubator, and the creators were solicited by investors (business angels). However, discussions were hampered by a lack of information on whether there was a genuine market for the product.

Lacking shareholders but driven by the dynamism of its creators, the company attempted to mobilize a crowd to fund its project by opting for RBCF. This was a perfectly valid choice as the project was well suited to CF:

- it had a social dimension;
- it was easy to understand (it could be explained in less than 30 seconds) without disclosing sensitive information;
- it had a clear business model;
- there was strong empathy toward the entrepreneurs;
- the entrepreneurs were able to exploit Web 2.0 communications.

What is remarkable in this case is the choice of a double RBCF campaign conducted successively on two of the world's leading platforms. One was the company initially named Indiegogo, an American reward platform whose fundraising model is based on the "keep it all" principle. The company would receive all the funds it raised even if it failed to achieve its fundraising goal. This platform was also chosen because it accepts projects even if they are not yet "technologically complete". This campaign aimed to mobilize a crowd and validate the company's technological and commercial proposal while the Catspad product was still in an experimental phase. For the reward, the entrepreneurs offered pre-orders at discounted prices. At the end of this first campaign, the company had not managed to reach its fundraising objective but had achieved more than 140 pre-orders worldwide. Thanks to this initial fundraising and the subsidies obtained, Catspad was able to complete an operational prototype of its product.

At the end of 2016, the company launched a second RBCF campaign on Kickstarter, the world's leading reward platform whose model is based on the "all or nothing" principle. In this case, the company would only receive the requested funds if its funding target was met. This second campaign was a success and exceeded the company's fundraising goal. The company was again seeking to validate a potential market and achieved more than 350 pre-orders of the product in more than 40 countries. The success of this campaign was also linked to a communication strategy that targeted both social networks and traditional media with a key focus on participating in international innovation fairs (including the CES in Las Vegas, where the company won an innovation award in January 2017). To add credibility to its offer, it approached the French National Order of Veterinarians, which helped the company to improve its mobile app.

After validating the existence of a global market during the two reward campaigns and taking into account the investment needed to ensure its future growth, the company adapted its funding strategy. The size and nature of its planned investments required a capital increase. The resources raised were intended to fund Catspad's manufacturing phase and the R&D necessary to develop new generations of connected distributors.

The entrepreneurs wanted to pursue CF to capitalize on the experience gained from the two previous reward campaigns. In 2017, they organized a fundraising campaign on a French ECF platform (SmartAngels) in co-investment with BAs. This BA co-investment aimed to strengthen the start-up's cognitive governance resources and leverage to support its future development (Bessiere *et al.*, 2019).

3. Discussion

This case study helps us to better understand the role of CF in the financing of entrepreneurial firms. RBCF has generated an important research stream because of the data available from the main Anglo-Saxon platforms, such as Kickstarter and Indiegogo.

Our primary observation is that CF is a key step in the validation of a start-up's entrepreneurial project. Because of its organizational model (selection procedures are relatively informal and the cost is linked to the platform's economic model), it is perceived as being faster, more "agile", and less formalized than BA or VC funding (Angere *et al.*, 2017).

It can even provide financial resources to fund the creation of a prototype. However, to obtain these resources, rewards are necessary which must be determined before the launch of the CF operation. The start-up is responsible for honoring these rewards which are an important element in establishing its reputation and its ability to mobilize the crowd for other fundraising rounds.

CF can be used to test an entrepreneurial idea or a value proposition. It gives the entrepreneur feedback on how the project is perceived by the crowd and can help measure the potential market for a product as well as provide certain answers relating to the project's implementation, such as the "time to market" (Ordanini *et al.*, 2011). As the Catspad entrepreneurs highlighted in the interviews conducted, the reward made multiple contributions to the project. It contributed, through pre-sales, to validating a global market study that the start-up could not have financed itself. The exchanges between the crowd and the entrepreneurs also helped to generate a set of solutions and opportunities for the future development of the product; the Catspad smartphone app was co-constructed based on proposals from the crowd, for example. In addition, it created a genuine interest in the product and the brand evidenced by the number of subscribers on the start-up's Facebook page. This recognition was international from the outset given the two platforms chosen.

RBCF, therefore, contributes to a set of cognitive resources that the company can exploit both for the design of its organizational model and for the future development of its entrepreneurial project. The exchanges with the crowd during the funding phase help to construct "recognition" capital, reinforcing the reputation of the project and the entrepreneur.

The success of a reward campaign is a signal that helps to limit the information asymmetry between the entrepreneur and future shareholders (BA, VC, or ECF). To be successful, it must mobilize two key aspects:

It must be observable and shared among the different actors. Several types of information and media are necessary: social network presence, the platform page where the company exchanges with the crowd, the number of sponsors, and expert funders (Kuppuswamy & Bayus, 2013; Mollick & Nanda, 2015). A successful reward campaign can strengthen an entrepreneur's reputation (Ibrahim, 2017).

It should be expensive for the issuer. Two approaches can be used to estimate the cost: the costs of the reward campaign (specific communication costs (video and customization of the web page, for example), the proposed rewards, and the percentage of funds retained by the platform) or the consequences of the failure of the reward campaign on the reputation of the entrepreneurial project. For RBCF, the failure rate for projects on platforms organized on the "all or nothing" principle is close to 50%. The failure of the CF operation may call into question the start-up's ability to conduct other types of fundraising in the future given the lack of confidence or the inability of the entrepreneur to mobilize the first funding cycle.

In the case studied, the success of the two RBCF cycles provided a convincing signal of the project's commercial potential and of the entrepreneurial team's communication skills. This type of signal can play an important role in the due diligence activities (consumer impact (Ordanini *et al.*, 2011), market potential, and product potential) and organization of subsequent ECF campaigns. This case study shows the ways in which a reward-based funding strategy can contribute to a project's reputation and social capital.

CF enables start-ups to rapidly raise funds with a set of simplified procedures. Reward-based campaigns combine these financial resources with a set of cognitive resources capable of solving certain significant problems for start-ups, including providing "sourcing" that creates opportunities for the development of the project. This case study helps us to better understand the latest interactions between seed capital players. The exploratory approach would benefit from additional observations in order to more fully understand the current, new funding trajectories pursued by start-ups.

4. Conclusion

RBCF highlights the major role of social networks and entrepreneurs' ability to co-construct their projects with key partners. As Block *et al.* (2018, p. 246) note,

> In winner-take-all markets, it is important to be fast and engage with the customer at an early stage. Some forms of crowdfunding like reward-based

crowdfunding allow for such early customer contact. It is also a way to test a product with customers and enable a form of customer co-creation. Insofar, crowdfunding reflects a general trend toward more open and flexible innovation processes.

Beyond RBCF, ECF is increasingly becoming an essential step in initiating a funding trajectory with BAs and/or VCs. These emerging studies call for new longitudinal contributions to better understand the diversity of start-up funding trajectories.

References

Bessière, V. and Stéphany, E. (2016). Equity crowdfunding: Start-up selection by the crowd. https://hal.archives-ouvertes.fr/hal-02013998.

Bessière, V., Stéphany, E., and Wirtz, P. (2020). Crowdfunding, business angels, and venture capital: An exploratory study of the concept of the funding trajectory. *Venture Capital*, 22(2): 135–160.

Block, J. H., Colombo, M. G., Cumming D. J., and Vismara, S. (2018). New players in entrepreneurial finance and why they are there. *Small Business Economics*, 50: 239–250.

Bruton, G., Khavul, S., Siegel, D., and Wright, M. (2015). New financial alternatives in seeding entrepreneurship: Microfinance, crowdfunding, and peer-to-peer innovations. *Entrepreneurship Theory & Practice*, 39(1): 9–26.

Davis, B. C., Hmieleski, K. M., Webb, J. W., and Coombs, J. E. (2017). Funders' positive affective reactions to entrepreneurs' crowdfunding pitches: The influence of perceived product creativity and entrepreneurial passion. *Journal of Business Venturing*, 32(1): 90–106.

Gurău, C. and Dana, L. P. (2020). Financing paths, firms' governance and corporate entrepreneurship: Accessing and applying operant and operand resources in biotechnology firms. *Technological Forecasting and Social Change*, 153: 119935.

Ibrahim, D. M. (2017). Crowdfunding signals. Working Paper, William & Mary Law School Research Paper No. 09-369. http://ssrn.com/abstract=3068323.

Kuppuswamy, V. and Bayus, B. L. (2013). Crowdfunding creative ideas: The dynamics of project backers in Kickstarter. DOI: 10.2139/ssrn.2234765.

Mollick, E. and Nanda, R. (2015). Wisdom or madness? Comparing crowds with expert evaluation in funding the arts. *Management Science*, 62(6): 1533–1553.

Ordanini, A., Miceli, L., Pizzetti, M., and Parasuraman, A. (2011). Crowdfunding: Transforming customers into investors through innovative service platforms. *Journal of Service Management*, 22(4): 443–470.

Wallmeroth, J., Wirtz, P., and Groh, A. P. (2017). Institutional seed financing, angel financing, and crowdfunding of entrepreneurial ventures: A literature review. https://ideas.repec.org/p/hal/wpaper/hal-01527999.html.

© 2023 World Scientific Publishing Company
https://doi.org/10.1142/9789811260483_0003

Chapter 3

CDS Approximation Accuracy Improvement with Cart and Random Forest Algorithms Based on a Time Span Including the COVID-19 Pandemic Period

Mathieu Mercadier

ESC Clermont Business School, CleRMa-UCA, Clermont-Ferrand, France

Abstract

This study uses decision tree and random forest regressions to improve the accuracy of an approximation of credit default swap (CDS) spreads called the Equity-to-Credit (E2C) formula based on a time span including the COVID-19 pandemic period. Certain sections are dedicated to explaining deeper important concepts in machine learning. Random forest regressions run with the E2C and selected additional financial data results in an accuracy in CDS approximations of 82% out-of-sample. The transparency property of these algorithms confirms that, for CDS spreads' forecasting, the most used feature is the E2C formula and to a lower extent companies' debt rating and size.

Keywords: Capital structure; credit default swap; COVID-19 pandemic; financial markets; machine learning

1. Introduction

The accuracy of the assessment of companies' credit risk concerns financial professionals and an extensive branch of literature is dedicated to this matter (e.g., Merton, 1974; Black & Cox, 1976; Vasicek, 1987; Finger *et al.*, 2002). Since the mid-90s, a derivative, the credit default swap (CDS), can be used as insurance against the uncertainty regarding the capacity of a debtor to fulfill its contractual obligations. Nevertheless, not all companies have actively traded CDS, leading to the development of estimations. Merton (1974) was the first to notice a relationship between the probability of default and the capital structure of a company. In brief, he used the option pricing framework to relate the three segments of the balance sheet: asset, debt, and equity. Other academics, Black and Cox (1976), integrated into the model the assumption that default can occur prior to maturity. But, when CDS started to be traded, it is in the private sector that many approximations flourished. In the midst of all these highly proprietary models, the CreditGrades model (Finger *et al.*, 2002) has been developed by practitioners and is available for use to everyone. This formula relies on the asset values of the companies modeled dynamically with a diffusion process and includes the concept of Black and Cox (1976) of a default barrier that can be crossed prior to maturity. Since then, academics have contributed to define further some input variables of the CreditGrades model to improve its accuracy (Zhou, 2001; Sepp, 2006; Stamicar & Finger, 2006; Escobar, Arian, and Seco, 2012).

In the literature, CDS is a topic of interest (Guarin, Liu, & Ng, 2011; Tomohiro, 2014; Cont & Minca, 2016; Chalamandaris & Vlachogiannakis, 2018; Koutmos, 2018; Irresberger *et al.*, 2018), but in practice, models for traded CDS spreads tend not to be popular among portfolio managers. Although the cited models provide very close estimations (Imbierowicz & Cserna, 2008), they are perceived as too complex. It is in this context that Mercadier and Lardy (2019) (from now on, this original paper is referred to as ML2019) develop a concise, transparent, and broad-based approximation assessing CDS spreads. This Equity-to-Credit (E2C) formula is a pared-down elementary equation inspired by the CreditGrades model (Finger *et al.*, 2002). After an empirical confrontation of the E2C formula to the actual CDS to evaluate its reliability, the authors propose to improve its accuracy using machine learning, which has become more prevalent in the financial sector.

In fact, they highlight that the E2C formula and structural models, in general, exclude some parameters influencing credit spreads. Thus, the accuracy of their model is improved by running a supervised learning algorithm on a multi-variate universe. The E2C formula and selected complementary features are set as independent variables and the dependent variable is the 5y CDS spread. The random forest regression algorithm (Breiman, 2001) is selected for its intelligibility: broadly speaking, this methodology averages multiple randomly bootstrapped decision trees constructed with subsets of the features randomly chosen at each node. Ultimately, the goal is to obtain high out-of-sample accuracy. An additional interesting property of this algorithm is linked to its transparency. In fact, one can observe how the decision is made at each node; it is thus straightforward to display the feature chosen to reduce the error. This allows to quantify the contribution of each feature in predicting the CDS spreads and confirms that the decision trees mainly select the E2C formula. Additionally, it identifies the next best source of improvements as the credit rating and the size of the companies.

In this study, my aim is to replicate this empirical process based on a time span including the COVID-19 pandemic period with two non-linear methods: decision trees and random forest regressions. I choose to add decision trees to the algorithm picked in the original paper as they are the underlying components of the random forests and thus, they help in the understanding of the latter. In the empirical part of their paper, Mercadier and Lardy (2019) dealt with 308 listed companies during the 2016–2018 period. However, we currently are in a peculiar period, the COVID-19 pandemic that had an impact on the financial markets (Ashraf, 2020a; Ashraf, 2020b; Ali *et al.*, 2020; Zhang *et al.*, 2020; Albulescu, 2021). Here, the study is conducted on 326 listed companies and almost twice the number of dates reaching 298 dates (from 155 dates in ML2019) from February 3, 2016 until September 24, 2021. According to the National Bureau of Economic Research (NBER[1]), the COVID-19 crisis heavily affected the financial market from February to April 2020.

The remainder of this study is organized as follows. In the next section, I present the literature review on the selected algorithms and define important words from the machine learning jargon. I then present the formula on which this study is based and the additional attributes that are used in the empirical part. Additionally, I introduce how the pruned

[1] https://www.nber.org/research/data/us-business-cycle-expansions-and-contractions.

decision tree regressions and random forest regressions should be used and their hyper-parameters tuned. Before the conclusion, the results for the accuracies of the models and the features' importance are discussed.

2. Literature Review

Originally, decision trees are decision support tools based on a tree-like model of decisions that explicitly represent decisions. Broadly speaking, it is a flowchart tree-like model in which each node stands for a test on an independent variable, and the first node is called the root node. Each outcome of the test is represented by a branch. Finally, a node at which there is no further split is called a leaf node. The entire path that records the set of classification rules goes from the root node to the leaf node and is composed of internal nodes (cf. Figure 1). On the one hand, decision trees are transparent non-linear models that are easy to understand. On the other hand, they are sensitive to a small change in the data and can lead to inaccurate out-of-sample results. Therefore, one may prefer running other algorithms like random forests of decision trees.

The ability to perform well out-of-sample is at the core of the field of supervised learning and is linked to the "bias–variance trade-off" (Geman, Bienenstock, & Doursat, 1992; Kohavi & Wolpert, 1996; Fortmann-Roe, 2012; Neal, 2019) (Figure 2). In fact, the expected error on an unseen sample, the square difference between the actual and predicted values, can be decomposed between the bias, variance, and irreducible errors. The bias is the difference between the average prediction of the model and the actual values, and it quantifies the error induced by oversimplification: models with high bias may not pay enough attention to the data in-sample

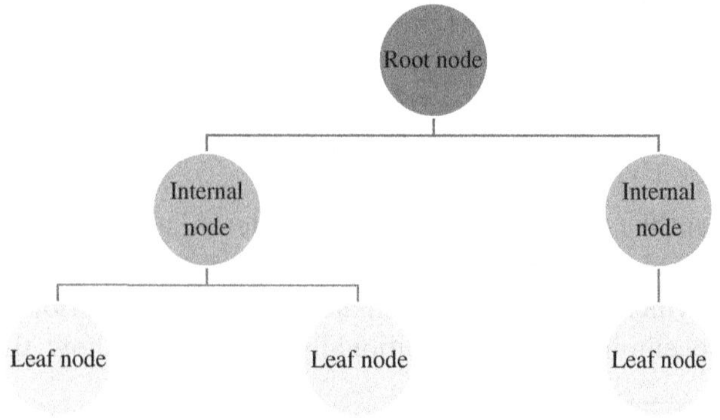

Figure 1. Main components of a decision tree.

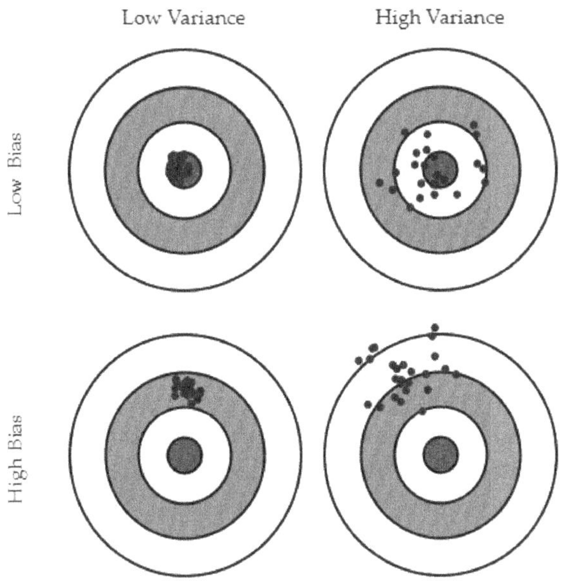

Figure 2. Graphical illustration of bias–variance trade-off.

Source: Fortmann-Roe (2012). Understanding the bias–variance trade-off.

called a training set in machine learning. On the opposite, models with high variance are based on too complex models that pay too much attention to the data sample but do not generalize well on the out-of-sample data called a test set in machine learning. A model that depicts very well the training set but does poorly on the test set is said to overfit. The role of data scientists is to choose and set the parameters of a model that represents well the training set (low bias) but not too much to avoid a high variance and thus are generalizable (low variance).

In this chapter, I run non-linear supervised learning algorithms on the E2C and other independent variables to improve CDS approximations. The first algorithm is a simple decision tree that is pruned to avoid overfitting. Pruning a decision tree means that we do not let it grow until the leaf nodes (Quinlan, 1986; Breslow & Aha, 1997). It is a data compression method that reduces the size of the trees aiming to remove the non-essential and redundant parts. In other words, it reduces the complexity of the model. Various decision tree algorithms exist; Quinlan (1986) developed the Iterative Dichotomer 3 (ID3). ID3 generates a multi-way tree which finds at each node the categorical variable that yields the maximum information gain for the targets. Then, with C4.5, Quinlan (1993) removed the restriction that the features must be categorical variables in partitioning the values of continuous attributes into a discrete set of intervals. In addition, C4.5 introduces pruning technology (Pang & Gong, 2009). Finally, Quinlan improved the efficiency of C4.5 with C5.0 that was released under a proprietary license (now available under the GNU General Public License (Quinlan, 2007)).

In statistical learning, classification and regression define different numerical types of the independent variable called in machine learning a label or target variable. Classification deals with discrete labels and regression with continuous labels. All the previously mentioned decision tree algorithms only handle categorical targets; thus, they belong to classification supervised learning. Classification and Regression Trees (CART, cf. Breiman *et al.*, 1984) work for regression as they were developed to support numerical targets. For instance, the predicted class for classification trees is the class that accumulates the most votes while an averaged value is computed for the regression version. CART builds binary decision trees choosing the features and thresholds maximizing the information gain at each node. Decision trees are generally using binary splits, splitting each node into two groups. In fact, multi-way splits exist but are not generally a good strategy as they fragment the data too quickly. Moreover, multi-way splitting can be achieved by a series of binary splits according to Hastie *et al.*, 2009. Nowadays, decision tree algorithms are generally referred to as classification and regression trees. And in this study, I use an optimized version of the CART algorithm.

Decision trees operate as follows, at each node, they must choose an independent variable called a feature in machine learning, and the splitting condition is applied to the chosen feature in order to get the highest homogeneity for the child nodes. When dealing with regression, the reduction in variance can be used to split the node. The idea is to compute the homogeneity of the node and an entirely homogeneous node as a variance of zero. For each split, the variances of the child nodes are computed, and the variance of each split is the weighted average variance of the child nodes. The split that achieves the lowest variance is selected, and this process is repeated until completely homogeneous nodes are achieved for unpruned trees.

Another important concept is the stopping criterion that checks whether a node is an internal or a leaf node. It is common to set a

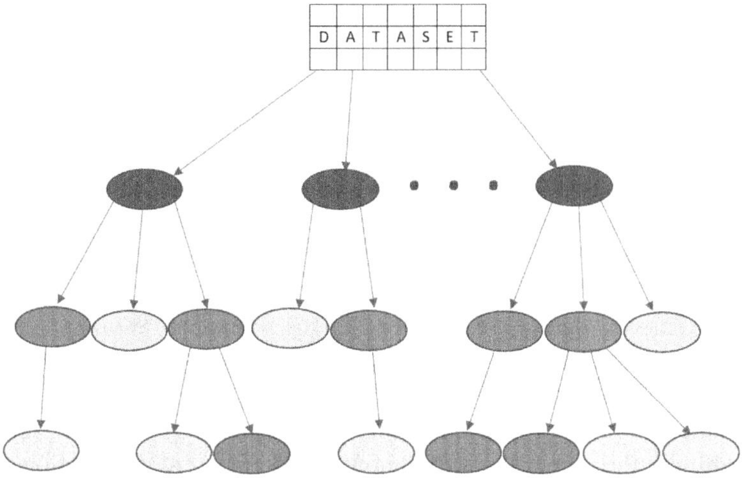

Figure 3. Graphical illustration of random forests.

minimum count on the number of training instances assigned to each leaf node. If the count is less than the defined threshold, there is no further split and it is then a leaf node. The more the splits in the tree, the more complex the decision tree. Thus, it is by tuning the stopping criterion that one can prune the tree and avoid overfitting.

However, it is still possible to decrease the variance while keeping unpruned trees. A solution is to rely on the strong law of large numbers (Bernoulli, 1713) and to run multiple decision trees that are averaged together. This ensemble method (Opitz & Maclin, 1999), called a random forest, was developed by Breiman (2001). Earlier work on random forests had been undertaken at Bell Laboratories by Ho (1995, 1998). The multiple CARTs are generated by bootstrap aggregating ("bagging", cf. Breiman, 1996). In brief, multiple trees are generated from sub-samples of the training set that are randomly drawn with replacement (Figure 3). Random forests integrate an additional property that also contributes to decrease the variance. In fact, at each node, the splitting criterion is chosen from a subset of the available features. An important property of the random forests, used in this article, is that it is easy to distinguish the features the most used by the algorithm, a computation called a feature importance.

Machine learning algorithms are used in many research fields, with a significant expansion in economics over the last decade. As early as 2007,

Tso and Yau empirically emphasized decision trees and neural networks as viable alternatives to stepwise regression models. Malliaris and Malliaris (2015) used a C5.0 decision tree to investigate the drivers of gold prices amongst financial variables. A summary of the improvements machine learning can provide to econometrics may be found in Varian (2014). Within the fields of economics and finance, random forests have recently been used to predict economic recessions (Nyman & Ormerod, 2016), to predict the direction of stock market prices (Khaidem, Saha, & Dey, 2017), and to produce an early warning system for predicting bank failures (Tanaka, Kinkyo, & Hamori, 2016). Behr and Weinblat (2017) have also applied random forest to study the out-of-sample default propensities of firms in seven European countries. Furthermore, the features' importance property of random forests has been used by Yeh *et al.* (2012) to highlight the main features among market-based information and Moody's KMV model (cf. Vasicek, 1987; Crosbie & Bohn, 2003). The validity of the use of random forests among a wide choice of learning algorithms has been studied, and confirmed, by Fernandez-Delgado *et al.* (2014). Brummelhuis and Luo (2017) further verify this in the context of CDS proxy construction.

Even though recent machine learning research is more oriented toward deep learning algorithms (Badrinarayanan, Kendall, & Cipolla, 2017; Sun, Yen, & Yi, 2018; Sangineto *et al.*, 2018), recent papers in applied machine learning have shown that the outputs of deep learning and ensemble-based methods are comparable, at least for reasonable sample sizes. An argument in favor of deep learning is its marginally better accuracy (Ahmad, Mourshed, & Rezgui, 2017) although random forests have in some cases outperformed neural networks (Liu *et al.*, 2013; Rodriguez-Galiano *et al.*, 2015; Krauss, Do, & Huck, 2017).

In line with ML2019, I want to keep the chosen methods as simple and understandable as possible, leading me to lean in favor of decision trees and random forests. The latter can deal with unbalanced and small sample data without deep pre-processing procedures (Liu *et al.*, 2013). Beyond performing internal cross-validation, random forests require less parameter tuning (Ahmad *et al.*, 2017), an advantage compared to support vector machines (SVM) that require the tuning of the regularization parameter and the determination of the right kernel, among other parameters. As far as transparency goes, random forests are also preferable to neural networks which are often considered to be black boxes (although see Shwartz-Ziv & Tishby, 2017, for a recent improvement).

3. Methodology

3.1. *The E2C formula*

The elementary CDS approximation equation used in this study is borrowed from Mercadier and Lardy (2019) and is called the Equity-to-Credit (E2C) formula. This equation is built defining default as the stock price dropping to zero, hence the financial insolvency of the firm, prior to maturity (Black & Cox, 1976). The upper bound of this probability of default is derived from the Gauss inequality (Gauss, 1821) which sharpens Chebyshev's inequality (Chebyshev, 1867) by a 4/9 factor, assuming that the relevant distribution is unimodal. Following Roy's (1952) conservative "principle of safety first", the inequality is converted to equality leading to the following E2C formula:

$$C = (1 - R).\frac{4}{9}.\frac{\bar{L}D}{S_0 + \bar{L}D}.\sigma^2_{S_0}$$

This formula is computed using both market-based and fundamental data. The current stock price (S_0), volatility (σ_0), and debt per share (D) of each company are extracted. The methodology of CreditGrades is used to compute the debt per share, and the average recovery on the debt ($\bar{L}$) is set at 0.5. The volatility is estimated as the median of various historical and implicit volatilities. The recovery rate (R) of the underlying CDS debt is set at 0.3 in a conservative manner. The authors emphasize that the E2C formula is very intuitive as the impact of the variables is consistent. Their CDS spread approximation is an increasing function of the corresponding stock volatility and the debt. Meanwhile, an increase in the share value decreases the credit spread value.

They then conduct diverse statistical tests and compare the E2C formula with its closest parent, CreditGrades, and with the actual 5y CDS. They notably identify the closeness between the two models and the actual CDS. Overall, they emphasize that the E2C is statistically slightly closer than CreditGrades to the actual CDS. These results are reinforced by positive results from regressions of the CDS, respectively, onto E2C and CreditGrades with fixed-effects models. Then, they analyze it further focusing on two universes: unsecured senior debt ratings and industrial sectors. To reduce the influence of outliers, they compare the medians and truncated means. After a presentation of the updated data, I display in the following the same kind of illustrations including the COVID-19 pandemic.

3.2. *Data and software*

The well-balanced panel data sample is a blend of market and fundamental reports information over 326 listed companies from various developed countries. Each company belongs to one out of 10 major sectors. The data set spans weekly every Friday over almost five years (i.e., 298 dates), from 2016-02-03 until 2021-09-24, and is based entirely on Bloomberg data. Data preparation and handling are entirely conducted in Python 3.6 (Python Software Foundation, 2016), relying on the packages "numpy" by Van der Walt, Colbert, and Varoquaux (2011), "pandas" by McKinney (2010), and for visual outputs on "matplotlib" by Hunter and Dale (2007), and Excel. In addition, I use "sci-kit learn" by Pedregosa *et al.* (2011) for the decision trees and the random forests.

3.3. *Updated rating and sectorial analysis*

As stated previously, I illustrate this study with two universes: one based on unsecured senior debt ratings and the other on industrial sectors (cf. Figures 4 & 5). The results of the E2C are compared, along with those of CreditGrades, to the actual CDS spreads using the median and truncated mean methods. More precisely, the average is computed after having dropped the extreme 10% top and bottom points. The senior unsecured debt ratings are provided by Standard & Poor's and Moody's. Their different rating scales are handled like in ML2019. In brief, if both agencies provide the same grades (based on Santos's (2008) comparison scale), the corresponding grade is selected; if only one agency gives a grade, this grade is chosen; and if the grades are different, the worst one is kept remaining conservative. The 10 major sectors are basic material, communications, consumer cyclical, consumer non-cyclical, energy, financials, industrial, utilities, technology, and diversified.

As in ML2019, the E2C formula provides a closer median (or almost like the double-B grade) to the CDS than CreditGrades before the COVID-19 pandemic. However, after the COVID-19 shock in early 2020, it seems for the safest rating that the E2C takes more time than CreditGrades to decrease back to the actual CDS. Although, the E2C

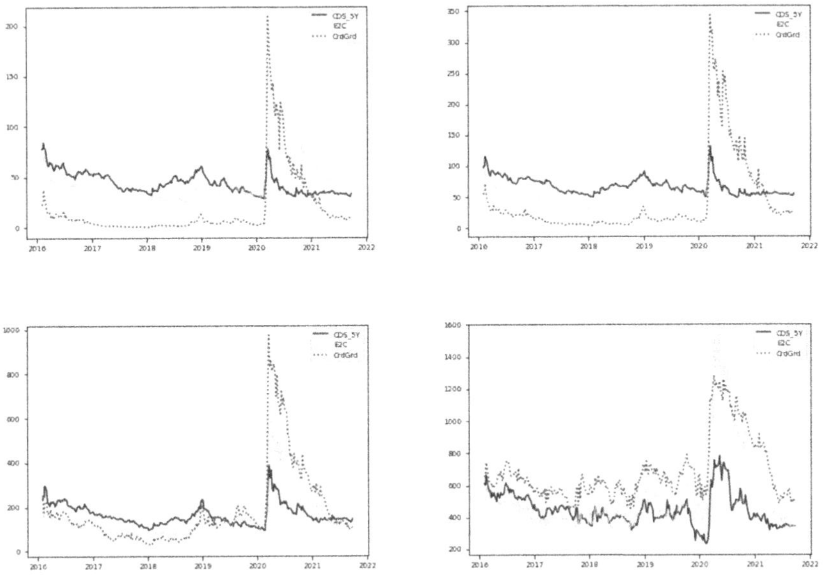

Figure 4. Median-based comparisons between original 5y CDS, E2C, and CreditGrades approximations in terms of senior unsecured debt rating (A: top left, BBB: top right, BB: bottom left, and B: bottom right).

seems to remain closer to the actual CDS, while CreditGrades goes beyond it. For the two riskiest clusters, the E2C is almost always closer than the CDS. It is also interesting to point out that the conservative E2C gives higher results for extreme moments compared to CreditGrades for the riskiest rating during the worst period of the pandemic. Regarding the truncated means, I find similar results to those of ML2019 until the end of 2018. And since 2019, close outputs to those of the medians' analysis are obtained. Additionally, structural models, like the E2C or CreditGrades, do not underestimate spreads for riskier companies (Teixeira, 2007).

In the original paper, Mercadier and Lardy found results before the crisis except for utilities and financials in line with Rodrigues and Agarwal (2011), Lardic and Rouzeau (1999), and Eom, Helwege, and Huang (2004), who emphasized that structural models generally under-predict the observed credit spreads, at least for low levels of risks. However, the COVID-19 shock increases the approximations well above

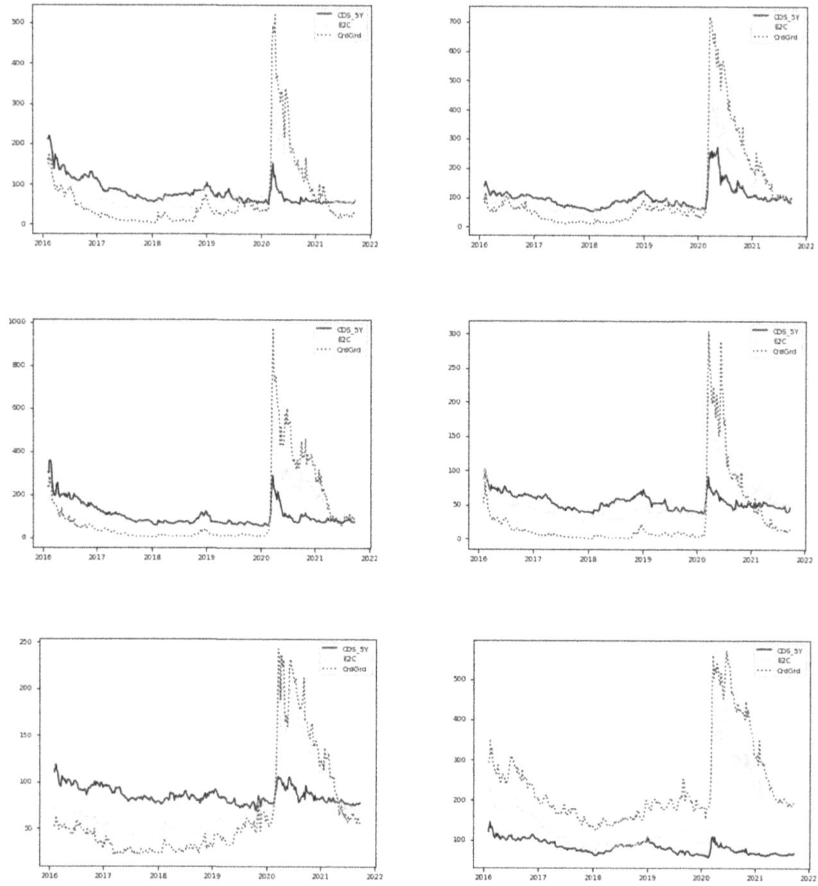

Figure 5. Median-based comparisons between original 5y CDS, E2C, and CreditGrades approximations in terms of industrial sectors (Basic Materials: top left, Consumer Cyclical: top right, Energy: middle left, and Industrial: middle right) and truncated mean based comparisons (Communications: bottom left and Financials: bottom right).

the actual 5y CDS in all sectors, playing their conservative role during stressed times. Even after the COVID-19 shock and according to the median, the E2C formula approximates the CDS spreads at least as well as CreditGrades and above all for basic materials, communications, consumer cyclical and non-cyclical, energy, and industrial.[2] Similar

[2]More results are available upon request to the authors.

conclusions are reached with the truncated mean. The E2C results are unquestionably better for basic materials, communications, consumer cyclical, industrial, utilities, energy, and financials. It is interesting to acknowledge the rather good estimate provided by the E2C for financials as CreditGrades and more generally "Merton" models are traditionally poor in assessing this sector.

3.4. *Feature engineering*

Feature engineering is a key step in machine learning, it is the process of mixing domain knowledge and data formatting to extract and transform relevant features from the original data set.

> To efficiently perform a basic machine learning algorithm, it is fundamental to pre-process the data, reduce dimensions, and extract hand-crafted, domain-specific features (LeCun, 2012).

In line with ML2019 but on a longer timeframe, my aim is to improve the CDS approximation given by the sole E2C formula, integrating additional meaningful input variables. The target variable is the 5y CDS spreads of the selected companies. Overall, I use four independent variables and 23 dummy variables. Although I expect the E2C formula to be a major independent variable in the model, it is based on equity information and lacks information on the credit market. The credit market is the one in which the CDS is traded. Thus, the most liquid index on the credit market, the Investment Grade CDS index (IG CDX), is set as a feature. In addition, credit rating agencies assess the debtors' probability of default assigning ratings to companies which are set as independent variables. As it is related to a level of stability and liquidity, I also consider the size of the studied companies, measured with the market capitalization. Companies' location and industrial sector are included in the model as well.

Once the features are chosen, they are handled as follows. First examples with at least one missing data are removed. Both decision trees and random forests are robust to instabilities and unaffected whether the data are scaled or not, thus I neither check for multi-collinearity nor standardize the data. However, I use label encoding for the ordinal variable and debt rating and one-hot encoding for the two nominal polytomous variables, i.e., locations and industrial sectors.

3.5. *Hyper-parameters' tuning*

3.5.1. *Decision tree regression*

Once the algorithm is chosen, the first task is to tune the hyper-parameters that must be distinguished from parameters. In machine learning, a parameter is optimized by the model, while a hyper-parameter is to be set by the user beforehand. For instance, the number of clusters for a k-means algorithm is set by the user and not modified by the algorithm. However, the user still needs to select a value for the hyper-parameter. To do so, the most common method is a heuristic called the elbow method. It consists in plotting on the y-axis the sum of squared errors corresponding to each setting plotted on the x-axis. The trade-off is as usual between the complexity and the tolerance to the remaining error of the model. The user will select the parameter that is at the inflection point. Hyper-parameters' tuning is performed on cross-validation sets. Generally, k-fold cross-validation divides the training set into k sub-samples. Then, the methodology alternatively uses the $k-1$ sample as a training set and the remaining one as a test set. The selected hyper-parameter is the one that minimizes the error or, as I do here, maximizes the accuracy.

For decision trees, three related parameters can be tuned: the maximum depth, the minimum samples split, and the minimum samples leaf. The first parameter indicates how deep the tree is allowed to grow. As usual, the deeper it is, the more information it holds but the more prone to overfit it is. Minimum samples split indicates the minimum number of samples required for a split to occur. Finally, the minimum samples leaf

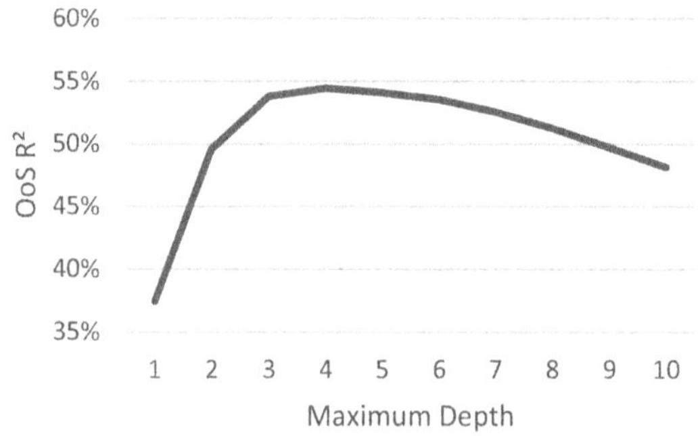

Figure 6. Maximum depth for the decision tree regression onto the E2C.

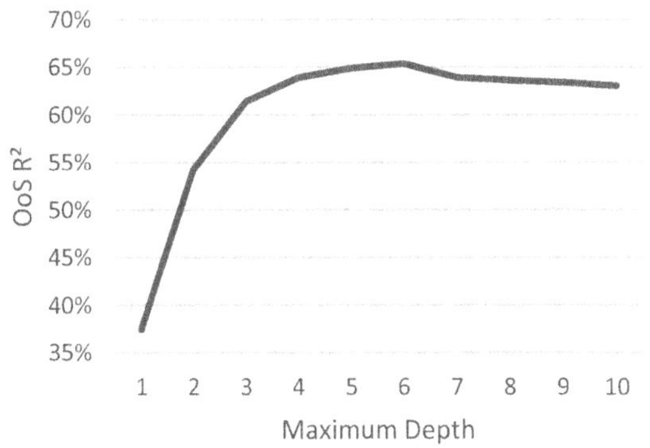

Figure 7. Maximum depth for the decision tree regression onto the entire universe.

specifies the minimum number of samples required to be at a leaf node. In other words, minimum samples leaf guarantees a minimum number of samples in a leaf while minimum samples split may create small leaves. In addition, it is possible to tune the maximum number of features used to split each node as for the random forests (cf. Section 3.5.2) but it is not used here.

In the following graphs, I draw the method by which the decision on the maximum depth tuning is taken considering as input the sole E2C or with the additional universe.

According to Figures 6 and 7, I allow the trees to, respectively, grow up to four and six nodes deep whether inputting the sole E2C or with the entire universe.

3.5.2. *Random forest regression*

As in the previous section, the first step is to tune the hyper-parameters. It is also possible for this algorithm involving decision trees to set a maximum depth, minimum samples split and leaf, but generally, the risk of overfitting is overcome by the number of trees and the number of features (cf. Section 2). Therefore, I use unpruned trees except when the input is the sole E2C for which I set a maximum depth of four nodes. In addition, one can consider pruning the trees to obtain quicker computations (as in ML2019 that targeted practitioners). Doing so the tree would make sense for someone frequently running the algorithm. The first parameter I deal with is the number of estimators to set the number of trees I want the algorithm to generate. As explained in Section 2, multiple decision trees are randomly drawn with replacement. One could think that producing more trees would give a more generalized output, but one may not forget that it would increase the time complexity of the model as well. Another hyper-parameter is the maximum features parameter that stands for the maximum number of features to consider when looking for the best split. As explained in Section 2, it also contributes to decrease the variance.

In the following graphs, I draw the method by which the decision on the number of features and the number of trees is taken considering as input the E2C with the additional universe.

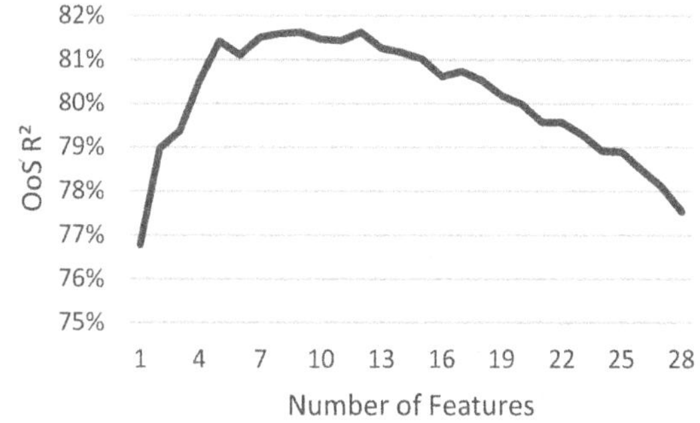

Figure 8. Number of features for the random forest regressions onto the entire universe.

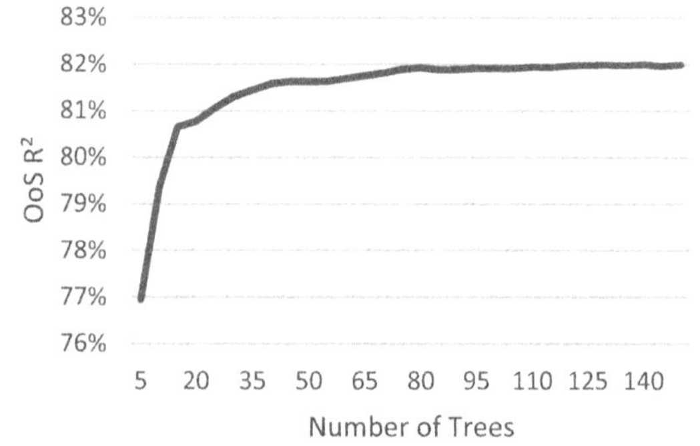

Figure 9. Number of estimators for the random forest regressions onto the entire universe.

According to Figures 8 and 9, I allow the trees to check nine features at each node for splitting, and the number of trees randomly generated is set at 80. From Figure 9, we see that one may consider building more than 80 estimators, which would needlessly increase computation time (although it will not degrade the output).

4. Results

4.1. *Accuracy improvement*

Like ML2019, I assess the accuracy with the widely known *R*-squared measure. Where

$$R^2(y,\hat{y}) = 1 - \frac{\sum_{i=1}^{N}(y_i - \hat{y}_i)^2}{\sum_{i=1}^{N}(y_i - \bar{y})^2}$$

I end up with the following results.

Running decision trees or random forests on only one input feature (E2C formula) provides similar out-of-sample results slightly above a 50% *R*-squared. But when I consider the entire universe, decision tree regressions furnish 65% *R*-squared and random forest regressions lead to an *R*-squared close to 82%. Only studying the pre-crisis period, ML2019 find an 87% *R*-squared. Thus, it seems that integrating the COVID-19 pandemic and almost doubling the considered number of dates only slightly decrease the accuracy, which vouches for the robustness of the method and the choice of the features.

To illustrate my point, I draw for seven large companies in Figure 10 the 5y CDS benchmarks (dotted line) and the various approximations (solid line), such as the sole E2C (left) and the multi-variate sample using decision tree regressions (middle) and using random forest regressions (right).

The early 2020 shock due to the COVID-19 pandemic has a tremendous impact on the sole E2C approximation. But as expected, adding relevant variables and running decision tree and random forest regressions contribute to improve the overall approximation. In line with the results from Table 1, the random forest regressions seem to highly improve the overall prediction regardless of the company.

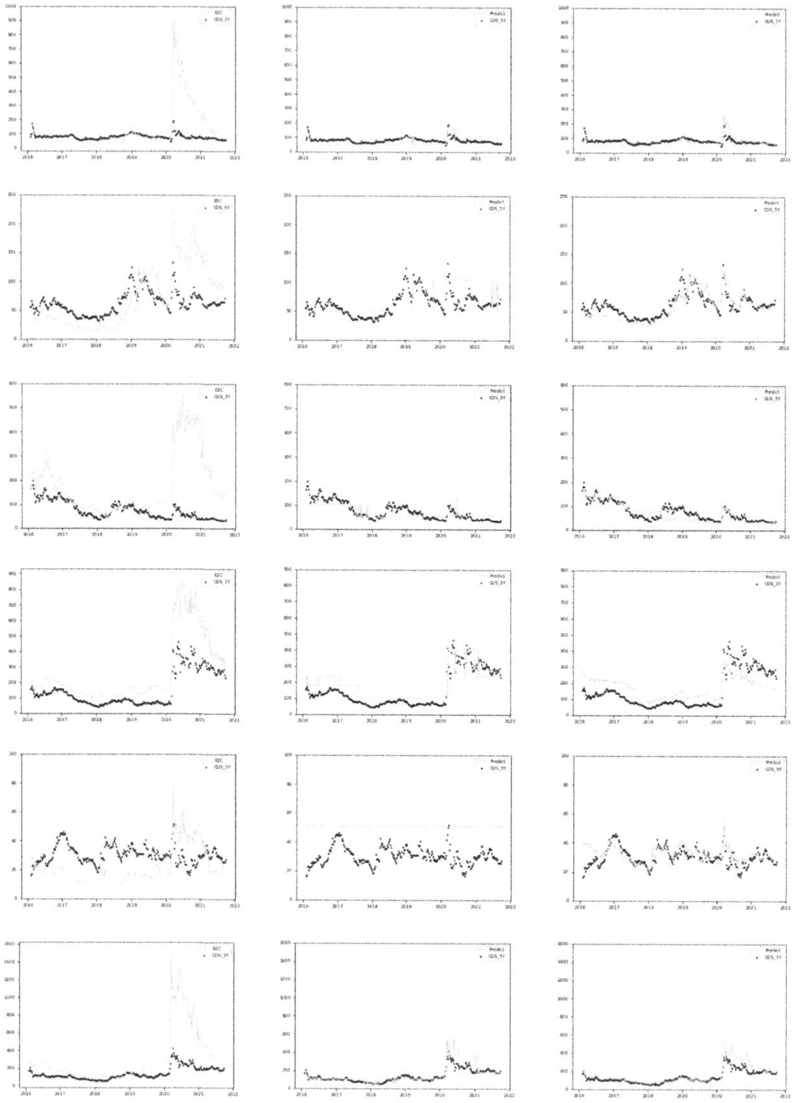

Figure 10. Goodness-of-fit comparison between the sole E2C approximations (left) and the multi-variate set-up handled with decision trees (middle) and random forests (left) for AIG (top), Bayer, BBVA, Deutsche Lufthansa, Pfizer, and Renault (bottom).

Table 1. Goodness-of-fit of averaged decision tree and random forest regressions using the sole E2C or with the additional universe.

R^2	IS Mean (%) (Std (%))	OoS Mean (%) (Std (%))
DecTree (E2C)	58.24 (1.82)	54.45 (3.26)
DecTree (All)	81.87 (1.10)	65.39 (9.36)
RndFrst (E2C)	58.74 (1.79)	55.20 (3.28)
RndFrst (All)	99.35 (0.06)	81.73 (6.26)

4.2. *Feature importance*

Random forest regressions inherit an interesting property from the decision trees highlighting the transparency of these algorithms. They both quantify the importance of each variable. This attribute allows me to evaluate the contribution of the variables to the improvement given by these algorithms. I use two methods for assessing this contribution. The first method called feature importance evaluates the contribution of a given variable to the trees. More specifically, it combines how frequently a variable is used for splitting and the overall improvement it brings each time it is used. For the random forests, the average over all trees of the total contribution of the variables is computed. The second method establishes the importance of a feature by how much permuting it (or shuffling the data) contributes to decrease the overall accuracy. Only using permutation this method does not affect the distributions and helps to distinguish the importance among correlated features.

In line with ML2019, Figures 11 and 12 confirm, as expected, the prominent contribution of the E2C formula to the approximation of the CDS. Additionally, the debt ratings of the companies play a role in this improvement. However, it is interesting to emphasize that their size, measured by the market capitalization, is only highlighted by the random forest regressions. This result is likely caused by the limited authorized depth of the decision trees as the size is the third-largest contributor if the maximum depth is set to 10 (cf. Figure A.1).

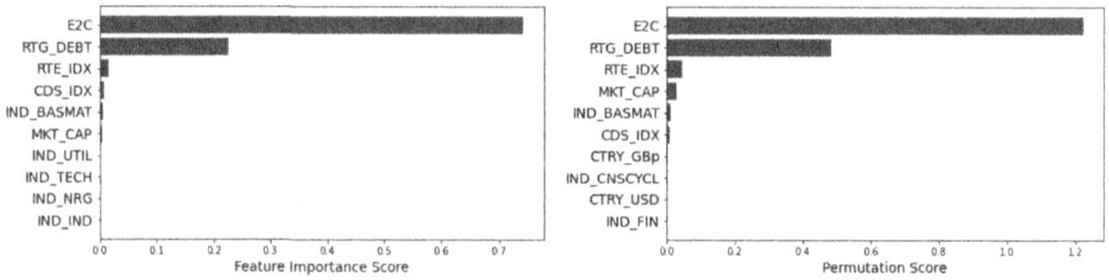

Figure 11. Feature importance assessment for the decision tree regressions using the entire universe.

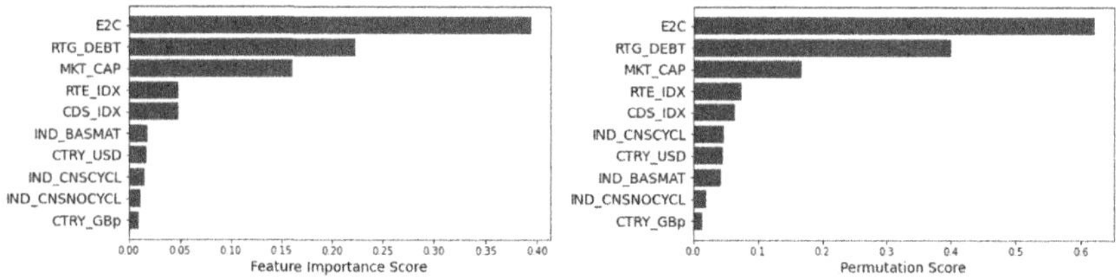

Figure 12. Feature importance assessment for the random forest regressions using the entire universe.

5. Conclusion

In this chapter, I use two non-linear supervised learning algorithms based on decision trees to improve the accuracy of an approximation of CDS spreads following the empirical process of Mercadier and Lardy (2019) based on a time span including the COVID-19 pandemic period. More precisely, both decision tree and random forest regressions are run on the sole E2C formula and on a dedicated multi-variate sample. After the introduction of the elementary E2C formula, I present the other features of interest. Certain sections are dedicated to explaining deeper important concepts in machine learning such as feature engineering and hyper-parameter tuning.

Once the algorithms are run, the accuracies provided for each method are discussed. By far, the random forest regressions on the entire universe give the highest accuracy, i.e., an out-of-sample *R*-squared around 82%. An accuracy that remains close to the one found by ML2019. Thus, integrating the COVID-19 pandemic and, therefore, almost doubling the number of dates considered only slightly decreases the accuracy, which vouches for the robustness of the method and the choice of the multi-variate sample.

Both methods studied here remain simple among non-linear supervised algorithms, yet the literature supports their efficiency. Moreover, they have the additional benefit of being transparent providing the possibility to enquire about the importance of the variables. In line with the original paper, it allows me to emphasize that the most used variable for this approximation is by far the E2C formula. Additionally, the debt rating has an impact on CDS along with the size to a lower extent.

This study partly answers to ML2019 that proposed for future research to rerun the experiment on a longer time span. Furthermore, this peculiar time span includes the highly volatile period observed at the beginning of the COVID-19 pandemic.

References

Ahmad, M. W., Mourshed, M., and Rezgui, Y. (2017). Trees vs neurons: Comparison between random forest and ANN for high-resolution prediction of building energy consumption. *Energy and Buildings*, 147: 77–89.

Albulescu, C. T. (2021). COVID-19 and the United States financial markets' volatility. *Finance Research Letters*, 38(101699): 1–4.

Ali, M., Alam, N., and Rizvi, S., A. R. (2020). Coronavirus (COVID-19) — An epidemic or pandemic for financial markets. *Journal of Behavioral and Experimental Finance*, 27(100341): 1–6.

Ashraf, B. N. (2020a). Stock markets' reaction to COVID-19: Cases or fatalities? *Research in International Business and Finance*, 54(101249): 1–7.

Ashraf, B. N. (2020b). Economic impact of government interventions during the COVID-19 pandemic: International evidence from financial markets. *Journal of Behavioral and Experimental Finance*, 27(100371): 1–9.

Badrinarayanan, V., Kendall, A., and Cipolla, R. (2017). Segnet: A deep convolutional encoder-decoder architecture for image segmentation. *IEEE Transactions on Pattern Analysis and Machine Intelligence*, 39: 2481–2495.

Behr, A. and Weinblat, J. (2017). Default patterns in seven EU countries: A random forest approach. *International Journal of the Economics of Business*, 24(2): 181.

Bernoulli, J. (1713). Ars Conjectandi: Usum & Applicationem Praecedentis Doctrinae in Civilibus, *Moralibus & Oeconomicis*, Chapter 4.

Black, F. and Cox, J. (1976). Valuing corporate securities: Some effects of bond indenture provisions. *Journal of Finance*, 31: 351–367.

Breiman, L. (1996). Bagging predictors. *Machine Learning*, 24: 123–140.

Breiman, L. (2001). Random forests. *Machine Learning*, 45: 5–32.

Breiman, L., Friedman, J., Stone, C. J., and Olshen, R. A. (1984). *Classification and Regression Trees*. Wardsworth, Belmont, CA.

Breslow, L. and Aha, D. (1997). Simplifying decision trees: A survey. *The Knowledge Engineering Review*, 12(1), 1–40.

Brummelhuis, R. and Luo, Z. (2017). CDS rate construction methods by machine learning techniques. pages 1–51. *SSRN Electronic Journal 2967184.*

Chalamandaris, G. and Vlachogiannakis, N. (2018). Are financial ratios relevant for trading credit risk? Evidence from the CDS market. *Annals of Operations Research*, 266: 395–440.

Chebyshev, P. L. (1867). Des valeurs moyennes. *Journal de mathématiques pures et appliquées*, 12: 177–184.

Cont, R. and Minca, A. (2016). Credit default swaps and systemic risk. *Annals of Operations Research*, 247: 523–547.

Crosbie, P. and Bohn, J. (2003). Modeling default risk. *Moody's KMV*.

Eom, Y. H., Helwege, J., and Huang, J.-Z. (2004). Structural models of corporate bond pricing: An empirical analysis. *The Review of Financial Studies*, 17: 499–544.

Escobar, M., Arian, H., and Seco, L. (2012). CreditGrades framework within stochastic covariance models. *Journal of Mathematical Finance*, 2: 303–314.

Fernandez-Delgado, M., Cernadas, E., Barro, S., and Amorim, D. (2014). Do we need hundreds of classifiers to solve real world classification problems? *Journal of Machine Learning Research*, 15: 3133–3181.

Finger, C. C., Lardy, J. P., Finkelstein, V., Pan, G., Ta, T., and Tierney, J. (2002). CreditGrades. Technical report, RiskMetrics Group.

Fortmann-Roe, S. (2012). Understanding the Bias-Variance Tradeoff. http://scott.fortmann-roe.com/docs/BiasVariance.html, Accessed date: 5 May 2019.

Gauss, C. F. (1821). Theoria combinationis observationum erroribus minimus obnoxiae (pars prior). *Gauss Werke*, 4: 3–26.

Geman, S., Bienenstock, E., and Doursat, R. (1992). Neural networks and the bias/variance dilemma. *Neural Computation*, 4(1): 1–58.

Guarin, A., Liu, X., and Ng, W. L. (2011). Enhancing credit default swap valuation with meshfree methods. *European Journal of Operational Research*, 214: 805–813.

Hastie, T., Tibshirani, R., and Friedman, J. (2009). *The Elements of Statistical Learning*. Springer, New York, Second edition.

Ho, T. K. (1995). Random decision forests. In *Proceedings of the Third International Conference on Document Analysis and Recognition*, pages 278–282.

Ho, T. K. (1998). The random subspace method for constructing decision forests. *IEEE Transactions on Pattern Analysis and Machine Intelligence*, 20: 832–844.

Hunter, J. and Dale, D. (2007). The matplotlib users guide. Technical report, R Cran.

Imbierowicz, B. and Cserna, B. (2008). How efficient are credit default swap markets? an empirical study of capital structure arbitrage based on structural pricing model. In 21st Australasian Finance and Banking Conference.

Irresberger, F., Weiss, G., Gabrysch, J., and Gabrysch, S. (2018). Liquidity tail risk and credit default swap spreads. *European Journal of Operational Research*, 269: 1137–1153.

Khaidem, L., Saha, S., and Dey, S. R. (2017). Predicting the direction of stock market prices using random forest. arXiv:1605.00003, pages 1–20.

Kohavi, R. and Wolpert, D. (1996). Bias plus variance decomposition for zero-one loss functions. *ICML*, 96.

Koutmos, D. (2018). Interdependencies between CDS spreads in the European Union: Is Greece the black sheep or black swan? *Annals of Operations Research*, 266: 441–498.

Krauss, C., Do, X. A., and Huck, N. (2017). Deep neural networks, gradient-boosted trees, random forests: Statistical arbitrage on the S&P 500. *European Journal of Operational Research*, 259: 689–702.

Lardic, S. and Rouzeau, E. (1999). Implementing Merton's model on the French corporate bond market. In *AFFI Conference*.

LeCun, Y. (2012). Learning invariant feature hierarchies. *Lecture Notes in Computer Science (including subseries Lecture Notes in Artificial Intelligence and Lecture Notes in Bioinformatics) 7583 LNCS, PART 1*.

Liu, M., Wang, M., Wang, J., and Li, D. (2013). Comparison of random forest, support vector machine and back propagation neural network for electronic tongue data classification: Application to the recognition of orange beverage and Chinese vinegar. *Sensors and Actuators B: Chemical*, 177: 970–980.

Malliaris, A. G. and Malliaris, M. (2015). What drives gold returns? A decision tree analysis. *Finance Research Letters*, 13: 45–53.

McKinney, W. (2010). Data structures for statistical computing in python. *Proceedings of the Ninth Python in Science Conference*, 445: 51–56.

Mercadier, M. and Lardy, J.-P. (2019). Credit spread approximation and improvement using random forest regression. *European Journal of Operational Research*, 277(1): 351–365.

Merton, R. (1974). On the pricing of corporate debt: The risk structure of interest rates. *Journal of Finance*, 29: 449–470.

Neal, B., (2019). On the bias-variance tradeoff: Textbooks need an update. arXiv:1912.08286: 1–63.

Nyman, R. and Ormerod, P. (2016). Predicting economic recessions using machine learning algorithms. arXiv:1701.01428: 1–14.

Opitz, D. and Maclin, R. (1999). Popular ensemble methods: An empirical study. *Journal of Artificial Intelligence Research*, 11: 169–198.

Pang, S., L. and Gong J., Z. (2009) C5.0 classification algorithm and application on individual credit evaluation of banks. *Systems Engineering – Theory & Practice*, 29(12): 94–104.

Pedregosa, F., Varoquaux, G., Gramfort, A., Michel, V., Thirion, B., Grisel, O., Blondel, M., Prettenhofer, P., Weiss, R., Dubourg, V., Vanderplas, J., Passos, A., Cournapeau, D., Brucher, M., Perrot, M., and Duchesnay, E. (2011). Scikit-learn: Machine learning in python. *Journal of Machine Learning Research*, 12: 2825–2830.

Python Software Foundation. (2016). Python 3.6.0 documentation.

Quinlan, J. R. (1986). Induction of decision trees. *Machine Learning*, 1: 81–106.

Quinlan, J. R. (1993). C4.5: programs for machine learning. Morgan Kaufmann.

Quinlan, J. R. (2007). C5.0. https://www.rulequest.com/.

Rodrigues, M., and Agarwal, V. (2011). The performance of structural models in pricing credit spreads. *Midwest Finance Association 2012 Annual Meetings Paper*: 1–26.

Rodriguez-Galiano, V., Sanchez-Castillo, M., Chica-Olmo, M., and Chica-Rivas, M. (2015). Machine learning predictive models for mineral prospectivity: An evaluation of neural networks, random forest, regression trees and support vector machines. *Ore Geology Reviews*, 71: 804–818.

Roy, A. D. (1952). Safety first and the holding of assets. *Econometrica*, 20: 431–449.

Sangineto, E., Nabi, M., Culibrk, D., and Sebe, N. (2018). Self-paced deep learning for weakly supervised object detection. *IEEE Transactions on Pattern Analysis and Machine Intelligence*, 1.

Santos, K. (2008). Corporate credit ratings: A quick guide. Treasurer's Companion, pages 45–49.

Sepp, A. (2006). Extended CreditGrades model with stochastic volatility and jumps. *Wilmott Magazine*: 50–62.

Shwartz-Ziv, R. and Tishby, N. (2017). Opening the black box of deep neural networks via information. arXiv:1703.00810, pages 1–19.

Stamicar, R. and Finger, C. C. (2006). Incorporating equity derivatives into the CreditGrades model. *Journal of Credit Risk*, 2(1): 3–29.

Sun, Y., Yen, G. G., and Yi, Z. (2018). Evolving unsupervised deep neural networks for learning meaningful representations. *IEEE Transactions on Evolutionary Computation*, 1.

Tanaka, K., Kinkyo, T., and Hamori, S. (2016). Random forests-based early warning system for bank failures. *Economics Letters*, 148: 118–121.

Teixeira, J. C. A. (2007). An empirical analysis of structural models of corporate debt pricing. *Applied Financial Economics*, 17(14): 1141–1165.

Tomohiro, A. (2014). Bayesian corporate bond pricing and credit default swap premium models for deriving default probabilities and recovery rates. *Journal of the Operational Research Society*, 65: 454–465.

Tso, G. K. F. and Yau, K. K. W. (2007). Predicting electricity energy consumption: A comparison of regression analysis, decision tree and neural networks. *Energy*, 32: 1761–1768.

Van der Walt, S., Colbert, S., and Varoquaux, G. (2011). The NumPy array: a structure for efficient numerical computation. *Computing in Science & Engineering*, 13: 22–30.

Varian, H. R. (2014). Big data: New tricks for econometrics. *The Journal of Economic Perspectives*, 28: 3–27.

Vasicek, O. A. (1987). Probability of loss on loan portfolio. *KMV Corporation.*

Yeh, C. C., Lin, F., and Hsu, C. Y. (2012). A hybrid KMV model, random forests and rough set theory approach for credit rating. *Knowledge-Based Systems*, 33: 166–172.

Zhang, D., Hu, M., Ji, Q. (2020). Financial markets under the global pandemic of COVID-19. *Finance Research Letters*, 36(101528): 1–6.

Zhou, C. (2001). The term structure of credit spreads with jump risk. *Journal of Banking & Finance*, 25: 2015–2040.

Appendix

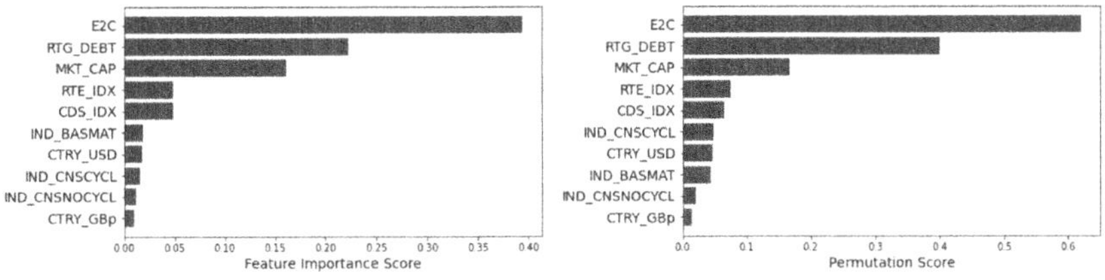

Figure A.1. Feature importance assessment for the decision tree regressions using the entire universe and a maximum depth set at 10.

Part 2

Issues in Financial Engineering

© 2023 World Scientific Publishing Company
https://doi.org/10.1142/9789811260483_0004

Chapter 4

Green Bond Market vs. Carbon Market in Europe: Two Different Trajectories but Some Complementarities

Yves Rannou*, Pascal Barneto†, and Mohamed Amine Boutabba‡

**ESC Clermont BS & CleRMa, Clermont-Ferrand, France*

†*University of Bordeaux (IAE) & IRGO, Bordeaux, France*

‡*Université Paris-Saclay, Univ Evry, EPEE, 91025, Evry-Courcouronnes, France*

Abstract

Europe was the first continent to create concomitantly a large-scale carbon market to reduce the level of carbon emissions and to create a green bond market to finance the transition to low-carbon economies. In this chapter, we study the respective roles of these instruments, their price trajectories, their interaction, and their potential complementarities over a six-year period (2014–2019). We enrich the literature on environmental markets in several respects. First, we report significant short-run and long-run persistence of shocks to the conditional correlation between the European carbon and the European green bond markets. Second, we detect bidirectional shock transmission effects between those markets but no significant spillover effects. Taken together, these results suggest that a green bond issued in Europe may be used to hedge against the carbon price risk.

Keywords: Green bond, European allowance, spillover effects, asset complementarity

1. Introduction

Creating a green and low-carbon economy represents a global market opportunity for all investors, financial institutions, and firms. In Europe, the European Green Deal's Investment Plan, unveiled in January 2020 by Ursula von der Leyen, aims to mobilize €1 trillion of investments in the next decade at least. Two months later, the European Commission (EC hereafter) presented its proposal for the European Climate Law, part of the European Green Deal, to serve EC's vision to be climate neutral by 2050. With this European Green Deal Package, Europe remains at the forefront of climate change mitigation and adaptation.

Europe has been the first (and the only) continent to promote the use of carbon markets to reduce the level of carbon emissions and of a green bond market to finance the transition to low-carbon economies quasi simultaneously. The European Union Emission Trading Scheme (EU ETS hereafter) that resulted in the European carbon market was used to achieve both greater environmental effectiveness and lower overall cost of mitigation. The Stern–Stiglitz High-Level Commission on Carbon Prices, while recognizing that *A well-designed carbon price is an indispensable part of a strategy for reducing emissions in an efficient way*, called in 2017 for "explicit price trajectories." Carbon pricing provides mitigation incentives and indirectly reduces the vulnerability of the economy to climate change. Since a breakthrough in fiscal policy is unlikely, additional financing resources like green bonds are necessary.

Issuing green bonds is another solution for financing climate change mitigation, an innovation that has been implemented in Europe. Since the first green bond issued by the European Investment Bank (EIB) in 2007, the European green bond market has grown quickly and is now valued at 118.6 billion dollars of issuances in 2019 (CBI, 2020).

Green bonds are used for mitigation issues to a large extent but also for adaptation to climate change impacts. However, some studies have pointed out that they may be cheaper than conventional bonds thus reducing the cost of debt (Zerbib, 2019). Bachelet, Becchetti, and Manfredonia (2019) found that the act of certifying a green bond reduces its yield so issuers can reduce *de facto* debt costs for green investments. Another reason to issue green bonds is the diversification of the investor base (Thang & Zhang,

2018) and its communications role. Many corporates have made long-term climate commitments. Issuing green bonds can help signal (implicit) carbon pricing. Unlike carbon pricing, green bonds do not provide the needed marginal incentives for corporates to optimally factor carbon costs into their decision-making. Furthermore, the signal reflected by carbon pricing may be disturbed by a major concern among practitioners and investors, namely, greenwashing. This concern is explained by the absence of legal enforcement mechanisms to ensure compliance with the use of proceeds laid out in the green bond prospectus.

This chapter examines the roles of these instruments, their price trajectories, their interaction, and their potential complementarities over a six-year period (2014–2019).

When carbon markets and green bonds are jointly implemented, they interact in two ways at least. First, holders of green bonds may be interested in reacting against the tightening of ETS caps. An ETS sets a cap on emissions, and emissions leakage[1] can occur if green bonds finance climate change mitigation projects for industries covered by the ETS. Mitigation effects obtained via green bonds decrease the scarcity of European Union Allowances (EUAs hereafter) under the cap, reducing the carbon price. To prevent this decrease, the emissions cap should be tightened when green bonds are introduced. A second interaction effect between green bonds and carbon prices works through price volatility. Green investment projects can more easily attract green bond financing if returns on investment are less volatile. As the returns to these projects depend on carbon prices, a more stable carbon price also generates a more stable return on investment and greater demand for green bonds simultaneously.

The financial engineering techniques operate at two levels for both carbon assets (EUAs) and green bonds. In terms of product innovation, green bonds can be issued with specific attributes (fixed/variable coupons and callable features), whereas EUAs can be traded via spot contracts or

[1] Emissions leakage is the situation in which, as a result of stringent climate policies, companies move their production abroad to countries with less ambitious climate measures, which can lead to a rise in global greenhouse gas emissions. For the 3rd trading phase from 2013 to 2020, companies are supposed to purchase their emissions allowances under the EU ETS through auctioning as the default allocation method. However, the production from European industrial sectors that is deemed to be exposed to a significant risk of carbon leakage is getting protection by receiving their allowances to emit CO_2 for free.

a large range of derivatives contracts (futures, options, strips of futures, and swaps). In terms of risk management, green bonds and EUAs are volatile assets that require accurate estimation of their volatility (risk) so investors can adapt their hedging policies in consequence.

In the literature, few attempts have been made to model portfolio and/or risk strategies including a carbon asset and a green bond. For instance, Rannou (2019) builds a model of two assets traded in a continuous double auction market: (i) an EUA traded at the prevailing price and (ii) a green bond that pays out a fixed payoff at the end of maturity.

However, to the best of our knowledge, no paper has yet compared the price dynamics of the European green bond market and that of the European carbon market notably during the Phase III of EU ETS (2013–2019), where the EUA (auctioned) has an initial price. The difficulty here is that the carbon market and the green bond market in Europe are not directly comparable through their primary or their secondary market. Regarding the primary market, the issuance of EUAs that are auctioned is strictly managed by the EC while the issuance of green bonds is only subjected to the approval of stock exchanges once they are certified or labeled (Bachelet *et al.*, 2019). Regarding the secondary market, the European carbon market enjoys a liquid secondary market (Medina and Pardo, 2013; Stefan & Wellenreuther, 2020) in contrast to the European green bond market that suffers from an illiquid secondary market (Zerbib, 2019).

To remedy these difficulties, we proceed in two steps.

First, we employ the European green bond and EUA carbon indices rather than using prices from stock exchanges. Second, we develop a VAR BEKK GARCH model, which is particularly adequate to capture volatility shocks as well as volatility spillover effects between the European carbon market and the European green bond (GB (EUR) hereafter) market and vice versa.

Three important results emerge from our empirical work. First, we observe significant short-run and long-run persistence of shocks to the dynamic conditional correlation between EUA and GB (EUR) markets but not between EUA and green bond global (GB Global hereafter) markets. Second, the dynamic conditional correlation coefficient between EUA and GB (EUR) markets is low fluctuating in the range 0.01–0.12 from 2014 to 2018. Since the beginning of 2019, it becomes slightly negative. This result can be explained by the good carbon market performance in 2019 due to the drop in emissions of electricity producers and the use of the Market Stability Reserve, a sort of central allowance bank intended to reduce excess supply of EUAs in order to maintain EUA prices at a certain level. Third, we detect bidirectional shock transmission effects between EUA and GB (EUR) while a one-way positive volatility spillover effect from GB (Global) to EUA is reported.

Taken together, these results suggest that the green bond instrument issued in Europe may be used to hedge against the EUA carbon price risk. This finding is important for investors and for fund managers that may invest in green bonds and in EUA futures to create a portfolio of environmental assets. Henceforth, these financial assets can be considered complementary.

The rest of this chapter is organized as follows. Section 2 presents the role and the evolution of the European carbon market. Section 3 reviews the role and the development of the European green bond market. Section 4 analyses the interaction of the price dynamics of both the European carbon market and the European green bond market. Section 5 concludes.

2. The Carbon Market in Europe

> *"Carbon trading is set to become the world's largest commodity market. The world emits 35 billion tons; priced at $20; that's $700 billion. Put a 10–20 multiple [...] you're talking about $10 trillion at maturity."*
>
> R. Sandor (2010), founder of the European Climate Exchange (ECX)

2.1. *Economic concept of the carbon market (EU-ETS)*

There are two ways to establish a carbon price. First, a country can levy a tax on carbon content, i.e., the CO_2 emissions caused by its production. Second, a government or a supranational authority can establish a system in which the aggregate level of emissions covered by the quotas is set equal to the desired level of total emissions, and the quotas are tradable — an ETS (e.g., the EU-ETS in Europe). A carbon tax provides certainty about the price of carbon, whereas an ETS can lead to high price volatility because the inelastic supply of permits combines with inelastic demand for them in the short run. But the volatility is reduced by allowing 'banking and borrowing' of quotas across time periods and/or by introducing hybrid schemes in which sharp price movements trigger a change in the authorities' supply of quotas (e.g., Market Stability Reserve) (Monast, 2010).[2] More importantly, both a carbon tax and an ETS can raise revenue as long as, in the latter case, the quotas are auctioned.

2.2. *Current framework of the European carbon market*

Issued by the Directive 2003/87/EC, the EU-ETS is a cap and trade scheme that controls the CO_2 emissions of more than 12,000 regulated installations that mainly come from industrial and power sectors and from aviation since 2012 (European Commission, 2013). The principles of the carbon market as a cap-and-trade scheme are two-fold. First, a global cap of emissions is set; an equivalent number of EUAs (i.e., quotas to emit 1 tCO_2 equivalent) is issued and allocated to the regulated installations. An installation must comply by surrendering the number of EUAs equal to its verified emissions. This is the cap. The level of emissions reductions essentially depends on the cap and not on the trade: the incentives to reduce emissions depend on the allocation since emissions cannot exceed the number of EUAs issued. Second, polluting firms are required to purchase EUAs for each ton of carbon dioxide lacking by trading them on secondary spot or futures markets. In Phase I (2005–2007) and Phase II (2008–2012) of EU ETS, nearly all EUAs were given away for free. In Phase III (2013–2020), the EU objective of 21% reduction of greenhouse gases (GHGs hereafter) in 2020 relative to the 1990 level forced the 27 EU member states to introduce gradually auction sales for EUA so that the free allotment has been reduced significantly. From 2013 onward, the shift toward an auction-based allocation process should have created a larger primary market for EUAs, with investors paying more attention paid to the long term. This also raises the importance of futures markets as an effective tool to hedge against unexpected changes in the carbon price. In fact, the European carbon market has encountered a recurrent problem of low and volatile prices since the beginning of EU ETS. During Phase I

[2] In the carbon market, in the absence of a "safety valve", a rocketing carbon price could seriously damage the economy. In this way, capped entities may also use offsets that have been created outside the EU ETS scheme.

(2005–2007), the EUA price fell because of a significant overallocation of EUAs. During Phase II (2008–2012), the EUA market experienced a significant price drop because of the economic crisis that impacted industrial production and, therefore, the level of carbon emissions (Alberola, Chevallier, & Chèze, 2008). At the beginning of Phase III in 2013, the EUA price fell below €5 — a level that was too low to favor switching to low-carbon technologies.

Medina and Pardo (2013) document the existence of heavy tails, volatility clustering, and asymmetric volatility in EUAs' returns. They also provide evidence of negative asymmetry, positive correlation with stock indexes and higher volatility levels typical of financial assets, and the existence of an inflation hedge and a positive correlation with bonds which are characteristics of commodity futures. In this way, EUAs may be viewed as a new asset class. Other studies have highlighted the influence of two other distinctive attributes of the EUA market.

Information asymmetry: In the financial market, issuers are responsible for the information released to the public under the supervision of the regulator whose task is to design and check the rules so that all investors have transparent information as to the risks involved. In the carbon market, the public authority is the only issuer of EUAs, and EUA transactions are tracked by the registries' network. Thus, the registries could provide the market with exhaustive information on spot trades almost in real time. This information remains "private" because it cannot be released to the public for five years. Such private information is held by EU ETS compliant ("informed") firms. This information is closely monitored by market participants. In addition, Rannou (2019) identifies a second important source of information asymmetry, namely, adverse selection costs that uninformed traders bear when they trade EUAs with informed counterparty traders through an exchange-based platform (i.e., limit order book).

Risk aversion: Chevallier, Ielpo, and Mercier (2009) detected lower volatility after the amount of verified emissions corresponding to the 2006 compliance period was disclosed to the public. They also estimated that risk aversion is higher on the EUA market than on equity markets in Phase I and Phase II. It is directly related to the uncertainty around the compliance events and political decisions related to the future of EU ETS (e.g., level of the emission cap in the next phase).

2.3. *Market segments in the EU ETS*

As is the case with stock or commodity markets, we can distinguish the EUA primary market (issuance of new EUAs that are auctioned in Phase III) from the EUA secondary market that offers EUA spot or futures contracts for trading.

Primary market: From a theoretical point of view, the EU-ETS is a compliance market where regulated installations seeking to cover their emissions can purchase an equivalent number of EUAs on a primary market. In Phase III, the primary (auction) market only takes place at the EEX exchange (except in the UK where the auction occurs on the ICE ECX exchange).

Figure 1 plots the evolution of EUA prices traded on the primary market of EEX along almost the entire Phase III (Jan 2013–Dec 2019). We observe that the EUA price has increased five-fold in spite of a slight increase of EUAs issued. This significantly higher price should clearly encourage power and industrial companies to switch to low-carbon technologies.

Secondary market: In practice, the EUA market is also a financial market to the extent that EUA derivatives (i.e., futures and options) are traded by market participants searching to hedge or speculate. Interestingly, Lucia *et al.* (2015) found that the influence of speculators in the EUA futures market is higher than that of hedgers after the disclosure of

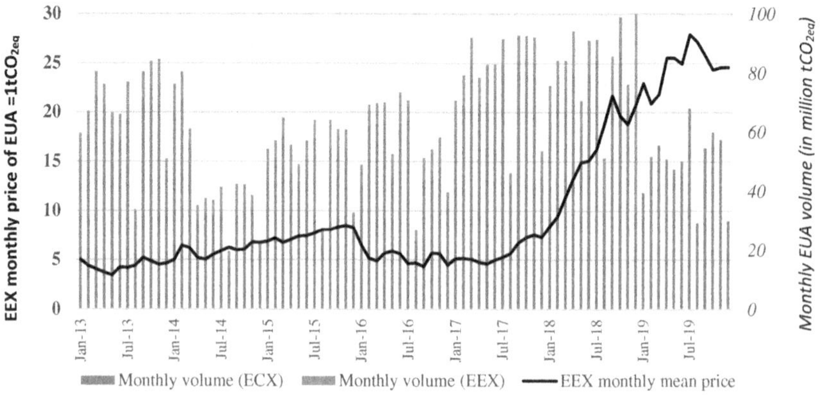

Figure 1. Price evolution and volume of EUAs issued on the primary market (2013–2019).

verified emissions to the public in May. Spot contracts and options on EUA futures are also available for sale representing less than 10% each of the EUA trading volume recorded on exchanges (Mizrach, 2012). The European Climate Exchange (ECX) has dominated the trading of EUA futures that represents 80% of EUA trading volume in Phase II (Rannou & Barneto, 2016).

Accordingly, an important strand of research has investigated the price discovery function of EUA futures markets. Rittler (2012) shows that the carbon price discovery mainly occurs in this market. Rannou and Barneto (2016) find that flows of private information are controlled and lagged by informed traders by executing large trades on the OTC market, while flows of public information are constrained on exchanges encouraging mimetic (speculative) trading by uninformed traders who fuel higher price volatility (risk). In Phase II, Boutabba (2009) shows that the ICE-ECX is more influential in the information transmission process even if prices traded on the European Energy Exchange (EEX) affect those of the ICE-ECX. In the current Phase III, the ICE-ECX in London and the EEX in Leipzig are the two most active exchanges where EUA futures with similar contract specifications are traded (Stefan & Wellenreuther, 2020).

2.4. *Market participants*

In Table 1, we can note that power and industrial companies covered by EU ETS account for 29% of the ICE-ECX market participants. Neuhoff *et al.* (2012) identify and characterize three main trading strategies that they could follow:

- Hedging by rollover EUA (December) futures contracts to minimize trading costs.
- Making arbitrage between different maturities of EUA futures contracts (*strip futures*) on the ECX in priority because it is the most liquid platform.
- Speculating by contracting or maintaining open positions (Lucia *et al.* 2015). Because speculative buyers of EUAs carry more risk, they require higher returns.

Institutional investors (e.g., fund managers, portfolio managers, and insurance companies) represent 20% of ICE-ECX members, much less

Table 1. Market participants trading EUA spot and futures contract on ICE-ECX (2013–2019).

EU-ETS compliant firms	**Institutional investors**	**Banks**	**Brokers**	**Other financial intermediaries**
Arcelor Mittal	ADM	ABN Amro	Aurel BGC	Five Rings Capital
BG International	Alpiq	Banco Santander	Axpo Trading	Infinium CM
British Petrol. Gas	Citadel	Barclays	Cantor CO2e	Jane Capital
Centrica Energy	European Inv. Bank	BNP Paribas	Consus	Jefferies Bache
CEZ A.S	FCStone	CA CIB	EDF Man Trading	Jump Trading
EDF	Fortum	Credit Suisse	Evolution Markets	Knight CA
EGL Energia	Galp Power	Deutsche Bank	GFI Group	KFW Banken
Electrabel	GH Financials	Goldman Sachs	ICAP Energy	REN
Endesa	Macquarie Futures	HSBC	Marex Spectron	RNK Capital
E.On	Man Investment	JP Morgan Sec	Newedge	Saxon Finance
Energa-Obrót	Nomura International	Merrill Lynch	Orbeo	Sempra Energy
Gazprom	Nordea	Mizuho	Tradition Financial Services (TFS)	Susquehanna
PetroChina Int.	OTC Europe	Morgan Stanley	Tullett Prebon	Tibra Trading
PGNiG	Optiver VOF	Natixis	Vitol	XR Trading
Polska Energ.	Proxima	RBC	Virtu	
RWE	SEB Futures	RBS		
Scottish Power	Smartest Energy	Société Générale		
Sempra Energy	Wells Fargo	UBS		

Table 1. (*Continued*)

EU-ETS compliant firms	**Institutional investors**	**Banks**	**Brokers**	**Other financial intermediaries**
Shell				
Solvay				
Statkraft Energi				
Tauron Polska				
ThyssenKrupp				
Total				
Vattenfall				
Verbund AG				
26	**18**	**18**	**15**	**14**

Note: This personal categorization is based on the updated list of ICE-ECX members published in January 2019.

than in stock and bond markets. They may arbitrage the spot/futures basis or hedge their exposure to (spot) carbon price volatility by trading EUA futures. Also, they may have followed speculation strategies like momentum strategies to continue a given price direction and make profits (Rannou & Barneto, 2016). Also, they may have pursued diversification strategies by investing in carbon in a portfolio together with other assets including energy, stock, ETFs, bonds, or by investing in EUAs as part of a larger "green" portfolio including green bonds (De Croce *et al.*, 2011).

20% of ICE-ECX members are (investment) banks. They provide a wide range of services including order and trade execution, clearing of exchange-based or OTC trades, and also research on carbon markets (fundamental analysis and chart analysis to determine price trends). They also engage in arbitrage and in hedging carbon strategies by trading EUA futures.

Brokers represent 16% of ECX members. According to Mizrach (2012), there are nine active brokers on the EUA secondary market of ICE-ECX (Aurel BGC; CantorCO2e; Evolution Markets; GFI Group; ICAP; Marex Spectron; MF Global; TFS; and Tullett Prebon). With the exception of MF Global, they are all members of the London Energy Brokers Association. They benefit from invaluable information related to the order flow (i.e., price and volume of orders) of their clients thanks to their dual role (principal–agent). Finally, the remaining 15% of ICE-ECX members are financial intermediaries (other than brokers). They have either market making activity (e.g., Five Ring Capital, Jump Trading) and/or behave as day traders (arbitrage and speculation).

3. The Green Bond Market in Europe

> *"I do think there are a number of investors who would love to have sovereign green bonds in their portfolios. What I would like to see is what are they going to pay me for it?"*
>
> Sir Robert Stheeman, Head of the UK Debt Management Office

3.1. *Green bond definition and label*

Green bonds are among the most popular debt instrument used in which the proceeds will be exclusively and formally applied to projects or activities that promote climate or other environmental sustainability purposes. By purchasing, these bonds (also called climate bonds[3]), investors lend a fixed amount of capital to the issuer which repays the capital (principal) and accrued interest (coupon) over a set period of time. The difference with a conventional bond lies in the channeling of the investments to projects that generate environmental benefits, for instance, in renewable energy, energy efficiency, sustainable waste management, sustainable land use (forestry and agriculture), biodiversity conservation, clean transportation, and clean water. It is a common practice for issuers to rely on independent experts to validate the environmental quality of the proposed projects.

On the one hand, benefits for green bond issuers include reputational gains (Thang & Zhang, 2018) as well as upgraded risk management processes due to their commitments to better inform about their exposure to climate change. On the other hand, the main benefit for bondholders, especially long-term and responsible investors, is related to the opportunity provided to diversify their portfolios with green bonds that respect ESG (Environmental, Social, and Governance) criteria.

---

[3]Climate bonds are a type of green bond which specifically are supposed to address climate change problems, though the two terms are often used interchangeably.

At present, the most common way to ensure that bonds claiming to be "green" can do so is to comply with the Green Bond Principles (GBP). These are voluntary guidelines elaborated by key market participants, and coordinated by the International Capital Markets Association (ICMA). The GBP cover four key mandatory principles: (i) the description of the use of proceeds which need to finance assets and projects with positive environmental impacts; (ii) the requirement of a clear process for the selection of projects; (iii) a description how the funds are allocated or tracked; and (iv) reporting on the use of proceeds with, if possible, information on the environmental impact of the projects. Accordingly, the green credentials of green bonds can be structured into four categories. Bonds related to tax revenues (use-of-proceeds revenue bonds) represent a large segment of green bond market. Green project bonds and green securitized bonds constitute relatively small niche markets that have recently attracted more attention with the first green bond being issued in the Eurozone by Berlin Hyp in 2015.

The EU is leading the effort to formalize regulations. The first set of rules, called the Green Bond Standard, building on the GBP, was planned for 2020. A second — a 414-page taxonomy that will set definitions for sustainable activities or projects — is expected to be in place by 2022. These rules ultimately should eliminate any uncertainty about how proceeds can be used and how issuers should manage the green bond designation process.

3.2. *Current framework of the EU green bond market*

The green bond market originated in 2007 when the EIB issued its "Climate Awareness Bond" which focused on renewable energy and energy efficiency. From 2008 to 2013, green bond issuance was mainly dominated by Sub-sovereign, Supranational and Development Agency actors (SSA or MDBs).[4] Various corporates such as Bank of America, EDF, Vasakronan,

[4]In 2008, the World Bank (International Bank for Reconstruction and Development or (IBRD)) began its marketing of green bonds with approximately USD 440 million in response to specific demand from Scandinavian pension funds seeking to support climate-focused projects. Since then, Multilateral Development Banks (MDBs) such as the European Bank for Reconstruction and Development (EBRD) and the International Finance Cooperation have been key players in developing the global green bond market and helping it to become a mainstream capital market (European Commission, 2016).

Toyota[5] as well as municipalities and local governments such as Ile de France (Paris) and Gothenburg (Sweden) regions have more recently joined the market. Annual issuance of green bonds in Europe has nearly quadrupled from USD 11 billion in 2013 to USD 47.8 billion in 2015 with issuance from 14 of the G20 countries. This expansion continued in 2016 with an amount of USD 54.1 billion issuance estimated at the end of September. As a result, the outstanding amount of green bonds issued has totaled USD 694 billion of which USD 118 billion are due to labeled green bonds and USD 576 billion to unlabeled green bonds, as reported in July 2016 (CBI/HSBC, 2016).[6] The European market continues to dominate global issuance reaching USD 116 billion in 2019, which accounted for 45% of global issuance. KfW, the German state-owned development bank, and the Dutch State Treasury Agency (DSTA) were ranked as the second and the third largest global issuers in 2019, respectively.

3.3. *Market segments and liquidity*

As for the European carbon market, two complementary markets of green bonds in Europe can be distinguished: the primary (issuance) market and the secondary market.

The primary market is the marketplace where issuers offer their *bonds* to investors. According to CBI (2019), green bonds experienced significant demand in the primary market during the first semester of 2019, with larger book cover and spread compression than vanilla equivalents on average. CBI (2019) has built yield curves on the issue date of a selected sample of green bonds to determine whether or not there was a new issue premium called a "greenium." The report of CBI (2019) concludes that the new issue premium paid by investors was unlikely.

The secondary market can be characterized as the trade of already issued green bonds. Stock exchanges play an important role in the

---

SSA provided critical leadership by priming the market with low risk issuance and educating investors.

[5]Toyota's 2014 sale of securities with proceeds used for investment in electric vehicles and hybrids.

[6]Labeled green bonds are bonds that earmark proceeds for climate or environmental projects and have been labeled as "green" by the issuer, while unlabeled green bonds refer to bonds whose proceeds are used to finance environmentally friendly projects but do not yet carry the green label yet (CBI/HSBC, 2016).

secondary market to increase green bond visibility and promote transparency and market integrity. In 2007, the Luxembourg Stock Exchange became the first stock exchange to list a green bond following the launch of the European Investment Bank's "Climate Awareness" bond. To date, this platform leads the European green bond market, listing 170 green bonds from over 40 different issuers with a collective value of USD 45 billion. In 2019, USD 167 billion (€150 billion) worth of green bonds were listed on various stock exchanges, representing 65% of the total green bonds issued worldwide. Green bonds issued on the over-the-counter (OTC) markets account for 16% of total in 2019, while 19% were not listed or for which information was not available (CBI, 2020).

In spite of the rapid growth in green bond issuance over the past few years, the supply of green bonds may be insufficient due to a lack of fiscal incentive for green investment (Zerbib, 2019) and a missing global classification system for green bonds in relation to the widely used market-based best practices like the Green Bonds Principles. However, green bonds may in some cases be more attractive on the secondary market than conventional bonds. According to the fund manager Mirova (2018), there is sufficient liquidity in the European green bond market. Thus, investors are able to actively manage portfolios and take profit from arbitrage opportunities. Febi *et al.* (2018) find that green bonds traded on the two largest dedicated European market platforms, namely, the Luxembourg Green Exchange and London Stock Exchange, are, on average, more liquid than conventional bonds over the period 2014–2016. In particular, the two employed liquidity measures, the LOT liquidity and the bid-ask spread, are positively related to the yield spread. However, their results suggest that the influence of liquidity risk for green bonds on yield spread vanishes over time which indicates that the European green bond market is mature.

3.4. *Market players*

Six main categories of market players are active in the green bond market and interact: issuers, underwriters, external reviewers, intermediaries, index providers, and investors.

The issuers borrow the money and define the credit risk of the bond. In 2019, the largest issuers were non-financial corporates (27% of cumulative issuance) followed by government-backed entities (22%), financial institutions (21%), sovereigns (17.5%), development bank (9.5%), and local government (1.5%).

The underwriters manage the issuance process of the bond to the public. They work closely with the issuers to determine the bond-offering price at which the underwriters purchase the green bond from the issuer and sell them to investors. In 2019, some of the largest underwriters in terms of volume were Credit Agricole CIB, HSBC, SEB, BNPParibas, Barclays, Société Générale, Deutsche Bank, Natixis, Santander, and ING.

Institutional investors are typically insurance companies and pension funds which prefer investing in green bonds with maturity between 8 and 12 years. They follow buy and hold strategies in order to minimize trading costs in a context of a very illiquid secondary market.

External reviewers confirm alignment with specific guidelines or standards. They are specialized consultants, verifiers, certifiers, and rating agencies.

Other (financial) intermediaries include brokers, market makers, or liquidity providers.

Index providers track the green bond market performance by focusing on bonds where proceeds finance environmental projects. The Bloomberg Barclays MSCI Euro Green Bond Index is the dedicated index that tracks the performance of the green bonds issued in Europe.

4. Interaction Between European Carbon and Green Bond Markets

4.1. *Data set description*

Our empirical work focuses on the dynamic correlation and risk transmission between the green bond market and the carbon market in Europe. We use the S&P GSCI Carbon Emission Allowances (EUA) index (Total Return index) and the Bloomberg Barclays MSCI Euro Green Bond Index (Total Return Index Value Hedge). The former (EUA hereafter) reflects the performance of European Union Allowance Futures and is calculated in Euro (EUR). The latter (GB (EUR) hereafter) is a market value-weighted index designed to measure the performance of green-labeled bonds issued in Europe. We also use the Bloomberg Barclays MSCI Global Green Bond Index (Total Return Index Value Hedge (GB (Global) hereafter) in order to assess volatility interaction between EUA market and global green bond market.

Table 2. Summary statistics of EUA and GB returns.

	EUA returns	GB returns (EUR)	GB returns (Global)
Panel A: Descriptive statistics			
Mean	0.0007	0.0008	0.0002
Maximum	0.0427	0.0196	0.0212
Minimum	−0.055	−0.0164	−0.0282
Standard deviation	0.0122	0,0045	0.0072
Skewness	−0.323	−0.1957	−0.4729
Kurtosis	5.0336	5.3772	4.3729
Jarque–Bera test	60.524	77.151	36.9429
Probability	0.0000	0.0000	0.0000
Panel B: Unit root tests			
Augmented DF	−17.9501***	−17.5712***	−19.338***
PP	−17.967***	−17.6088***	−19.3974***
KPSS	0.2119***	0.168***	0.1314***
Panel C: Unconditional correlations			
EUA returns	1	−0.0345	−0.016

Note: Unit root tests (constant model) are performed on levels. The 1% critical values are −3.4507, −3.4507, and 0,739 for the Augmented DF, PP, and KPSS tests, respectively;
*** denote statistical significance at the 1% level.

From January 10, 2014, to February 14, 2020, the sample contains 315 weekly observations. The logarithmic returns are used in this paper to depict the market volatility. Table 2 presents the summary statistics of EUA and GB returns.

Broadly speaking, the returns of EUA and GB (EUR and Global) indices vary over time (see Figure 2) and behaved in an opposite manner on the whole (Figure 3).

Moreover, Figure 2 depicts the derived EUA and GB returns as having significant volatility agglomeration characteristics. According to the mean or the standard deviation of each return series (Table 2), we can see that the volatility of EAU returns appears more significant than that of green bonds. All the skewness coefficients are not equal to zero and all the kurtosis coefficients are above three, which indicate that EUA and GB returns series here all follow the fat-tailed non-normal distribution. Not all time series satisfy the normality assumption as supported by the Jarque–Bera test. Besides, the Augmented Dickey-Fuller (ADF),

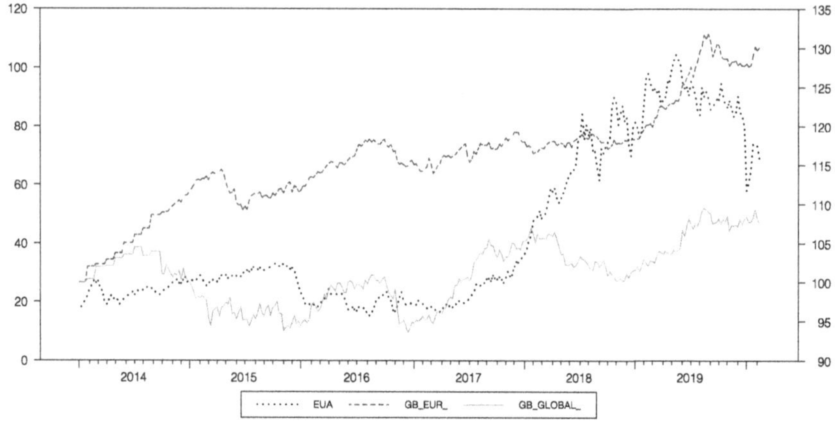

Figure 2. Evolution of weekly prices of Carbon and Green Bond indices (2014–2020).

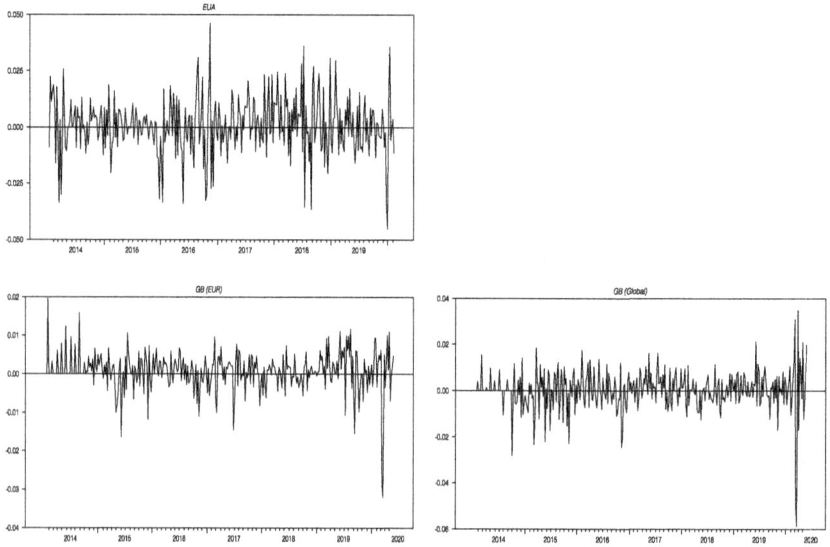

Figure 3. Evolution of weekly returns of Carbon and Green Bond indices (2014–2020).

Kwiatkowski–Phillips–Schmidt–Shin (KPSS), and Phillips–Perron (PP) tests are employed in this paper, and the results suggest that the three returns series are all stationary at the 1% significance level. The correlation values between EUA returns and the green bond returns are low and negative illustrating the benefits of diversification in the short term. The highest correlation is between EUA returns and GB (EUR) returns.

4.2. *Methodology*

The VAR model has been used to capture the linear interdependencies among multiple time series. In this study, the VAR model is used to investigate the conditional mean which provides the foundation for further volatility spillover research.

This bivariate VAR model for the EUA and green bond indices is written as follows:

$$r_t^E = u_t^E + \sum_{m=1}^{M} a_m^E r_{t-m}^E + \sum_{n=1}^{N} b_n^E r_{t-m}^G + \varepsilon_t^E \quad (1)$$

$$r_t^G = u_t^G + \sum_{m=1}^{M} a_m^G r_{t-m}^G + \sum_{n=1}^{N} b_n^G r_{t-m}^E + \varepsilon_t^G \quad (2)$$

where r_t^E and r_t^G are the logarithmic returns of EUA and GB indices at time t, respectively, while u_t^E and u_t^G are their respective conditional mean series. Lag orders are m and n with maximum lag values being M and N, respectively. Mean spillover coefficients a^E and a^G are for their own market and b^E and b^G are for across market. The residuals of Eqs. (1) and (2) are, respectively, ε_t^E and ε_t^G.

We then apply the dynamic conditional correlation generalized autoregressive conditional heteroskedasticity (DCC-GARCH) model (Engle, 2002) to investigate the time-varying correlations between EUA and GB returns. The major advantage of the DCC-GARCH model is to examine time-varying market volatility spillover effects and possible changes in conditional correlation over time, implying dynamic portfolio behaviors in response to cross-market news. The DCC model is estimated in two steps: (1) we estimate a series of univariate GARCH parameters and (2) we assess their correlation estimations that vary over time.

Thus, the conditional covariance matrix can be decomposed as follows:

$$H_t = D_t R_t D_t \quad (3)$$

where $D_t = diag\left\{\sqrt{h_{i,t}}\right\}$ is a 2 × 2 matrix containing the time-varying standard deviations from the univariate GARCH model, and where $R_t = \rho_{ij}, t\ (i,j = 1,2)$ is the 2 × 2 matrix comprising the conditional correlations.

The generalized autoregressive conditional heteroskedasticity (GARCH) model captures two important market features: time-varying variance and leptokurtic distribution.

The standard deviations in D_t are presented by the following GARCH (1, 1) process:

$$h_{it}^2 = \gamma_i + \sum_{p=1}^{P_i} \alpha_{ip} \varepsilon_{i,t-p}^2 + \sum_{q=1}^{Q_i} \beta_{iq} h_{i,t-q}^2, i = 1,2 \tag{4}$$

where ε_t follows an independently and identically standard normal distribution with mean 0 and variance of 1, and α_i, β_i are the coefficients of the GARCH and ARCH terms. The coefficients must satisfy $\sum_{i=1}^{p} \alpha_i + \sum_{j=1}^{q} \beta_j < 1$, and α_i, $\beta_j \geq 0$.

The conditional correlation matrix R_t is defined as follows:

$$R_t = Q_t^{*-1} Q_t Q_t^{*-1} \text{ with} \tag{5}$$

$$Q_t = \left(1 - \sum_{k=1}^{K} \theta_{1k} - \sum_{l=1}^{L} \theta_{2k}\right) \overline{Q} + \sum_{k=1}^{K} \theta_{1k} \left(\varepsilon_t - k\varepsilon_{t-k}\right) + \sum_{l=1}^{L} Q_{t-1} \tag{6}$$

where $\bar{Q}$ is the unconditional variance-covariance matrix from the model estimated in Eq. (4) and Q_t^* is a 2 × 2 matrix containing the square root of the diagonal elements of Q_t.

The dynamic conditional correlations are then given by

$$\rho_{ij,t} = q_{ij,t} \Big/ \sqrt{q_{ii,t} q_{jj,t}} \qquad (i,j = 1,2) \tag{7}$$

Finally, we perform the BEKK model of Engle and Kroner (1995) which permits the interaction of the conditional variances and covariances of several time series. It, therefore, allows us to identify volatility transmission effects.

The conditional covariance matrix of the BEKK model, H_t, is expressed as follows:

$$H_t = W'W + A'\varepsilon_{t-1}\varepsilon_{t-1}' A + B' H_{t-1} B \qquad \text{with}$$

$$C = \begin{bmatrix} c^{EE} & 0 \\ c^{GE} & c^{GG} \end{bmatrix}, \quad A = \begin{bmatrix} a^{EE} & a^{EG} \\ a^{GE} & a^{GG} \end{bmatrix}, \quad B = \begin{bmatrix} b^{EE} & b^{EG} \\ b^{GE} & b^{GG} \end{bmatrix} \tag{8}$$

where C is a 2 × 2 lower triangular matrix of constants and C' is its transposed matrix. a^{EG} and b^{EG} capture shocks and volatility spillover from

EUA market to GB market. a^{GE} and b^{GE} capture shocks and volatility spillover from GB market to EUA market. a^{EE} and b^{GG} capture the impact of past shocks of EUA market and EUA on their own current volatility, respectively, and b^{EG} and b^{GE} capture the impact of past volatility of EUA and GB markets on their own current volatility, respectively.

4.3. *Empirical results*

4.3.1. *Dynamic correlations*

As stated earlier, the coefficients of the VAR-DCC-GARCH (1,1) model are estimated in two steps: the first step is to estimate the VAR model, while the second step is to evaluate the conditional correlation on the basis of residual errors estimations from the VAR model.

Table 2 shows the estimated coefficients of VAR-DDC-GARCH (1,1) with maximum likelihood (BFGS) and correlation targeting estimation between the return of EUA and GB indexes and the findings are shown as follows.

First, we observe significant short-run persistence of shocks to the dynamic conditional correlation between EUA and GB (EUR) markets as well while it is not significant between EUA and GB (Global) markets. The finding provides some evidence of short-run predictability in the correlation changes between EUA and GB (EUR) market returns. Second, we document significant long-run persistence of shocks to the dynamic conditional correlation between EUA market and GB (EUR) and GB (Global) markets.

Table 3 shows that all the values of *b* are statistically significant and close to one, which indicates that the long-run persistence of shocks is quite important for the long-run change prediction on the dynamic conditional correlation in the two cases.

Meanwhile, according to the values of θ_2 in Table 3, we find that the long-run persistence of shocks on the dynamic conditional correlation between EUA and GB (EUR) returns is the highest. Finally, we find that the sum of estimated parameters θ_1 and θ_2, which indicates the volatility persistence of index increase, is close to one. The result suggests that the shocks of index increase play an important role in all the predictions on the EUA and GB (EUR) indices.

Table 4 summarizes the descriptive statistics of these dynamic correlation coefficients, while Figure 4 presents a plot of dynamic conditional

Table 3. Estimated coefficients of the VAR-DDC-GARCH (1,1) model.

	EUA and GB (EUR)	**EUA and GB (Global)**
Panel A: Conditional mean equation		
u^E	9.8211e^{-04} (0.1283)	9.8090e^{-04} (0.1681)
u^G	5.7218e^{-04}*** (0.0000)	4.1457e^{-04} (0.2994)
a_1^E	−0.0314 (0.6168)	−0.0213 (0.7190)
a_2^E	−4.5138e^{-03} (0.9342)	0.0117 (0.8385)
a_3^E	−0.0150 (0.7641)	−0.0183 (0.7361)
a_4^E	−0.0915* (0.0626)	0.1172** (0.0302)
a_1^G	9.9931e^{-03} (0.7594)	−0.1187** (0.0473)
a_2^G	−4.2354e^{-03} (0.8159)	−0.0753 (0.1684)
a_3^G	0.0307 (0.5386)	5.1319e^{-05} (0.9993)
a_4^G	0.1665*** (0.0000)	0.1602*** (0.0052)
b_1^E	−0.0436 (0.7694)	0.2374*** (0.0031)
b_2^E	−0.0169 (0.8858)	0.0263 (0.7512)
b_3^E	0.2401 (0.1529)	0.0290 (0.7273)
b_4^E	0.0963 (0.5497)	−0.0231 (0.7826)
b_1^G	0.0319 (0.1248)	0.0122 (0.7209)
b_2^G	8.2978e^{-03} (0.6625)	0.0297 (0.3715)
b_3^G	−0.0207*** (0.0000)	−8.5926e^{-03} (0.8075)
b_4^G	−0.0213 (0.2609)	0.0108 (0.7445)
Panel B: Variance mean equation		
γ^E	5.5411e^{-05}***(0.0000)	4.7232e^{-06} (0.2228)
γ^G	6.4753e^{-06}*** (0.0000)	4.1025e^{-05}*** (0.0046)
α^E	0.0727** (0.0128)	0.0882** (0.0131)
α^G	0.1163*** (0.0024)	0.0906 (0.2868)
β^E	0.5497*** (0.0000)	0.8852***(0.0000)
β^G	0.5474*** (0.0000)	0.1002 (0.7311)
Panel C: Correlation		
θ_1	0.0364*** (0.0000)	0.0274 (0.3647)
θ_2	0.9622***(0.0000)	0.9171*** (0.000)

(*Continued*)

Table 3. (*Continued*)

	EUA and GB (EUR)	EUA and GB (Global)
Log likelihood	2232.539	2079.1
Akaike info criterion	−13.9282	−12.9661
Schwarz criterion	−13.7983	12.8363

Note: γ, α, and β are the estimated parameters of the univariate GARCH (1,1) model, and p-values are reported in the parentheses. θ_1 measures the short-term average adjustment ratio of the correlation coefficient between two indices, and θ_2 measures the long-term persistence of the correlation coefficient between two indices. *, **, and *** indicate significance at the 10%, 5%, and 1% levels, respectively.

Table 4. Descriptive statistics of correlation coefficients.

	Mean	Max	Min	Median	Std. Dev.
r^E & r^{GE}	−0.0345	0.2734	−0.2325	−0.0375	0.0846
r^E & r^{GG}	−0.0117	0.1265	−0.1601	−0.0015	0.0595

Note: r^E, r^{GE}, and r^{GG} refer to the returns of EUA, GB (EUR), and GB (Global).

correlations between EUA and GB indices. Two observations from the analysis of Table 4 and Figure 4 are given in the following.

The correlation between EUA and GB returns is slightly less than zero according to the mean values in Table 4. The standard deviation of their dynamic correlations is similar to zero, which implies that the volatility of EUA market has a lower effect on the volatility of the green bond market. Specifically, the correlation degree between EUA and GB (EUR) appears the highest on average based on the mean values. Moreover, the correlation between EUA and GB is highly time-varying both within the timeframe of one year (e.g., 2014, 2016, and 2019) and across the full sample period. The correlation coefficient oscillated at a low level at the beginning of 2014, but the coefficient declined from February 2014 to reach a peak of −0.04 (EUA and GB (EUR)) and −0.17 (EUA and GB (Global)) at the end of 2014. The slowdown in economic activity which has exacerbated the surplus of emission allowances and the carbon market crisis is reflected in the decline of the correlation coefficient at the beginning of 2014: it varies in the range of 0.01–0.12 from 2014 to 2018. Since the beginning of 2019,

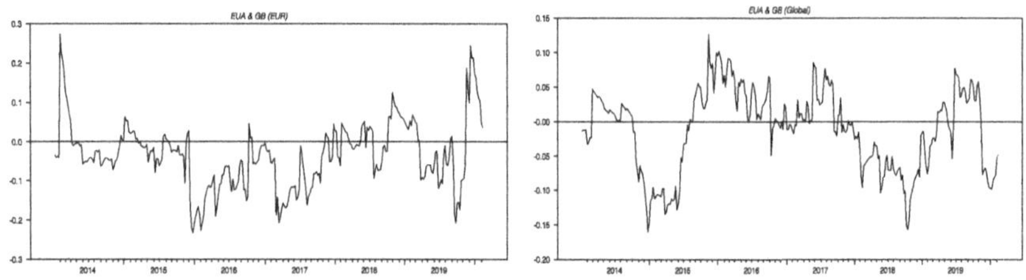

Figure 4. Dynamic conditional correlations of returns (2014–2020).

the dynamic conditional correlations between EUA and GB indices fluctuate around negative correlations. This can be explained by the good performance of the carbon market in 2019 due to the fall in emissions in electricity production and the commissioning of the Market Stability Reserve mechanism (MSR), a sort of central allowance bank, which is intended "to dry up" the excess supply of quotas and to support prices. When comparing Figures 1–3, we note that the correlation between markets tends to increase as the market becomes more volatile.

In addition, EUA and GB markets, confronted with uncertain information, reveal a risk complementarity effect. In particular, as shown in Figure 2, we can find that in addition to a few positive values, the dynamic conditional correlations between EUA and GB market returns are negative. This is an indication of consistency in the changes of time-varying variances between these two markets. Consequently, the risk separation may also change based on the rise or decline of the dynamic correlation coefficient.

4.3.2. *Spillover effects*

Table 5 provides the estimated results of the full BEKK-GARCH (1,1) model. The majority of conditional variances have been found to be statistically significant. This indicates that the current volatility of the EUA and GB markets depends on past shocks (a^{EE} and a^{GG}) and the past volatilities (b^{EE} and b^{GG}, except for GB (Global)). It implies that any unexpected events in the EUA market or green bond market can increase the implied volatility of their own markets.

Investigating the off-diagonal elements of matrices A and B, a^{ii} and b^{ij}, $i \neq j$, which capture cross-market effects, namely, shock and volatility spillovers, respectively, between EUA and GB indices, we find evidence of bidirectional shock transmission effects between EUA and GB (EUR), since

Table 5. Estimation results of BEKK-GARCH model.

Panel A: EUA and GB (EUR)

$$C=\begin{bmatrix} c^{EE} & 0 \\ c^{GE} & c^{GG} \end{bmatrix} \qquad A=\begin{bmatrix} a^{EE} & a^{EG} \\ a^{GE} & a^{GG} \end{bmatrix} \qquad B=\begin{bmatrix} b^{EE} & b^{EG} \\ b^{GE} & b^{GG} \end{bmatrix}$$

0.00189**	0	−0.2382***	0.0433**	0.9450***	0.0122
(0.0134)		(0.0001)	(0.0181)	(0.0000)	(0.1535)
0.0015***	0.0000	0.2570**	0.3115***	−0.2819***	0.8863***
(0.0000)	(0.9998)	(0.0475)	(0.0000)	(0.0000)	(0.0000)

Panel B: EUA and GB (Global)

$$C=\begin{bmatrix} c^{EE} & 0 \\ c^{GE} & c^{GG} \end{bmatrix} \qquad A=\begin{bmatrix} a^{EE} & a^{EG} \\ a^{GE} & a^{GG} \end{bmatrix} \qquad B=\begin{bmatrix} b^{EE} & b^{EG} \\ b^{GE} & b^{GG} \end{bmatrix}$$

0.0006	0	0.38505***	0.0753	0.8645***	−0.0154
(0.6735)		(0.0000)	(0.1541)	(0.0000)	(0.7423)
−0.0065***	−0.0000	−0.4019***	0.1951**	0.3897**	0.3265
(0.0000)	(0.9998)	(0.0006)	(0.0715)	(0.0152)	(0.2241)

Note: Log likelihood values are 2231.4752 and 2067.1764 for EUA and GB (EUR) and EUA and GB (Global) models, respectively. Values between parentheses are p-values.
*** and ** denote rejection of null hypothesis at 1% and 5% significance level, respectively.

the off-diagonal parameters, a^{EE} and a^{GG}, are both statistically significant. However, since b^{GE} is significantly negative, while b^{EG} is insignificant, past conditional volatility of GB (EUR) negatively affects the current level of EUA volatility.

Regarding the relationship between EUA and GB (Global), the significant a^{GE} coefficient estimate and insignificant a^{EG} parameter estimate suggest the existence of a unidirectional shock spillover from the GB (Global) market to the EUA market. Consequently, previous shocks of GB (Global) have a negative impact on the current volatility of EUA. Moreover, we find evidence of a one-way positive volatility spillover effect from GB (Global) to EUA since b^{GE} is significantly positive and b^{EG} is insignificant.

5. Conclusion

This chapter examines the interaction between the carbon market and the green bond market in Europe by comparing their price and volatility dynamics over a six-year period corresponding to the Phase III of EU ETS (2014–2019).

To the best of our knowledge, it is the first attempt to compare the price volatility dynamics of both the European green bond market and the European carbon market during this extensive period, where the EUA (auctioned) has an initial concrete price.[7]

Our methodological approach is based on two principles. First, we use the European prices of green bond and carbon indices rather than those of stock exchanges to track the evolution of prices and their returns. Second, we develop a VAR BEKK GARCH model that is revealed adequate to capture volatility shocks as well as volatility spillover effects from the European carbon market toward the European green bond market and vice versa.

Our contribution to the literature is three-fold. First, we report significant short-run and long-run persistence of shocks to the dynamic conditional correlation between European carbon and European green bond markets. By contrast, this persistence of shocks is insignificant in the short term and in the long term if we consider the case of European carbon and the Global green bond markets. Second, we find that the correlation coefficient between EUA and European green bond markets is really low approaching zero. It tends to be slightly negative from the year 2019 because of the good carbon market performance due to the drop in emissions of electricity producers and the use of the Market Stability Reserve, intended to reduce the excess supply of EUAs that maintain EUA prices at a certain level. Third, we document bidirectional shock transmission effects between EUA and GB (EUR) in contrast to the one-way positive volatility spillover effect from GB (Global) to EUA.

In sum, these results indicate that the green bonds issued in Europe may be used to hedge against the EUA carbon price (volatility) risk. This finding is important for investors and for fund managers who may purchase green bonds and EUA futures to create a portfolio of environmental assets. In this respect, these assets can be considered as complementary.

---

[7]Remind that the EU-ETS compliant firms received EUAs allocated on a free basis based on their historical emissions in Phase II (2008–2012) while most of EUAs were auctioned from Phase III (2013–2020), so EUAs have an initial concrete price in this period.

References

Alberola, E., Chevallier, J., and Chèze, B. (2008). Price drivers and structural breaks in European carbon prices: 2005–2007. *Energy Policy*, 36(2): 787–797.

Bachelet, M. J, Becchetti, L., and Manfredonia, S. (2019). The green bonds premium puzzle: The role of issuer characteristics and third-party verification. *Sustainability*, 11(4): 1–22.

Boutabba, M. A. (2009). Dynamic linkages among European carbon markets. *Economic Bulletin*, 29(2): 499–511.

CBI (2019). Green Bond Pricing in the Primary Market January - June 2019, Harrison, C.

Climate Bonds Initiative (CBI), 2020. Green Bonds Market Summary 2019. Research Report.

Chevallier, J., Ielpo, F., and Mercier, L. (2009). Risk aversion and institutional information disclosure on the European carbon market: A case study of the 2006 compliance event. *Energy Policy*, 37(1): 15–28.

Engle, R. F. and Kroner, K. F. (1995). Multivariate simultaneous generalized ARCH. *Econometric Theory*, 11: 122–150.

Engle, R. (2002). Dynamic conditional correlation: A simple class of multivariate generalized autoregressive conditional heteroskedasticity models. *Journal of Business and Economic Statistics*, 20(3): 339–350.

European Commission (2013). Commission Regulation No 389/2013 of 2 May 2013 establishing a Union Registry pursuant to Directive 2003/87/EC. Decisions No 280/2004/EC and No 406/2009/EC of the European Parliament and of the Council and repealing Commission Regulations (EU) No 920/2010 and No 1193/2011.

Febi, W., Schäfer, D., Stephan, A., and Sun, C. (2018). The impact of liquidity risk on the yield spread of green bonds. *Finance Research Letters*, 27: 53–59.

Lucia, J., Mansanet-Bataller M., and Pardo, A. (2015). Speculative and hedging activities in the European carbon market. *Energy Policy*, 82(C): 342–351.

Medina, V. and Pardo, A. (2013). Is the EUA a new asset class? *Quantitative Finance*, 13(4): 637–653.

Mirova (2018). Liquidity of the green bond market. Report published on February 20, 2018.

Mizrach, B. (2012). Integration of the global carbon markets. *Energy Economics*, 34(1): 335–349.

Monast, J. (2010). Climate change and financial markets: Regulating the trade side of cap and trade. *Environmental Law Reporter*, 40(1).

Neuhoff, K., Schopp, A., Boyd, R., Stelmakh, K., and Vasa, A. (2012). Banking of surplus emissions EUAs: Does the volume matter? Discussion Papers of DIW Berlin 1196.

Rannou, Y. and Barneto, P. (2016). Futures trading with information asymmetry and OTC predominance: Another look at the volume/volatility relations in the European carbon markets. *Energy Economics*, 53: 159–174.
Rannou, Y. (2019). Limit order books, uninformed traders and commodity derivatives: Insights from the European carbon futures. *Economic Modelling*, 81: 387–410.
Rittler, D. (2012). Price discovery and volatility spillovers in the EU emissions trading scheme: A high frequency analysis. *Journal of Banking and Finance*, 36(3): 774–785.
Stefan, M. and Wellenreuther, C. (2020). London vs. Leipzig: Price discovery of carbon futures during Phase III of the ETS. *Economics Letters*, 188, 108990.
Zerbib, O. D. (2019). The effect of pro-environmental preferences on bond prices: Evidence from green bonds. *Journal of Banking and Finance*, 98: 39–60.

© 2023 World Scientific Publishing Company
https://doi.org/10.1142/9789811260483_0005

Chapter 5

Innovative Public Sustainability-Oriented Financial Mechanisms: The Case of Social Impact Bonds

Vincenzo Buffa[*,†] **and Benjamin Le Pendeven**[*]

[*]*Audencia Business School, Nantes, France*

[†]*University of Angers, Angers, France*

Abstract

Emerged around 2010, social impact bonds (SIBs) are a multi-stakeholders' mechanism where private investors fund a social service experiment and are paid back by a public body if pre-defined social outcomes are achieved. This chapter presents a synthesis of the knowledge produced about SIBs by both academics and experts by the following: first, presenting the emergence of the SIB model in the UK and its diffusion; second, highlighting the different features of the SIB model according to rationales, goals, and risks; third, focusing on the different approaches and financial arrangements characterizing the SIB application around the world, before ending the chapter with a case study presentation focusing on the SIB development in France.

Keywords: Social impact bonds; financialization; social risks; impact investing

1. Introduction

The emergence of new social risks in modern societies (such as single-parent families, dependent seniors, youth unemployment, and refugees) that are largely ignored by the State, as well as pressure to keep social expenses under control, has provided rationales for several transformations in how social issues are addressed. The need to more efficiently use scarce public resources and the acceleration of previously implemented evidence-based policies in Western countries, where citizens and civil society demand more rationalized choices, are among the most visible expressions of this trend. Non-profit organizations have been identified, along with private sector organizations, as the main actors in operationalizing this demand based on the assumption that they are more innovative and responsive than the public sector.

One of the newest instruments that could accommodate these trends in the evolution of social policy are social impact bonds (SIBs). SIBs are a funding mechanism for experimental social services that aim to align the interests of private funders with those of non-governmental organizations (NGOs) or welfare organizations to test innovative social actions. The public sector repays the funders with interest if the pre-determined cost savings and social objectives are achieved. SIBs generally involve five different parties (Fraser *et al.*, 2018) which are as follows (see Figure 1):

- Commissioners who repay the program's investors if it succeeds (usually central or local public agencies).
- Service providers who deliver the commissioned services (NGOs or social firms).
- Investors who cover the costs of providing the service in exchange for an agreement with the commissioners to repay their initial investment plus a return if pre-defined target outcomes are achieved (private investors who are often philanthropists).
- Intermediaries who are involved in developing the project, organizing the contract with the commissioner, raising capital from the investors, and monitoring the project's delivery (mainly consulting firms that are specialized in social issues).
- Evaluators responsible for measuring the intervention's impacts.
- The target population (often accounting firms or university research teams).

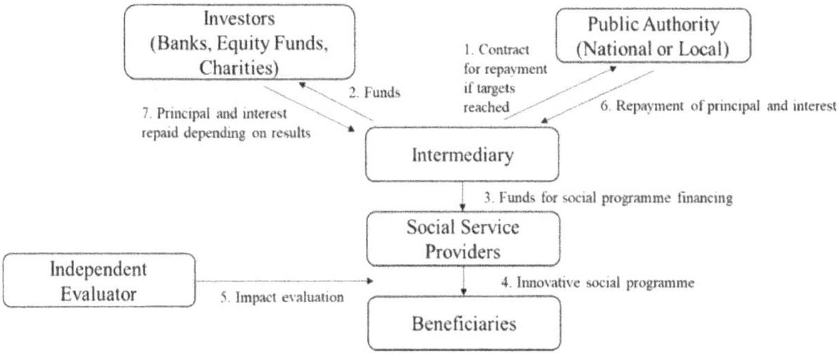

Figure 1. Typical SIB structure.

1.1. *The first experiments in the United Kingdom*

The SIB model was first developed by public and private UK-based organizations in the late 2000s. In 2007, Social Finance, a private organization, started working on the idea of special bond issues in which the funders of a specific social activity would be linked to the evaluation of results, which would trigger the related payments to investors (Social Finance, 2009). The idea was discussed in 2008 during the Prime Minister's Council on Social Action (CoSA). After this first discussion, the Cabinet Office, Her Majesty's Treasury, Social Finance, the Young Foundation, and New Philanthropy Capital started concretely testing the model.

Box 1. From contingent revenue bonds to social impact bonds.

The social impact bond model evolved from an earlier idea that never found a concrete application. In the late 1980s, the New Zealand-based economist Ronnie Horesh developed the idea of a special government bond issue dedicated to a social matter in which repayment would be linked to the evaluation of social outcomes. In this first configuration, the bond issue could have been traded in a financial market like any other financial product (Horesh, 2000).

(*Continued*)

(*Continued*)

In the 2000s, Ashoka, an organization that supports social entrepreneurs in developing countries, tried a so-called "Contingent Revenue Bond" in which the capital financing for work on the ground concerning a specific social activity would be provided by philanthropic foundations and reimbursed after an impact measurement (Social Finance, 2009). Combining these two ideas led to the creation of the social impact bond structure that Social Finance developed in 2007.

In 2010, the Peterborough Prison issued the first SIB in the world. The bond raised five million pounds from a group of social/philanthropic investors[1] to fund a pilot project that aimed to reduce rates of recidivism among short-term prisoners. The relapse or re-conviction rates of ex-prisoners released from Peterborough were to be compared with the relapse rates of a control group of prisoners over six years. If Peterborough's re-conviction rates were at least 7.5% below the rates of the control group for 3,000 ex-prisoners or 10% for 1,000 ex-prisoners, investors would receive a return that increases proportionally to the difference in relapse rates between the two groups. The return would be capped at 13% annually over an eight-year period. The Ministry of Justice and the City of Peterborough would pay the returns, and Social Finance (the first promoter of SIBs in the UK) was the intermediary for the contract. The program ended in 2015, two years before the seven years originally planned, due to a national reform which will extend similar rehabilitation services to all offenders in the country (the Transforming Rehabilitation program). In 2017, the Ministry of Justice announced that this first SIB successfully reduced recidivism and that the investors would receive repayment plus a return of 3% per year.

The emergence of SIBs can be explained in light of two main processes: they are presented as a hybrid instrument that seeks to develop evidence-based policy tools using a combination of some Impact Investing

[1]The investors in the Peterborough SIB were Barrow Cadbury Charitable Trust, Esmée Fairbairn Foundation, Friends Provident Foundation, the Henry Smith Charity, Johansson Family Foundation, Lankelly Chase Foundation, the Monument Trust, Panaphur Charitable Trust, the Tudor Trust, and Paul Hamlyn Foundation (https://golab.bsg.ox.ac.uk/knowledge-bank/project-database/hmp-peterborough-one-service/, accessed on 18/06/2020).

practices (such as private investors and risk-taking). Evidence-based policies focus on instruments that allow public authorities, in their contracts with private actors, to link payments for services with clearly defined objectives. Developed in English-speaking countries at the end of the 1990s, evidence-based policies were first used in the health field for payments related to outputs after having been tested in the field of social services with a payment-by-results approach (where payments are related to outcomes). In the case of SIBs, service providers are paid by the public authorities only if they are able to achieve the expected social results (such as a reduction in the incarceration rate and a reduction in nights spent sleeping rough for the homeless).

Impact investing practices were initiated in the United States and the United Kingdom by large non-profit and philanthropic organizations in the 2000s (Nicholls, Simon, & Gabriel, 2015). Since then, a diverse group of actors (foundations, think tanks, companies, and private funds) have been involved in their dissemination. In a 2015 article, Höchstädter and Scheck (2015) proposed a definition of this heterogeneous set of investment practices: "As to the definitional aspects of impact investing, the typical definition centers around two core elements: non-financial impact, typically in the form of social and/or environmental impact, and financial return, which requires at least the preservation of the invested principal but can allow for market-beating returns. Some of the definitions further require that the non-financial impact be intentional and/or measurable/being measured" (Höchstädter & Scheck, 2015, p. 460).

1.2. *The SIB landscape in 2020*

After the first Peterborough SIB in 2010, other SIBs have been developed in several English-speaking and European countries: the USA in 2012, the Netherlands in 2013, Australia in 2013, Belgium in 2014, Canada in 2014, and France in 2016. As of summer 2020, the SIB model has been tested in 26 countries with a total of 187 contracts signed, including 39 completed projects (see Figure 2) and with at least 69 projects under development. This movement has raised $441M to date, and the interventions have involved 1,711,902 beneficiaries.[2] The United Kingdom

[2]https://sibdatabase.socialfinance.org.uk/ and https://golab.bsg.ox.ac.uk/knowledge-bank/project-database/hmp-peterborough-one-service/, accessed on 18/06/2020.

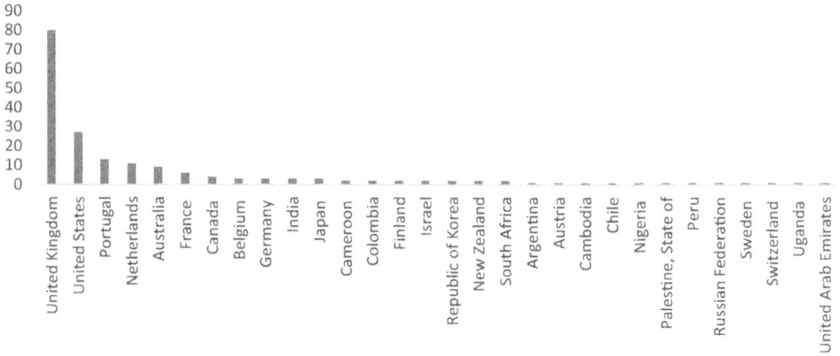

Figure 2. Number of social impact bonds launched per country between 2010 and June 2020.

remains the biggest market for SIBs with 80 contracts, followed by the United States (27), Portugal (13), and the Netherlands (11).

The SIB landscape is populated by a wide array of actors. On the investor side, a prominent role is played by UK-based impact investors. Bridges Fund Management, which has invested in 22 SIB projects, Big Issue Invest (eight SIB investments), and Big Society Capital (seven SIB investments) are among the most engaged investors in the SIB market.

The outcomes' funders are usually central government agencies (46 different central agencies have been involved in SIBs, such as the Ministry of Justice in the UK and Ministère de l'Agriculture in France), but we also find several local institutions, like city councils and regions (28, including Family and Community Services of the New South Wales Government in Australia and Actiris in the Brussels region in Belgium), and some clinical commissioning groups (six, including the Waltham Forest Clinical Commissioning Group and the Hillingdon Clinical Commissioning Group in the UK) among the outcomes funders. Social providers are the most diversified actors. While it is common for these providers to invest in more than one SIB (eight are engaged in two contracts), only one from the Netherlands has signed three SIBs (Buzinezzclub).

Concerning the social issues targeted (see Figure 3), SIBs have been analyzed by topic. The first two applications focused on criminal justice and recidivism, but subsequently, work-related activities have been the issues that received the most SIB funding with 44 contracts across the

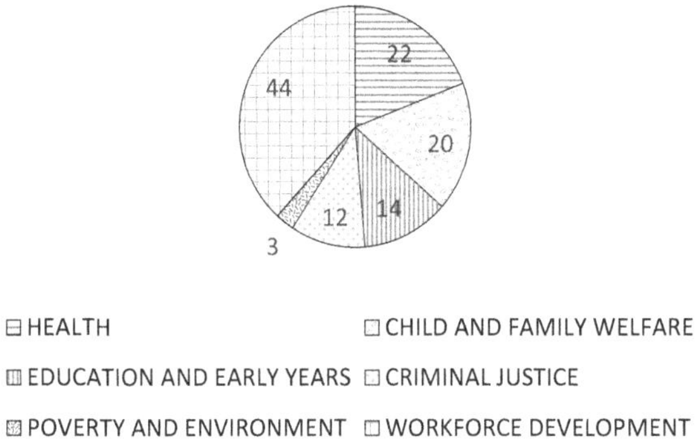

Figure 3. Social impact bonds by social sector in 2020

Source: Social Finance Database, https://sibdatabase.socialfinance.org.uk/, accessed on 29/06/2020.

world. We find also a strong focus on homelessness and housing policies with 23 contracts.[3]

2. The Social Impact Bond Model

2.1. *Rationales*

Over the past decade, a broad range of rationales have been invoked to justify the development of SIBs. They mainly concern inefficiencies encountered by the welfare sector and standard social public services related to both the administrative model and its financing structure. Some justifications specifically reflect financial actors' ambition to gain entry unto the impact investing market.

Starting from a general criticism of welfare services, which inefficiently address social problems, SIB promoters highlight the lack of collaboration in the design of social services and the lack of a culture of evaluation of welfare expenditures that is typical of public management of social issues. Notably, they denounce the "fee for service" approach that characterizes the dominant way that public authorities delegate the implementation of social services and thereby justify abandoning them.

[3] *Ibid.*

While the inefficiency of both social projects and the public financing model is profoundly linked to SIB's critique of the public welfare model, some purely financial reasons seem to arise: SIBs appeared during a period when there was strong pressure to limit or cut public social spending in some countries. Indeed, public institutions seem to have limited capacity or willingness to experiment with new social welfare practices. Moreover, players in the non-profit sector, who are increasingly involved in public action, also lack adequate and sustainable funding because of constraints in traditional public expenditure.

2.2. *Goals*

The main goals of the SIB mechanism are to address the supposed current inefficiencies in the delivery of public social services. The first goal concerns collaboration. SIBs are a new type of contract that links various stakeholders. Academic research shows how in the US the SIB implementation process brought early childhood education assistance into the policy and funding agenda by bringing together public and private actors, where they had previously worked mostly separately (Tse & Warner, 2018). Another important point about collaboration is the prominent role that investors played in accompanying social providers. That fact is highlighted in the SIBs for the homeless in London (DCLG, 2014, 2015) or for the DWP Innovation Fund in the UK where the direct "hands-on" involvement of investors in the management of projects was analyzed in the literature (Griffiths & Meinicke, 2014).

The second goal is to transfer risks from citizens and the public sector to private investors. This goal remains quite controversial in practice. All SIBs are organized to transfer risk to investors because they advance the working capital and could potentially lose all or part of their investment if the outcomes are not achieved. But we also find a large number of risk mitigation mechanisms. Notably, the US market offers many such mechanisms: the Rikers Island SIB, the first US SIB, has a 75% guarantee against loss for the senior investor (Goldman Sachs), and the Massachusetts recidivism SIB guarantee is provided by a philanthropic foundation. Other kinds of mitigation practices exist, like guarantees from the commissioner in the first Australian SIB.

Finally, the SIB is a tool for generating new solutions to social problems. For instance, the UK homelessness project promoted more individualized solutions for the homeless with a *Navigator* and spread a Housing

First approach, notably with social workers having a specific budget for each beneficiary. SIBs in education have pushed the development of early interventions aiming to take into account childhood educational issues. Nevertheless, we also find less innovative SIBs: for instance, the Innovation Fund SIB projects, the Essex SIB in the UK, or the Australian Newpin program, which finances programs that are already well established.

2.3. *Risks*

SIB development confronts three types of risk as follows:

- Operational risks that are related to the transaction costs and evaluation difficulties (Cooper, Graham, & Himick, 2016).
- Possible perverse and unintended effects associated with the SIB model may prevail such as "gaming" outcomes or beneficiaries of the program in order to achieve the objectives (Whitfield, 2015).
- The links between SIBs and other broader phenomena of contemporary capitalism: marketization and financialization (Dowling, 2017).

The first SIBs exhibited a limited capacity for economies of scale mainly due to separate contracts and the transaction costs characterizing each SIB. Moreover, the contracting process took a long time to complete, generating high transaction costs compared to the small size of SIBs. The evaluation methods used to measure SIBs' impact were another challenging issue similar to the implementation difficulties and high costs (Fox & Morris, 2019). The literature also highlights challenges with the effective attribution of social effects to the welfare program financed by an SIB (Vecchi & Casalini, 2019).

The SIB model can also generate uncertainty and information asymmetries between the public and private actors involved. The asymmetry may favor private actors who bias the contract by prioritizing financial actors' objectives. Public actors risk entering contracts that are too generous in terms of investors' remuneration (Saltman, 2017).

Among some participants, the SIB payment system may favor opportunistic behavior, which may also lead to pressure from private investors, or their intermediaries, to concentrate on easy-to-achieve social objectives. This risk could be also linked to social providers when they select the easiest beneficiaries to help or when they focus the social outcomes more strongly on the achievement of quantitative objectives set out in the contract (with the risk that some beneficiaries may leave the program too early) (Lowe *et al.*, 2019).

3. Diversity of Approaches, Diversity of Financial Arrangements

3.1. *Diversity of approaches*

The analysis of SIBs in operation indicates that there are three emerging structures that reflect differences in where governance and accountability lie: "direct," "intermediated," and "managed" (Bridges, 2017). These different configurations marginally change the positions of the different stakeholders according to the legal arrangement that links them, notably concerning the importance of service providers or the intermediary in the development of the deal. In addition, the performance management set-up changes according to the models (see Figures 4 and 5 for examples):

(1) *Direct*: The delivery contract is between the outcome funders and the service provider. Investors provide funds to the service provider to finance the delivery contract with returns linked to the successful delivery of outcomes. The service provider plays an important role, especially with internal performance management procedures.
(2) *Intermediated*: The delivery contract is between the outcome funders and investors who contract with the service provider(s). In this configuration, investors might be in closer contact with service providers. The intermediary also plays a role in developing the deal. This structure is particularly common in countries like the US or France, where SIBs are often developed without the presence of a Special Purpose Vehicle (SPV). In this case, senior lenders or lead investors are the first connection between providers and outcomes funders.
(3) *Managed*: The delivery contract is between the outcome funder and the prime contractor (often an intermediary) or the main contractor-owned SPV, which contracts with the service provider(s). In this arrangement, the intermediary has a major role in organizing the deal and follows the performance management process. The first SIBs developed in the UK, like the Peterborough SIB, were organized following this configuration, and an important role was played by the intermediary. The managed structure remains the most common way to structure SIBs.

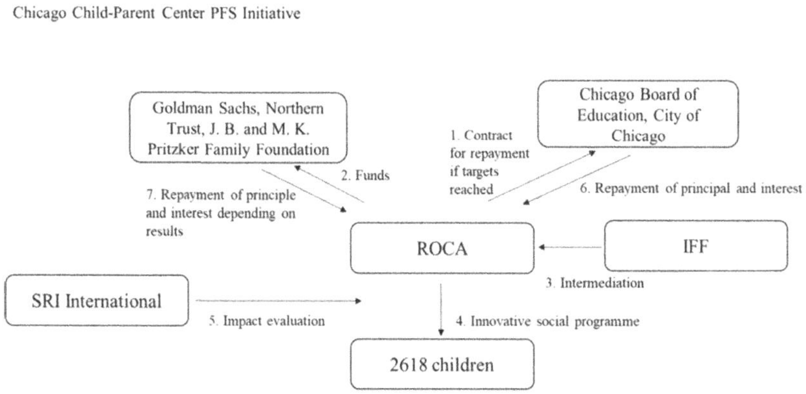

Figure 4. Intermediated social impact bond.

Source: Social Finance Database, https://sibdatabase.socialfinance.org.uk/, accessed on 29/06/2020.

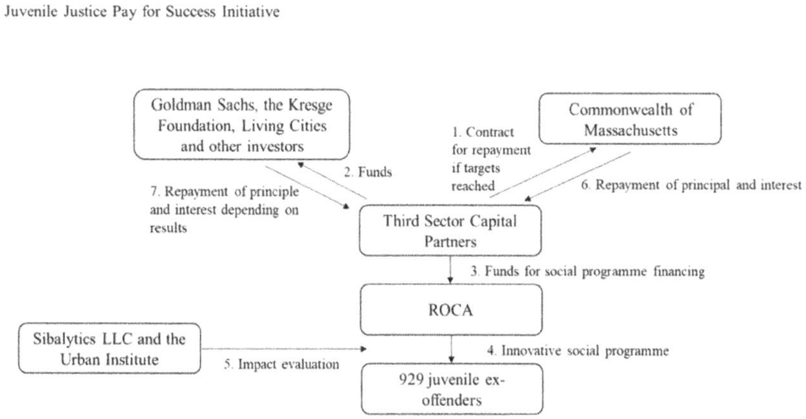

Figure 5. Managed social impact bond.

Source: Social Finance Database, https://sibdatabase.socialfinance.org.uk/, accessed on 29/06/2020.

The diversity of SIB approaches could also be reflected as differing in alignment with the core assumptions of the model (see Table 1). Starting with a fully compliant contract concerning the creation of a new social program that leads to an *ad hoc* social intervention that ensures flexibility in designing the program (Arena *et al.*, 2016), we can find different models of organizing SIBs (which are partially compliant or marginally

Table 1. Analysis of 20 SIB configurations according to their compliance with the standard SIB model.

Compliance-based configuration	Characteristics	Number of contracts
Full Compliance	Presence of an innovative and preventive program; transfer of risk to private investors; outcome evaluation	4
Partial Compliance	Funding the expansion of existing programs; inclusion of risk mitigation arrangements for private investors. Support for a particular intervention rather than the achievement of specific outcomes	9
Marginal Compliance	Funding the expansion of existing programs; inclusion of risk mitigation arrangements for private investors. Support for a particular intervention rather than the achievement of specific outcomes	7

Source: Arena *et al.* (2016).

compliant). The Peterborough SIB is a paradigmatic example of a model in which a special intervention is made by a network of social providers organized within the "One Service" created for the SIB. An example of the high level of flexibility and customization is the DWP Innovation Fund SIB, where an outcome rate had been suggested in advance by outcome funders that social providers and investors could then use when choosing the outcome that they want to include in the evaluation.

Partially compliant SIBs are those that only partially cohere with the SIB prototype. They are implemented at the local or regional level, so their ability to transform the public–private engagement paradigm remains limited. Consequently, the flexibility of the programs is often also limited.

Some contexts where welfare policies are strongly regionalized, like in the Netherlands, Belgium, or Germany, tend to develop localized interventions (sometimes only at the city level) that are difficult to scale up to broader contexts. The SIBs included in this group, compared to the prototype, are characterized by the inclusion of risk mitigation arrangements for private investors. A wide range of mitigation mechanisms exist like those presented in the previous section of the chapter (Section 2.2), but these practices seem to be of particular concern to the US SIB market.

The marginally compliant SIBs generally fund the expansion of an existing program and are usually carried out by a single service provider. Despite being based on a payment-by-results logic, the actors agree to support a particular intervention rather than the achievement of specific outcomes. Therefore, the capacity for service providers to organize the work as they would like is very limited.

3.2. *Diversity of financial arrangements*

The financial syndication of an SIB is also characterized by specific features, and it can take different forms in terms of the financial products employed (see Figure 6). SIBs are hybrid investments, which include debt, equity, and derivative components. SIBs operate over a fixed time period, similar to traditional bonds, and returns are contingent and vary according to the successful delivery of pre-agreed outcomes. Coupled with the lack of liquidity at present, this makes the risk profile of SIBs more linked to equity or quasi-equity products. Finally, given that investor returns are contingent on the successful delivery of outcomes, SIBs differ from bonds or equity investments and can be compared to a derivative product in which the financial values are linked to external and further evaluations.

The investment structures of existing SIBs vary in their similarity to debt (investment with a fixed repayment timeline and interest rate) and equity (repayment and interest are dependent on performance) (Gustafsson-Wright, Gardiner, & Putcha, 2015). Most of the deals have characteristics of both debt and equity, and offer variable returns based on outcomes as in an equity investment. Many deals have caps on returns and set interest

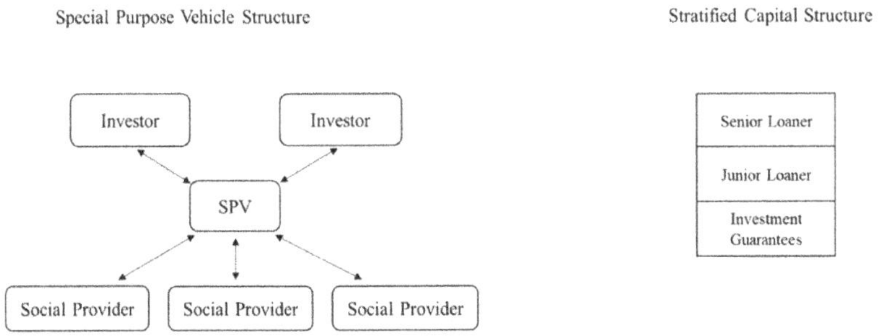

Figure 6. Different financial SIB configurations.

rates for given outcomes, which is more like debt. A common structure is represented by the development of an SPV that centralizes the invested capital and the financial flows linked to the outcome payments. In the case of an SIB, an SPV will receive capital from investors and receive payments from outcome funders based on the evaluation of the program. The first SIB in Peterborough was implemented via the creation of an SPV (in the form of a limited company). SPVs are the most common way for UK players to organize the financial structure of SIBs.

Other SIB deals have been financed by stratified capital structures which may include senior investment, subordinate investment, and investment guarantees. Junior investors are repaid after senior investors making the subordinated investment riskier. Subordinated investment is often structured as an equity investment, while senior investment is often structured as debt (Gustafsson-Wright *et al.*, 2015). Non-recoverable grants are not repaid, and investment guarantees are triggered to pay investors only if the program is unsuccessful. This configuration is used in many US-based SIBs, for example, the Massachusetts Juvenile Justice Initiative SIB in which the senior lender (Goldman Sachs) received 5% annual interest and junior lenders (Living Cities and the Kresge Foundation) received 2% annual interest.

4. Case Study: SIB Implementation in France

France joined the SIB movement in 2016. The publication of an interministerial call for proposals launched by Martine Pinville, Secretary of State for Trade, Crafts, Consumption and the Social and Solidarity Economy, with the strong support of the Ministry of Economic Affairs symbolizes the original way that France tried to translate the model to its institutional context. This call for proposals was issued under a centralized strategy with job-based welfare financing and a focus on social innovation instead of cost saving. Emerging from this first initiative of the Ministry of Economic Affairs and operationalized by the central agency dedicated to promoting the social economy, the SIB movement began in France as a governmental strategy for stimulating social innovation.

This first push to develop SIBs by the French public authorities led to about 60 proposals from diverse social organizations. The selection committee for the call for proposals finally chose 13 applications. Among these organizations, there were both small, emerging associations (a minority of the selected organizations), and well-established social providers, including some for-profit social enterprises. The project promoters then began to pursue a contract with the state with the support of the public authorities. However, the call for proposals did not lead to a public financial commitment, but only to a label attesting to the alignment of the proposed projects with the SIB model and the official beginning of a process to establish a contract.

Among the selected projects, the project led by the ADIE was the first SIB signed in France in May 2017. It was financed by a group of investors (BNPParibas, the Caisse des Dépôts, AG2R La Mondiale, the Fondation Avril, and Renault Mobiliz Invest) with ADIE as a service provider, the Ministère de la Transition Ecologique et Solidaire as the outcome payer, and the consulting firm KPMG as the evaluator. Since then, six other SIBs have been signed, all from the initial call for projects.

In 2019, two actions marked the development of SIBs in France, both at the initiative of the High Commission for the Social and Solidarity Economy and Social Innovation (HCESSIS). The first action was the creation of a working group chaired by the President of the ADIE to analyze the barriers in France for expanding SIBs. The second action was the announcement of the opening of an Outcome Fund ("Fonds de Paiement au Résultat," FPR) which should systematize and simplify the financial commitment of the public authorities in the French SIBs.

Box 2. The French Outcome Fund.

In September 2019, the High Commissioner for Social and Solidarity Economy and Social Innovation announced the creation of the first outcome fund for SIBs in France. This fund will centralize public funds dedicated to the SIBs in order to simplify contracting protocols. The fund will be endowed with €30 million divided into three axes of €10 million. Three central departments will be responsible for the various axes:

- The Ministry of Territorial Cohesion: fighting homelessness.
- The Ministry of Labour: Inclusion: lifting back-to-work barriers for unemployed people, including childcare and mobility.
- The Ministry of Ecological and Solidarity Transition: circular economy, fighting waste, promoting the reuse, and reduction of waste.

Table 2. French SIB characteristics.

Project leader	Social sector	Program	Investment	Max rate of return (%)	Investors	Duration	Benefi-ciaries
ADIE	Workforce development	Microcredit in rural areas	1.3 M€	4.6	BNPParibas; Caisse des Dépôts; Renault Mobiliz Invest; AG2R La Mondiale; Fondation Avril	2017–2013	320
IMPACT PARTENAI-RES	Workforce development	Creation of franchised businesses in working-class neighbor-hoods	0.8 M€	4.3	Bpifrance; Fonds Européen d'Investissement (FEI); BNPParibas; Française Des Jeux; Revital'emploi; Conseil Régional IDF	2017–2023	1,000
WIMOOV	Workforce development	Access to mobility advice for job seekers	0.7 M€	5.5	BNPParibas; Caisse des Dépôts; Ecofi Investissements; Aviva Impact Investing France	2018–2019	1,000

LA CRAVATE SOLIDAIRE	Workforce development	Access to professional outfits for people excluded from employment	0.4 M€	5	MAIF Investissement Social et Solidaire; Caisse des Dépôts; Aviva Impact Investing France; Inco Investissement	2019–2022	900
APPRENTIS D'AUTEUIL (two contracts)	Early childhood	Alternative to child placement	2.3 M€ + 2.5 M€	Below 4	BNPParibas; Caisse des Dépôts; IDES; FEI; Inco (only in the one contract)	2019–2026	68
FONCIÈRE CHÊNELET	Housing	Renovate housing for people in precarious situations	3.4 M€	—	—	2019–2025	—
ARTICLE 1	Education	Help agricultural high school students to pursue studies	1M€	3	BNPParibas; Citizen Capital	2018–2023	1,130

All the SIBs signed since 2017 have emerged from those projects labeled under the initial call for proposals (see Table 2 for details). Active employment policies have received most of the financing, but different approaches have been tested in order to help job seekers. For instance, rural access to microcredit, coaching and providing professional outfits, or facilitating the return to employment of people who lack transportation have been tested with employment-focused SIBs in France.

References

Arena, M., Bengo, I., Calderini, M., and Chiodo, V. (2016). Social impact bonds: blockbuster or flash in a pan? *International Journal of Public Administration*, 39(12): 927–939.

Cooper, C., Graham, C., and Himick, D. (2016). Social impact bonds: The securitization of the homeless. *Accounting, Organizations and Society*, 55: 63–82.

DCLG (2014). https://www.gov.uk/government/publications/qualitative-evaluation-of-the-london-homelessness-social-impact-bond-first-interim-report (accessed on 10/06/2020).

DCLG (2015). https://assets.publishing.service.gov.uk/government/uploads/system/uploads/attachment_data/file/414787/Qualitative_evaluation_of_the_London_homelessness_SIB.pdf (accessed on 10/06/2020).

Dowling, E. (2017). In the wake of austerity: Social impact bonds and the financialisation of the welfare state in Britain. *New Political Economy*, 22(3): 294–310.

Fox, C. and Morris, S. (2019). Evaluating outcome-based payment programmes: Challenges for evidence-based policy. *Journal of Economic Policy Reform*, 1–17.

Fraser, A., Tan, S., Lagarde, M., and Mays, N. (2018). Narratives of promise, narratives of caution: A review of the literature on Social Impact Bonds. *Social Policy & Administration*, 52(1): 4–28.

Griffiths, A. and Meinicke, C. (2014). Introduction to social impact bonds and early intervention. *Early Intervention Foundation*, 28. https://www.eif.org.uk/resource/social-impact-bonds-and-early-intervention (accessed on 10/06/2020).

Gustafsson-Wright, E., Gardiner, S., and Putcha, V. (2015). The potential and limitations of impact bonds: Lessons from the first five years of experience worldwide. Global Economy and Development at Brookings.

Höchstädter, A. K. and Scheck, B. (2015). What's in a name: An analysis of impact investing understandings by academics and practitioners. *Journal of Business Ethics*, 132(2): 449–475.

Horesh, R. (2000). Injecting incentives into the solution of social problems: Social policy bonds. *Economic Affairs*, 20(3): 39–42.

Lowe, T., Kimmitt, J., Wilson, R., Martin, M., and Gibbon, J. (2019). The institutional work of creating and implementing Social Impact Bonds. *Policy & Politics*, 47(2): 353–370.

Nicholls, A., Simon, J., and Gabriel, M. (2015). *New Frontiers in Social Innovation Research.* Springer Nature.

Saltman, K. J. (2017). The promise and realities of Pay for Success/Social Impact Bonds. *Education Policy Analysis Archives*, 25: 59.

Social Finance (2009). *Social Impact Bonds: Rethinking Finance for Social Outcomes*. London: Social Finance. https://www.socialfinance.org.uk/resources/publications/social-impact-bonds-rethinking-finance-social-outcomes (accessed on 10/06/2020).

Tse, A. E. and Warner, M. E. (2018). The razor's edge: Social impact bonds and the financialization of early childhood services. *Journal of Urban Affairs*, 1–17.

Vecchi, V. and Casalini, F. (2019). Is a social empowerment of PPP for infrastructure delivery possible? Lessons from Social Impact Bonds. *Annals of Public and Cooperative Economics*, 90(2): 353–369.

© 2023 World Scientific Publishing Company
https://doi.org/10.1142/9789811260483_0006

Chapter 6

A Multi-Criteria Comparison of Financial Performance between Sustainable and Non-Sustainable Companies

Marianna Eskantar[*], Michalis Doumpos[*], Aggeliki Liadaki[*], and Constantin Zopounidis[*,†]

[*]*Technical University of Crete, Chania, Greece*

[†]*Audencia Business School, Nantes, France*

Abstract

The purpose of this study is to examine whether Greek companies that apply Environmental, Social, and Governance (ESG) criteria in their activities show better financial performance than companies that do not apply such criteria. The analysis considers 10 financial indicators for a sample of 56 Greek companies. With the application of the multi-criteria UTADIS method, the differences between the two groups of companies are examined. The results show that companies that apply ESG criteria seem to show a better financial performance in certain financial ratios, while the other indicators show indifference between the two categories of companies.

Keywords: ESG performance; corporate social responsibility; financial performance; multi-criteria analysis; ESG criteria; financial indicators

1. Introduction

The trend towards environment, social, and governance (ESG) practices has evolved into an issue of major importance for various stakeholders, such as employees, local communities, regulators, shareholders, investors, customers, and suppliers, among others (Jasch, 2006). For instance, shareholders and investors use these practices as a means of risk management while for businesses it has become an emerging part of their competitive strategy (Galbreath, 2013). However, in the academic literature, sustainable practices related to the three pillars of ESG have been discussed as this issue has occupied the academic community for over 50 years (Eccles & Viviers, 2011), proving the enormous importance of this issue.

ESG indicators quantify aspects of corporate performance, which are not covered by accounting data (Bassen & Kovács, 2008). For instance, financial statements do not provide information about the value of various qualitative issues, such as reputation, quality, security, workplace culture, and a range of other issues that are crucial for creating long-term value for shareholders and investors (Galbreath, 2013).

Companies now understand that disclosing ESG data is vital. ESG activities can enhance management practices resulting in improved company financial performance (Tarmuji, Maelah, & Tarmuji, 2016). This is supported by empirical research, with various studies demonstrating the positive effect that ESG has on the financial performance of companies, although the exact extent of this effect is still unknown.

Environmental aspects are the first of the three pillars in the ESG framework. Environmental issues involve among others air emissions, waste, hazardous material, water consumption, and biodiversity. The company must use proper practices to its environmental footprint, optimize the use of natural resources in the production process, and employ innovative technologies to improve its environmental performance. Stronger environmental performance could improve the value of a firm, while appropriate environmental practices can create cost savings and avoid negative business implications due to environmental issues (International Federation of Accountants, 2005).

The social practices of companies cover issues like corporate social responsibilities (financial, legal, ethical, and discretion), corporate social responsiveness (defense, response, residence, and pre-action), and social issues (consumers, environment, product safety, differentiation/employee safety, and shareholders). Social performance refers to the shaping of the principles of social responsibility, social response processes and policies, programs, and tangible results of a business organization, as they relate to the social relations of the company (Wood, 2010). Corporate Social Performance (CSP) can also be defined as a structure that emphasizes a company's responsibilities to many stakeholders, such as employees and the community, in addition to its traditional responsibilities to financial shareholders. As a result, companies with high social returns find it easier to attract eligible employees (Turban & Greening, 1997). Social responsibility and responsiveness involve a range of issues, such as product responsibility, human rights, diversity and opportunities, quality of employment, health and safety, training and development.

Governance is the third pillar of ESG. The implementation of a proper corporate governance system is of major importance for the performance of a company (Fama & Jensen, 1983). Corporate governance enhances business prosperity and corporate responsibility with the goal of recognizing the long-term value of shareholders, while also accounting for the interests of all stakeholders. The management board is of fundamental importance in the context of corporate governance (Said, Hj Zainuddin, & Haron, 2009). Moreover, shareholders must be treated equally and have certain privileges. Corporate governance means that the company has special systems for managing sustainability (Klettner, Clarke, & Boersma, 2014). Several studies have shown that corporate governance affects corporate performance (Giannarakis, Konteos, & Sariannidis, 2014; Zabri, Ahmad, & Wah, 2016).

The financial materiality of ESG factors is a key issue. Financial management focuses on a series of economic principles to maximize wealth, i.e., the total value of a firm. Maximizing the wealth of a firm means achieving as much profit as possible with the least risk. Proper management and decision-making result in higher expected returns and lower risk, a fact recognized by investors, for whom the value of the business is likely to increase. Therefore, financial analysis supports corporate management in designing and implementing strategies that strengthen the financial health of a company and create long-term value for shareholders. Therefore, the examination of the relationship between ESG practices and financial performance is of major research and practical interest. Existing studies have shown that ESG practices can have a positive effect on the financial soundness of the firms (Aragón-Correa *et al.*, 2008).

Despite the rich international literature on the relationship between ESG and corporate financial performance, such studies are lacking for

Greece, which has faced a severe economic crisis since 2009. The adverse economic environment has placed a significant burden on firms, thus affecting the adoption of new business practices such as ESG. However, recently there has been a growing interest among Greek companies in adopting the principles of ESG. This study presents a first attempt to analyze the financial characteristics of Greek companies that follow the principles of ESG and compare them to companies that do not. The analysis is based on a multi-criteria decision-making approach, which allows the analysis of the differences between the two groups of companies. Empirical results are reported for a sample of 56 large Greek companies.

The rest of the chapter is organized as follows. Section 2 outlines the multi-criteria methodology used in the analysis, whereas Section 3 describes the application data. Section 4 is devoted to the presentation and discussion of the results. Finally, Section 5 concludes the chapter and presents some future research directions.

2. Multi-criteria Methodology: The UTADIS Method

The UTADIS multi-criteria method comes from the preference disaggregation approach of the multi-criteria decision aid (MCDA). Its first presentation was made in the early 1980s by Jacquet-Lagreze and Siskos (1982) and Zopounidis and Doumpos (1999).

According to this method, initially, a reference set is used, consisting of alternatives (e.g., firms) that are evaluated by the decision maker and classified into performance categories according to the purpose of the analysis. The categories (classes) are defined in an ordinal manner such that $C_1 \succ C_2 \succ \ldots \succ C_Q$, where $\succ$ denotes the preference relation between the classes.

Using linear programming techniques, an additive function is developed in order to achieve the classification of the alternatives in the groups to which they belong with the lowest classification error. The additive value model has the following form:

$$V(a)=\sum_{j=1}^{m} v_j[g_j(a)] \tag{1}$$

where g_1, g_2, …, g_m are the evaluation criteria, $g_j(a)$ is the description of alternative a on criterion g_j, $v_j[g_j(a)]$ denotes the marginal value of alternative a on criterion g_j, and $V(a)$ is the global value (i.e., performance score) of alternative a. With the additive model (1), the assignment of an alternative a to one of the predefined categories can be performed through the following classification rules:

$$t_\ell < V(a) < t_{\ell-1} \Rightarrow a \in C_\ell \tag{2}$$

where $t_0 = 0 < t_1 < \ldots < t_{Q-1} < t_Q = 1$ are thresholds that distinguish the categories.

To construct the additive model using the data and classifications of the reference alternatives, for each evaluation criterion g_j, its range $[g_{j*}, g_j^*]$, defined by the least and the most preferred values of the criterion, is divided into $b_j - 1$ intervals $[g_j^k, g_j^{k+1}], k = 1, 2, \ldots, b_j - 1$. The aim is to estimate the marginal values at each of these points. Suppose that the evaluation of an alternative on a criterion g_j is $g_j(a) \in [g_j^k, g_j^{k+1}]$. Then, its marginal value is specified through linear interpolation:

$$v_j\left[g_j(a)\right] = v_j\left(g_j^k\right) + \frac{g_j(a) - g_j^k}{g_j^{k+1} - g_j^k}\left[v_j\left(g_j^{k+1}\right) - v_j\left(g_j^k\right)\right] \tag{3}$$

The marginal value functions are assumed to be monotone. Thus, for a benefit criterion g_j (e.g., financial profitability), the following constraints should be satisfied:

$$v_j(g_j^{k+1}) - v_j\left(g_j^k\right) \geq 0, \forall k$$

The monotonicity constraints are simplified by setting $w_{jk} = v_j(g_j^{k+1}) - v_j(g_j^k) \geq 0$. With this transformation, the weights of each criterion can be computed as $v_j(g_j^*) = \sum_{p=1}^{b_j-1} w_{jp}$, whereas the marginal value of an alternative a on criterion g_j according to (3) is rewritten as follows:

$$v_j[g_j(a)] = \sum_{p=1}^{k-1} w_{ip} + \frac{g_j(a) - g_j^k}{g_j^{k+1} - g_j^k} w_{jk} \tag{4}$$

With this modeling of the additive model (1), there are two possible classification errors with respect to rules (2). On the one hand, the overestimation error $\sigma^+(a)$ involves cases where an alternative is classified to a class of lower performance than the class that it belongs to (e.g., an alternative is classified in class C_2 while belonging to class C_1). On the other hand, an underestimation error occurs when an alternative is classified to a higher-performing class than the class that it belongs to (e.g., an alternative is classified in class C_1 while belonging to class C_2).

Introducing the above-mentioned errors to the classification rules (2) leads to the following inequalities for each reference alternative a:

$$\begin{aligned} &\sum_{j=1}^{m} v_j\left[g_j(a)\right] + \sigma^+(\alpha) \geq t_\ell + \delta \qquad \forall a \in C_\ell, \ell = 1,\ldots,Q-1 \\ &\sum_{j=1}^{m} u_j\left[g_j(a)\right] + \sigma^-(\alpha) \leq t_{\ell-1} - \delta \quad \forall a \in C_\ell, \ell = 2,\ldots,Q \end{aligned} \tag{5}$$

where δ is a small positive real constant used to ensure the strict inequalities in the classification rules (3). These inequalities are used in the following linear programming problem for inferring the additive value model (1) from a set of assignment examples:

$$\begin{aligned} \min \quad & \sum_{\ell=1}^{Q} \frac{1}{n_\ell} \sum_{a \in C_\ell} [\sigma^+(a) + \sigma^-(a)] \\ \text{subject to} \quad & (4), (5) \\ & \sum_{j=1}^{m} \sum_{p=1}^{b_j-1} w_{jp} = 1 \\ & w_{jp}, t_\ell, \sigma^+(a), \sigma^-(a) \geq 0 \end{aligned}$$

where n_ℓ represents the number of reference alternatives from class C_ℓ. This linear program minimizes the overall weighted classification error,[1] subject to constraints (4) and (5), which define the additive model and the classification errors, whereas the third constraint ensures that the additive model is scaled between 0 and 1 (i.e., the weights of the criteria sum up to 1).

3. Application

In this study, the multi-criteria methodology UTADIS was used to examine the differences between large Greek companies that adopt the principles of

[1]The total weighted error is used to account for cases whether there is an imbalance in the number of alternatives from each class, which could lead to biased classification results.

ESG and others that do not. The data used in the analysis involve the financial performance of the companies measured through a set of financial ratios derived from the financial statements of the companies.

3.1. *Data*

The data used to carry out the analysis concern 56 large Greek companies and they involve two samples of firms. The training sample consists of 39 large Greek companies (approximately 70% of the data), whereas the test sample includes the remaining 17 companies. The purpose of considering the test sample is to evaluate the predictability of the model.

The sample is classified into two classes: (i) companies that apply ESG criteria (class C_1) and (ii) companies that do not apply ESG criteria (class C_2). The sample of 56 companies contains 28 companies that belong to class C_1, i.e., that apply ESG criteria, and 28 companies from class C_2, i.e., that do not apply ESG criteria. Tables 1 and 2 show the names of all the companies in the sample as well as the industry to which they belong.

3.2. *Financial criteria*

The purpose of financial analysis is to assess the solvency, liquidity, and profitability of companies through the examination of various financial ratios that quantify the financial situation of a company.

The data used for this study are based on a financial analysis carried out for the year 2019. The 56 companies were evaluated based on 10 financial criteria. In this study, we consider the following financial ratios, as described in Zopounidis (2013):

G1. *Financial profitability* (FP): It shows whether the goal of achieving a satisfactory result for shareholders has been achieved (i.e., return on equity):

Net income after taxes/Equity

G2. *Industrial profitability* (IP): It measures the operational profitability of a firm and its ability to use its assets in an efficient manner for generating strong operating profits (i.e., return on assets):

Earnings before interest and taxes/Total asset

Table 1. Companies that apply ESG criteria.

No	Company Name	Sector
1	Alumil	Metal production
2	Elval Halcor	Metal production
3	Enel	Energy
4	Eunice Trading	Energy
5	European Reliance	Insurance
6	Genesis Pharma	Pharmaceutical
7	Hellas Gold	Mining
8	Hellenic Petroleum	Oil and gas
9	Hellenic Telecommunications Organization (HTO)	Telecommunications
10	Heracles	Cement production
11	Hygeia	Health services
12	Imersys	Mining
13	Megadis	Hygiene products
14	Merck	Healthcare research
15	Mitsis	Hotels
16	Motor Oil	Oil and gas
17	Mytilineos	Industrial conglomerate
18	Greek Organisation of Football Prognostics (OPAP)	Sports betting
19	Paegae	Logistics
20	Polyeco	Waste management
21	Public Gas Corporation (DEPA)	Energy
22	Public Power Corporation (PPC)	Energy
23	Quest Holdings	Information technology
24	Terna Energy	Energy
25	Toyota Hellas	Automotive distribution
26	Uni Pharma	Pharmaceutical
27	Volterra	Energy
28	Volton	Energy

G3. *Asset turnover* (AT): It indicates how intensively a company uses its assets to generate revenue:

$$\text{Turnover/Total assets}$$

Table 2. Companies that do not apply ESG criteria.

No	Company Name	Sector
1	Bayer	Chemical and pharmaceutical
2	Cretan Holidays	Travel
3	Vianex	Pharmaceuticals
4	Sklavenitis	Retail
5	Eltrak	Manufacturing
6	ENET Solutions	Technology
7	Forthnet	Telecommunications
8	Fraport Regional Airports of Greece A[a]	Air transport
9	Fraport Regional Airports of Greece B[b]	Air transport
10	Karelia Tobacco Company Inc	Tobacco
11	Anonimi Naftiliaki Etairia Kritis (ANEK)	Shipping
12	ION	Food industry
13	Piraeus Port Authority (PPA)	Marine facilities
14	Jumbo	Retail
15	Papastratos	Tobacco
16	Mellon Technologies	Hardware and software technology
17	Plaisio	Electronics retailing
18	Nestle	Food industry
10	Plastika Kritis	Plastics industry
20	Novartis International	Pharmaceuticals
21	Pfizer Inc.	Pharmaceuticals
22	Praktiker	Retail
23	SYN.KA Supermarkets	Retail
24	SGB S.A.	Retail
25	Vodafone	Telecommunications
26	Helliniki Halyvourgia	Steel industry
27	Wind	Telecommunications
28	ANEDIK Kritikos	Retail

Notes: [a]Fraport Greece consists of two concession companies with their corporate seats in Athens, one company for Cluster A named "Fraport Regional Airports of Greece A S.A." ("Fraport Greece A").
[b]Fraport Greece consists of two concession companies with their corporate seats in Athens, one company for Cluster B named "Fraport Regional Airports of Greece B S.A." ("Fraport Greece B").

G4. *Equity turnover* (ET): It indicates whether the equity is employed in an efficient manner to generate revenue:

Turnover/Equity

G5. *Financial expenses ratio* (FE): This last ratio represents the burden that a company faces due to financing expenses in relation to its sales:

Financial expenses/Turnover

G6. *Total debt capacity* (TDC): It represents the ratio between the liabilities and the assets of the company, with higher values indicating a heavy debt burden:

Total liabilities/Total assets

G7. *Long-term debt capacity* (LDC): In contrast to the TDC ratio, LDC focuses on the reliance of a company on long-term debt to finance its activities in relation to the total long-term capital sources (i.e., equity and long-term debt):

Equity/(Equity + Long-term liabilities)

G8. *Current ratio* (CR): It is a liquidity indicator indicating the ability of a company to cover its short-term liabilities through its current assets:

Current assets/Current liabilities

G9. *Quick ratio* (QR): It extends the CR by excluding inventories from the measurement of a company's liquidity status because inventories often do not generate cash in a timely manner to cover short-term obligations:

(Current assets – Inventories)/Current liabilities

G10. *Working capital ratio* (WC): This ratio indicates the ability of a firm to cover its fixed assets through long-term sources of capital (long-term liabilities and equity):

(Equity + Long-term liabilities)/Net fixed assets

4. Results

In this section, we present the results of the UTADIS method. We start the analysis with the classification performance of the developed model. Figure 1 presents the classification accuracy results for the training and test sets. It is evident that the accuracy of the results for the companies that apply ESG criteria (i.e., companies belonging to class C_1) is quite high (81% and 86% for the training and test sets, respectively). Therefore, we can conclude that indeed the companies that apply ESG criteria show better financial performance than companies that do not apply ESG criteria. On the other hand, it is observed that the companies that do not apply ESG criteria (i.e., companies from class C_2) do not show very high accuracy (72% and 70% for the training and test sets, respectively). The overall accuracy of the results for both training and test samples ranges at satisfactory levels, namely, 77% and 76%, respectively. The performance of the model was also tested with the area under the receiver operating characteristic curve (AUC), which was found to be 73% and 70% for the training and test samples, respectively.[2]

Regarding the contribution of the financial ratios in the model, Table 3 presents the weights of financial ratios, which reveal that ratios G2, G6, and G10 are the most important for the performance of the companies. Figure 2 illustrates the marginal value functions of the three most important ratios, namely, the working capital ratio (G10), total debt capacity (G6), and industrial profitability (G2), with weights of 51.24%, 40.8%, and 6.51%, respectively.

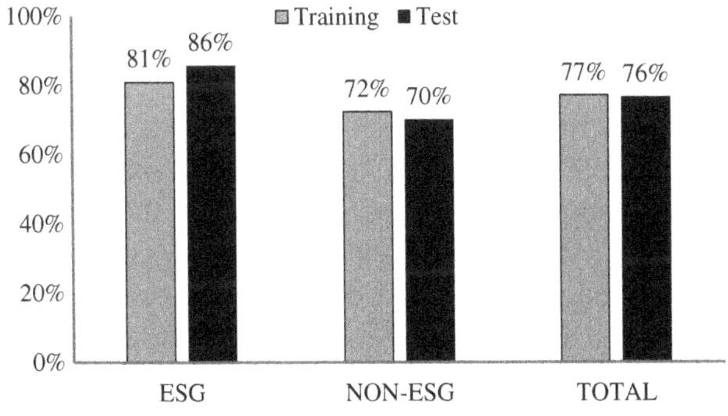

Figure 1. Classification accuracies.

[2]The closer the AUC results are to 1, the higher the discriminating power of the model.

Table 3. The weights of the financial ratios.

Ratio	**Weight (%)**	**Ratio**	**Weight (%)**
G1	0.12	G6	40.80
G2	6.51	G7	0.78
G3	0.15	G8	0.12
G4	0.14	G9	0.11
G5	0.04	G10	51.24

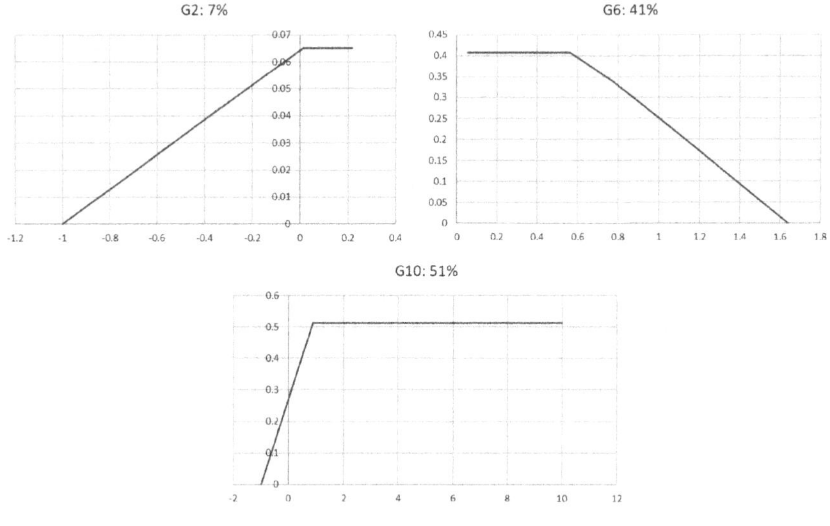

Figure 2. Marginal values of the most important criteria.

Based on the developed model, Table 4 presents the evaluations for the top and bottom five companies in the sample. We observe that three out of the top five performing companies are those that apply ESG criteria. For the other two companies, we note that they perform satisfactorily, and it would be good to pursue an ESG policy that would improve their overall (not only financial) image. On the contrary, four out of the bottom five companies are those that do not apply ESG criteria. The only company that presents a bad financial image is Hellas Gold and this is because the financial performance is mediocre to poor.

Table 4. Evaluation results for the top and bottom five performing companies.

Firms	Global Value	Estimated Class	Original Class
Top 5			
Toyota Hellas	0.992	C_1	C_1
Motor Oil	0.991	C_1	C_1
Karelia	0.991	C_1	C_2
Europaiki Pisti	0.991	C_1	C_1
Pfizer Inc.	0.991	C_1	C_2
Bottom 5			
Halivourgia	0.703	C_2	C_2
Hellas Gold	0.626	C_2	C_1
Anonimi Naftiliaki Etairia Kritis	0.593	C_2	C_2
Forthnet	0.265	C_2	C_2
Novartis International	0.116	C_2	C_2

5. Concluding Remarks and Future Research

This research focused on the investigation of the relationship between ESG criteria and financial performance in Greek companies. To our best knowledge, this is the first research that carries out such an analysis for Greek data. The analysis examined whether companies that apply ESG criteria perform better (in financial terms) than companies that do not apply ESG criteria. The examination of the present problem was carried out with the UTADIS multi-criteria methodology.

Two main findings can be identified from the obtained results. First, it seems that companies that apply ESG criteria show better financial performance. But a small percentage shows that companies that do not apply ESG criteria can have just as good a financial performance. In addition, the conclusion that can be drawn is that the financial ratios that show significant differences between these two categories of companies are the working capital ratio, industrial profitability (return on assets), and total debt capacity. That is, these indicators show the portion of fixed assets used to finance the operating cycle of the business, control the performance of the funds invested by the shareholders, and reveal the degree of coverage of the assets (total assets of the company from the loan funds).

In conclusion, the Greek companies that apply ESG criteria seem to be slowly taking the lead from the rest. It is a pleasant fact since Greece is very immature in this area and the efforts made are significant. The next step to be done is to perform a similar analysis for more years for stronger results. It will also be interesting to evaluate companies on specific ESG criteria as well as the evaluation of financial ratios. Thus, the analysis will be more valid in terms of evaluating companies that make the same level of effort in terms of ESG criteria. Moreover, examining the Greek evidence in comparison to similar international studies would also be interesting.

References

Aragón-Correa, J. A., Hurtado-Torres, N., Sharma, S., and García-Morales, V. J. (2008). Environmental strategy and performance in small firms: A resource-based perspective. *Journal of Environmental Management*, 86(1): 88–103. https://doi.org/10.1016/j.jenvman.2006.11.022.

Bassen, A. and Kovács, A. M. (2008). Environmental, social and governance key performance indicators from a capital market perspective. *Zeitschrift Für Wirtschafts- Und Unternehmensethik*, 9(2): 182–192. https://doi.org/10.5771/1439-880X-2008-2-182.

Eccles, N. S. and Viviers, S. (2011). The origins and meanings of names describing investment practices that integrate a consideration of ESG issues in the academic literature. *Journal of Business Ethics*, 104(3): 389–402. https://doi.org/10.1007/s10551-011-0917-7.

Fama, E. F. and Jensen, M. C. (1983). Separation of ownership and control. *The Journal of Law and Economics*, 26(2): 301–325. https://doi.org/10.1086/467037.

Galbreath, J. (2013). ESG in focus: The Australian evidence. *Journal of Business Ethics*, 118(3), 529–541. https://doi.org/10.1007/s10551-012-1607-9.

Giannarakis, G., Konteos, G., and Sariannidis, N. (2014). Financial, governance and environmental determinants of corporate social responsible disclosure. *Management Decision*, 52(10): 1928–1951. https://doi.org/10.1108/MD-05-2014-0296.

International Federation of Accountants. (2005). *Environmental Management Accounting: International Guidance Document*.

Jacquet-Lagreze, E. and Siskos, J. (1982). Assessing a set of additive utility functions for multicriteria decision-making, the UTA method. *European Journal of Operational Research*, 10(2): 151–164. https://doi.org/10.1016/0377-2217(82)90155-2.

Jasch, C. (2006). Environmental management accounting (EMA) as the next step in the evolution of management accounting. *Journal of Cleaner Production*, 14(14): 1190–1193. https://doi.org/10.1016/j.jclepro.2005.08.006.

Klettner, A., Clarke, T., and Boersma, M. (2014). The governance of corporate sustainability: Empirical insights into the development, leadership and implementation of responsible business strategy. *Journal of Business Ethics*, 122(1): 145–165. https://doi.org/10.1007/s10551-013-1750-y.

Said, R., Hj Zainuddin, Y., and Haron, H. (2009). The relationship between corporate social responsibility disclosure and corporate governance characteristics in Malaysian public listed companies. *Social Responsibility Journal*, 5(2): 212–226. https://doi.org/10.1108/17471110910964496.

Tarmuji, I., Maelah, R., and Tarmuji, N. H. (2016). The impact of environmental, social and governance practices (ESG) on economic performance: Evidence from ESG score. *International Journal of Trade, Economics and Finance*, 7(3): 67–74. https://doi.org/10.18178/ijtef.2016.7.3.501.

Turban, D. B. and Greening, D. W. (1997). Corporate social performance and organizational attractiveness to prospective employees. *Academy of Management Journal*, *40*(3), 658–672. https://doi.org/10.2307/257057.

Wood, D. J. (2010). Measuring corporate social performance: A review. *International Journal of Management Reviews*, 12(1): 50–84. https://doi.org/10.1111/j.1468-2370.2009.00274.x.

Zabri, S. M., Ahmad, K., and Wah, K. K. (2016). Corporate governance practices and firm performance: Evidence from top 100 public listed companies in Malaysia. *Procedia Economics and Finance*, 35: 287–296. https://doi.org/10.1016/S2212-5671(16)00036-8.

Zopounidis, C. (2013). *Basic Principles in Financial Management*. Klidarithmos (in Greek).

Zopounidis, C. and Doumpos, M. (1999). A multicriteria decision aid methodology for sorting decision problems: The case of financial distress. *Computational Economics*, 14(3). https://doi.org/10.1023/A:1008713823812.

Part 3

Reflections About Financial Engineering

© 2023 World Scientific Publishing Company
https://doi.org/10.1142/9789811260483_0007

Chapter 7

Transformations in Shareholder Activism: Past, Present, and Future

Carine Girard-Guerraud, Jennifer Goodman, and Céline Louche

Audencia Business School, Nantes, France

Abstract

Shareholder activism, the use of ownership rights to exert influence on investee companies, is not new but is an evolving phenomenon that has made its way into mainstream investment approaches as a powerful means of inciting change in companies. In this chapter, we review not only the past and present of shareholder activism, going back to its origins and mapping the development of both financially and socially motivated activism, but also go further to identify future trends and challenges. Drawing on interviews with international experts from key organizations in the activism universe, we tease out the newest issues, actors, and tactics to give a forward-looking account of where shareholder activism will go next. We identify four new trends, the beneficiary revolution, refining collaboration, a holistic approach, and technological innovation, which stand out as significant shapers of the future direction of shareholder activism. Our analysis of these empirical trends combined with recent research and practical examples indicate some key challenges on the horizon that demand further attention in both research and practice. These challenges are the diversity of demand, democratization, temporality, and increasing polarization between leaders and laggards. These findings have implications not only from a practical investment or management perspective but also for future research in terms of identifying and analyzing potentially unintended consequences of the new trends.

Keywords: Shareholder activism; financial activism; social activism

1. Introduction

A series of recent events herald a new era for shareholder activism. Among them, we find evidence of a new generation of active investors, such as Engine No. 1, an exchange traded fund (ETF) that invests in 500 of the largest U.S. publicly listed stocks. It tracks a market cap-weighted index, provided by Morningstar that is diversified across all sectors and represents more than 80% of the U.S. equity market. After a short voting campaign promoted on a dedicated website named reenergizexom.com[1] in early 2021, this small fund with USD 272 million in assets under management obtained the appointment of three directors at the annual general meeting (AGM) of shareholders with the aim of pushing the oil giant EXXON (market cap of more than USD 267 billion) to reduce its carbon footprint.

Another example is the emergence of gamer activists to counter short selling funds. In early 2020, a gamer on Reddit and more specifically on the r/WallStreetBets forum (8.6 million subscribers) relayed a letter from a prominent investor, Michael J. Burry,[2] announcing that he had taken a 3% stake in GameStop and encouraged small investors to purchase the stock to create a short squeeze. In the trading frenzy that followed, two Wall Street hedge funds lost billions as small investors bought up the stock and forced short sellers to liquidate their positions.

There is also the transformation initiated by professional activist investors, such as BlackRock, whose Chairman Larry Fink stated in his 2021 letter to chief executive officers (CEOs) that a tectonic shift related to climate risk is now being reflected in its more customized index

[1] https://reenergizexom.com/.

[2] Michael J. Burry is a hedge fund manager and was one of the first to speculate on the unfolding sub-prime crisis. This episode is recounted in a 2015 film bibliography *The Big Short*.

portfolio offering to meet a demand for sustainability from much broader groups of people.[3] To these examples we could add the case of Danone, whose CEO and Chairman Emmanuel Faber was ousted due to his apparent overinterest in sustainability at the expense of shareholder interests.[4] The American and British minority investors, respectively, Artisan Partners and Bluebell Capital, had led an intense campaign in the press and with the board of directors.

Increasingly, investors are raising their voices by engaging in conversations with management or attending meetings with boards. If consensus is not reached, then they may adopt more confrontational tactics, such as open letters, shareholder proposals, and proxy voting. Shareholder activism is a form of active ownership through which investors undertake a range of activities to influence companies in terms of their investment portfolios (Huimin & Talaulicar, 2010). Shareholder activism used to be the preserve of a small minority, but over the years, it has spread to all investors from hedge funds, private equity firms, pension funds, and mutual funds to individual investors. Goranova and Ryan (2014) have described institutional investors as a "dynamic institutional force" playing a key role in changing companies' decision-making. According to a report published by Insightia (2021), in 2020, 810 companies worldwide were targeted by activist investors, a number that increases year after year despite a slowdown in 2020 due to COVID-19. The movement is also expanding geographically, going beyond the English-speaking world to reach various countries in Europe, Asia, and Latin America.

Shareholder activism has not only increased in terms of amount and influence but also in terms of form and focus, as the above examples reveal. If shareholder activism historically targeted corporate governance-related issues and revolved around questions of strategy and performance, the last decade has seen increasing interest in environmental and social issues. What were once seen as issues of concern for just a few social activists, such as climate change or diversity, have become systematic risks that cannot be ignored. Moreover, new digital tools have contributed to the development of new practices, such as online collaborative campaigns, and to attracting new shareholder activists, such as the beneficiaries of pensions. These new practices are transforming and will continue to transform the shareholder activism landscape.

---

[3] https://www.blackrock.com/corporate/investor-relations/larry-fink-ceo-letter.

[4] https://www.ft.com/content/8e7ae718-eb18-4d2f-bd18-59e6349540f2.

Based on insights from experts and practitioners in the field of shareholder activism, the objective of this article is to explore and discuss new trends in shareholder activism. The remainder of the paper is structured as follows. First, we provide some insights into what shareholder activism is in theory and practice. Second, we present a brief history of shareholder activism and distinguish between two main types of activist groups: financially driven activists and socially driven activists. Third, we explore new trends in shareholder activism. We conclude with a discussion of the challenges we have identified relating to these new trends.

2. Understanding Shareholder Activism

2.1. *Defining shareholder activism*

Shareholder activism goes by many names, such as shareholder engagement and shareholder stewardship, and has many definitions. However, they all have in common a focus on the active behavior of one or more minority shareholders who explicitly aim to influence a company's policies, practices, and performance by employing a range of tactics (Goranova & Ryan, 2014). As holders of equity stakes in companies and thereby as owners of those companies, shareholders have the right to engage with companies to express potential dissatisfaction with management decisions and to hold organizations accountable for their actions. The goals of activist shareholders range from short-term financial returns (Cheffins & Amour, 2011; Chung & Talaulicar, 2010) to significant change in corporate behavior (Lee & Lounsbury, 2011; Roberts *et al.*, 2006).

Shareholder activists have different objectives and motives for engaging with companies. Although they all seek changes in companies, those changes can differ greatly according to the activist. The literature on shareholder activism has identified two main types of activists, financially driven activists and socially driven activists (Chung & Talaulicar, 2010; Welker & Wood, 2011), that historically have different roots, paths, and tactics, as well as different theoretical foundations with divergent concerns. Financial shareholder activists tend to focus more on issues of financial interest to shareholders, such as profitability, growth, governance, mergers and acquisitions, and value per share to reach outcomes that positively influence the financial performance of companies. Social shareholder activists focus mainly on social and environmental issues to reach outcomes that positively influence the performance of companies. We discuss these in more detail in the following section.

While these two groups can be seen as complementary because they attempt to address corporate inefficiencies, the question of the primacy of shareholder logic over a social orientation has generated several controversies (Goranova & Ryan, 2014). Indeed, shareholders motivated by financial objectives alone may not share social objectives. However, with global and urgent challenges such as climate change and the need for clean energy, the boundary between the two begins to blur.

2.2. *Shareholder activism tactics*

There are various ways shareholders can engage in activism. We can classify the different tactics into four main categories: dialog, AGMs, divesting, and external tactics. These tactics can take a private often called "behind the scenes" approach in the form of discreet engagement between the company and the shareholder or a more public approach to gain the attention of a wider group of stakeholders. Activism can be done either individually, where investors engage with a company on their own, or collectively (or collaboratively), where several shareholders work together. Collective tactics are often used by formal investor networks or membership organizations, such as the Principles for Responsible Investment (PRI). By acting together, shareholders can achieve visibility and power, share information with each other, and spread the cost and effort. Table 1 provides an overview of the different tactics.

Dialog refers to a voice mechanism (Goodman *et al.*, 2014; Hirschman, 1970) through which shareholders use communication in an attempt to rectify performance lapses. Voice is presented as a long-term strategy (McNulty & Nordberg, 2016), as investors decide to hold their stocks and exercise their rights as shareholders to voice their concerns and attempt to change a company's practices. In other words, through voice investors become "active" campaigners for change. Dialog tactics include emails, writing letters, or holding meetings with the management, board of directors, or CEO. More confrontational tactics, such as media campaigns, issuing press releases, publishing reports, or writing open letters, may also be used. The more confrontational approaches aim to exert pressure on the company and eventually rally other shareholders and stakeholders to support the cause.

Table 1. Shareholder activism tactics.

Tactics			**Description**
Dialog	Private	Emails, phone calls Writing letters Meetings	Interactions between one or more shareholders and current or potential investees/issuers.
	Public	Media campaign Issuing press briefings Publishing reports Writing open letters	
Annual General Meeting (AGM)		Attending AGM	Participating actively during the AGM
		Filing shareholder proposals Voting on resolutions Proxy battle	Exercising voting rights on management/shareholder resolutions (and submitting resolutions) to formally express approval (or disapproval) on relevant matters.
		Calling an extraordinary general meeting (EGM)	Shareholders (under certain conditions) can call for an EGM to deal with urgent matters that arise in between the annual shareholders' meetings.
Divesting			Selling of shares
External tactics		Lawsuits	Using legal mechanisms to attack companies on specific litigation risks
		Engaging policymakers	Influencing policymakers.
		Investor-supported initiatives	Becoming member or signatory of initiatives (i.e., CDP and PRI).

Participating in the AGM and extraordinary general meetings (EGMs) is another public voice approach. It involves attending the investee company's AGM in person and actively participating by asking questions, raising concerns, and entering into debates with the company representatives. It also involves voting on resolutions linked to corporate matters, such as the election of directors to the board, approval of mergers and acquisitions, and operations relating to corporate social responsibility. However, because most shareholders cannot attend the annual meetings, companies have to provide shareholders with the option to cast a proxy vote, which allows a single person or firm (such as an asset manager) to vote on behalf of the shareholder. Shareholders can also propose resolutions, which are written demands sent to the company. If the shareholder proposal fulfills all the necessary requirements, it will be added and voted upon during the AGM. This mechanism provides all shareholders with an institutional means of informing corporate boards of certain issues or concerns they consider important. For example, in 2021, shareholders filed a resolution asking Amazon to report on plastic packaging and goals to reduce impacts of plastic pollution or HSBC to phase out the financing of coal and set targets aligned with limiting temperature rise to 1.5°C. Resolution proposals are particularly common in the US but are being increasingly used in other countries. Shareholders can decide to act collectively to gather enough shareholder proxy votes and engage in what is called a proxy battle. The objective is to secure the number of shareholder votes required to win a vote. This action is mainly used in corporate takeovers.

Divesting, also called exit strategy (Goodman *et al.*, 2014; Hirschman, 1970) and often referred to as the "Wall Street Walk" (Admati & Pfleiderer, 2009), consists of the selling of shares. The aim is to discipline underperforming management using a market-based mechanism. This tactic is characterized as being straightforward, impersonal, and indirect and can induce a reduction in the share price (if substantial enough), thereby pressuring managers to be more accountable to shareholders. Shareholders do not necessarily have to sell their shares; sometimes the mere threat of a divestment campaign can have the desired effect. For example, in 2012, the environmental organization 350.org launched the Go Fossil Free campaign through which they asked investors to divest from oil and coal companies and other fossil fuel industries. Finally, there are a number of other external tactics, such as lawsuits, engaging in policymaking, and joining investor-supported initiatives.

The tactics mentioned here are not exclusive, and there is no specific pathway or order that must be followed. Shareholders can gradually initiate a new tactic if the previous one fails or can use several tactics at the same time. For example, a shareholder may enter into private dialog with a company while threatening the company with divesting, or a shareholder can divest and keep dialoguing with the company through shareholder coalitions. Research shows that shareholders tend to use tactics in a dynamic and strategic manner (Goodman *et al.*, 2014) depending on the type of power they have (coercive, utilitarian, or symbolic) (Mitchell, Agle, & Wood, 1997), the results they want to obtain, the speed with which they want the change to happen, and the resources they have.

Shareholder activism has a cost (Gantchev, 2013; Goranova & Ryan, 2014), which can be substantial. For example, Albouy and Schatt (2009) calculated that €250 million of communication and share acquisition costs were spent by the Atticus fund and the US raider Guy Wyser-Pratte to succeed in their proxy battle with Vivarte, one of the leading French quoted companies in the retail industry. An investor's decision to engage in shareholder activism is based on a trade-off between the expected benefits (monetary or non-monetary) and the expected costs of these activities. The expected costs are related to the ownership structure of the target company and the possibility of collective action. However, there are sometimes problems relating to the free rider attitude of some shareholders. Some hope to benefit from the improved future value of the free cash flows generated by the activist shareholders without having to share in the costs linked to the initiated tactics (Milgrom & Roberts, 1997).

3. A Brief History of Financial and Social Shareholder Activism

As stated, there are two main types of shareholder activists, social and financial, each with different roots and historical development. Figure 1 provides an overview of the development of these two types of shareholder activism, focusing on the actors involved, the issues of concern, and the tactics used.

3.1. *Financial shareholder activism*

Shareholder activism began in the 1930s. After the Great Depression, numerous laws were passed to reform corporate governance. These reforms stemmed from an analysis of corporate inefficiency. According to Berle and Means (1932), this inefficiency is explained by the separation of ownership and control of the company. If company managers had interests that diverged from those of shareholders, they could make decisions contrary to shareholder value. At that time, individual owners did not monitor managers and were mostly absent from general meetings of

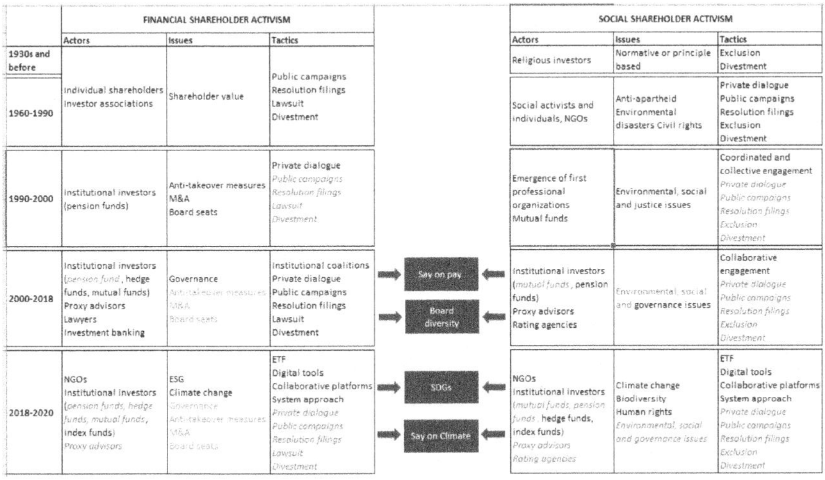

Figure 1. Historical development of social and financial shareholder activism.

Note: Items in gray and italics are items that continue from the previous period. The boxes in the center show examples of key issues financial and social shareholders have in common.

shareholders. In other words, they "voted with their feet" (Marens, 2002), meaning they simply sold their shares.

To remedy owners' passive position, in the US, the Securities Exchange Commission (SEC) Rule 14a-8 was drafted in 1942 (Gillan & Starks, 2000, 2009). This rule promulgated the first version of the shareholder resolution. It stipulates that management must authorize shareholder proposals that constitute appropriate subject matter for corporate action. In 1943, shareholders began to submit proposals to improve the governance and financial performance of companies.

Shareholder activism has been practiced by individual investors for many years, and some have formed associations (Strickland, Wiles, & Zenner, 1996). The first and most publicized association was the United Shareholders Association (USA). Created in 1986 and dissolved in 1996, the USA exercised an important counter-power to push for the development of minority shareholders' rights and improvements in the quality of information provided by companies. In the 1980s, this activism developed under the pressure of corporate raiders who used the market for corporate control to change boards and management (Brav *et al.*, 2008).

Shareholder activism became more important in the late 1980s and early 1990s as institutional investor ownership of companies increased (Monks & Minow, 2011). For example, Gillan and Starks (2009) found that between 1952 and 2006, the percentage of institutional investor ownership in U.S. stock markets increased from less than 10% to over 70%. As their ownership increased, these institutional investors realized that they could not sell their holdings, as easily without causing the stock price to fall and that they could no longer remain passive. As a result, these institutional investors, particularly public pension funds, began to exert pressure through various means (Guercio & Hawkins, 1999), such as the publication of a blacklist of the 10 worst performing companies in the S&P 500 index by the Council of Institutional Investors or a list of non-performing executives by the International Brotherhood of Teamsters pension fund. In 1992, the California Public Employees' Retirement System pension fund was one of the first to institute a "general voting policy" within American companies (Crutchley, Hudson, & Jensen, 1998), thus providing a guideline for each proposal submitted at AGMs.

The 1990s were also characterized by a very intense takeover market. In response, some companies adopted measures to protect themselves against hostile takeover attempts. Investors mainly contested these anti-takeover measures (e.g., the adoption of a supermajority clause to file a bid offer); activism was then positioned as an alternative control mechanism to align the interests of the managers (agents) with those of the shareholders (principals) (Smith, 1996).

In 1992, the SEC passed a new rule allowing shareholders to communicate with each other. This helped to reduce the cost of creating shareholder coalitions and encouraged dialog tactics rather than relying on proxy voting (Gillan & Starks, 2000).

In the early 2000s, hedge funds also appeared in the shareholder activism ecosystem (Gillan & Starks, 2009). Two groups of hedge funds emerged: event-driven hedge funds the objective of which was to create shareholder value by criticizing a specific aspect of a company's governance (such as changing the board) and short-seller hedge funds that used public campaigns to cause the share price to fall (a more aggressive approach). The number of companies criticized by these activist hedge funds steadily increased. Becht *et al.* (2017) found that between 2000 and 2010 of the 1,145 activist actions in North America, 381 in Europe (including 27 in France), and 214 in Asia, one quarter was coordinated by hedge funds.

2018 was a record year, according to Lazard (Lazard's Shareholder Advisory Group, 2019), as 131 investors initiated an activist tactic compared to 109 in the previous year. The Elliott Management Corporation in the US was by far the most aggressive with 22 new campaigns, including one against French spirits group Pernod Ricard. They were followed by ValueAct Capital (nine new campaigns) in the US and Cevian Capital (two new campaigns) in Sweden.

Some passive funds also became activists. This was particularly the case in 2019 when Wellington Management publicly expressed its opposition to the acquisition of Celgene by Bristol-Myers Squibb. When passive funds wish to influence the governance or strategy of companies in which they have invested, they are likely to do so indirectly by supporting activist campaigns. In an article in the *Financial Times* on 24 July 2018, the chairman of State Street Global Advisors explained that passive funds, such as ETFs (e.g., index funds), have a fiduciary duty to act as activists to improve company performance for the benefit of its investors. In the early 2000s, coalitions between the same class of institutional investors with the same investment horizon of 1–2 years were observed (Carrothers, 2017), while new interactions between index funds (and other mutual funds) and activist hedge funds are observed today (Gilson & Gordon, 2019). Index funds have a long-term investment horizon well beyond two years. For the fund manager, operational costs are reduced, as it is only a matter of adjusting the holding of stocks as they move in and out of an index. The fund is only exposed to the systematic risk of the index and not the risk of an individual company. The "big three" index funds (Blackrock, Vanguard, and State Street) have significantly increased their holdings in listed companies since the 2000s. Their growing presence in terms of the ownership of companies targeted by activist hedge funds can determine the success of a campaign (Brav *et al.*, 2021). Even if index fund managers are still inclined to support corporate managers (Bebchuk & Hirst, 2019), the voting recommendations made by proxy advisors such as Institutional Shareholder Services (ISS) nevertheless influence their votes against a resolution submitted by management (Dubois, McGinty, & Uchida, 2019). These new coalitions are the subject of much political and scientific debate, as they reveal a problem of decoupling between voting and a specific risk exposure not experienced by funds (Fisch, 2021). To the extent that an activist seeks to influence corporate governance issues, it is only legitimate if it assumes the consequences by being exposed to risk with shares held in its own name.

In the US, institutional investors subject to the ERISA Act are assumed to have an obligation to vote all shares under management. In the UK, the Stewardship Code encourages shareholder voting. In France, companies have long resisted institutional activism. However, faced with this growing pressure, a lively debate in the French public arena began with the publication on October 2, 2019 of the Woerth report on shareholder activism. This debate resulted in efforts to regulate shareholder activists' activities by drafting principles to reorient financial activism toward more social activism.

3.2. *Social shareholder activism*

Social shareholder activism evolved in parallel with the responsible investment (RI) movement. RI refers to the integration of environmental, social, and corporate governance (ESG) considerations into investment decisions and active ownership (Kurtz, 2008; Yan, Ferraro, & Almandoz, 2018). Shareholder activism is an integral and central strategy used by responsible investors. Three broad periods can be identified as shaping what social shareholder activism is today.

Before the 1960s, social shareholder activism referred mainly to excluding certain companies or sectors from an investment portfolio according to normative or principle-based criteria. This early form of RI dates back to the 18th century when religious institutions, such as the Society of Friends (Quakers) and the Methodists, started to question their own investment practices. They believed that investing was not a neutral activity but that it implied values. They started to exclude companies whose products conflicted with their fundamental beliefs. These so-called "sin" stocks were for the most part those of companies involved in alcohol, tobacco, gambling, and, in certain cases, weapons. One of the emblematic and first RI funds was the Pioneer Fund, launched in the US in 1928. During this period, the exclusion of certain unethical activities was the main form of social shareholder activism. There was no active engagement with companies.

The period of the 1960s–1990s marked a turn in social shareholder activism. Engagement activities really started toward the end of the 1960s when RI began in the contemporary sense of the term, taking on a more political connotation (Louche & Lydenberg, 2006). During this period, non-profits and activists — often with low budgets — leveraged, borrowed, or donated shares to file shareholder resolutions (King & Gish,

2015). Their actions were driven by values and ethics and emerged from social movements such as civil rights, anti-apartheid, feminism, LGBT rights, and environmental movements. This period was also marked by a number of major environmental disasters, such as the Seveso dioxin cloud in Italy (1976), the Amoco Cadiz oil spill (1978), the cyanide gas leak in Bhopal (1984), the Chernobyl nuclear disaster (1986), and the Exxon Valdez oil spill (1989), which not only helped raise environmental awareness generally but also increased concerns about corporations' activities. It was also during this period that the 1987 Brundtland Report introduced the concept of sustainable development and outlined how it could be achieved.

At this time, social shareholder activists were mainly individuals rather than investment professionals. They were ideologically driven and used the tools and rights of shareholders to exert pressure on specific companies. Their main tactic comprised dialogs behind closed doors but also included public dialog as a way to amplify the pressure. However, during this period, social shareholder activists started to exercise their right to communicate with both management and each other through a proxy statement. They bought shares in companies in order to file resolutions and attend companies' annual meetings. In 1968, the Medical Committee for Human Rights, an American social justice organization, filed the first social shareholder proposal with Dow Chemical that raised concerns about the company's production and sale of napalm for use during the Vietnam War against human beings. Although Dow Chemical initially refused to put the resolution on its proxy ballot, they were forced to do so by the Court of Appeals. This set the legal precedent for allowing shareholder proposals that dealt with social rather than strictly financial issues. Social shareholder activists' main objective was to exert pressure on companies to change their practices. Their leverage point was not financial, as the number of shares they held was too limited, but rather reputational. Moreover, their campaigns helped raise awareness among other shareholders and the general public, particularly when the confrontations were reported in the media. For example, in 1989, a number of religious organizations filed a resolution and raised their voices during Union Carbide's annual meeting to urge the company to take responsibility for the accident in Bhopal, India. Their message targeted the company's top management as much as the entire investor community, as evidenced by the voices of activists captured in the proceedings of Union Carbide's 1989 annual shareholder meeting: "I urge you to live up to your moral responsibility and vote 'yes' to the proposal [for compensation and health care for Bhopal victims]. Only then can we, the stockholders of Carbide, live down the shame epitomized in the slogan that environmentalists are raising repeatedly these days, the slogan that 'Exxon spills, Carbide kills'" (Dr. Clarence Dias, proxy for the Sisters of Charity, cited in Welker & Wood, 2011, p. S60).

A number of other emblematic campaigns targeted companies' irresponsible practices and behaviors and aimed at promoting corporate responsibility. Social activists, such as Ralph Nader and Saul Alinsky, bought shares in companies in order to confront them directly and openly, as in the Kodak case in the mid-1960s (civil rights) and the General Motors case in 1970 (safety issues). Although the resolutions tended to receive very little support, they raised interest, as noted by the reporter Jerry Flint, regarding the campaign against GM: "[T]he Campaign may not have won many votes, but it may have captured the high moral ground and the fight may just be beginning" (cited in Schwartz, 1971, p. 769). Another important campaign was the anti-apartheid divestment campaign, which focused on abolishing the political regime in South Africa and which used divestment to disestablish apartheid in that country (Hunt, Weber, & Dordi, 2017). It was during this campaign that the first shareholder resolution on a social responsibility issue was proposed and discussed at the AGM of a British company (the Midland Bank AGM in 1977) (John, 2000).

During the period of the 1960s–1990s, social shareholder activism also grew in terms of sophistication, and other professional organizations started to engage. Social activists realized that shareholder rights could be used to defend social and environmental concerns. A number of professional organizations were launched, initiating the start of more coordinated actions among social shareholder activists. In 1972, the Interfaith Center on Corporate Responsibility (ICCR), a consortium of religious organizations, started to engage collectively in social shareholder activism using a broad range of tactics. The Investor Responsibility Research Center, also established in 1972, was one of the first research and consultancy agencies dealing with social and environmental issues. Then followed several professional RI organizations — social rating organizations such as EIRIS in 1980 (UK), KLD in 1990 (US), Oekom in 1993 (Germany), Jantzi Research in 1992 (Canada), and Arese in 1997 (France) and associations such as the Social Investment Forum in 1984 in the US and in 1991 in the UK. Social shareholders started to mobilize collective forces and act together. For example, at the end of the 1980s, medical associations, medical schools, and religious groups started a campaign together against tobacco companies.

In the period of 2000–2020, social shareholder activism gained increased acceptance amongst mainstream investment practitioners (Dumas & Louche, 2016). A number of elements contributed to this acceptance. First, sustainability and corporate social responsibility became part of national and international agendas with the realization that business activities were fundamentally intertwined with global challenges (e.g., the Millennium Development Goals (MDGs) in 2000 replaced in 2015 by the Sustainable Development Goals (SDGs), the Paris Agreement in 2015, and more specific to the financial sector, the PRI). The PRI was set up by an international group of institutional investors backed by the United Nations to promote the adoption and implementation of six principles promoting ESG issues in investment practice, including active ownership. As of November 2021, the PRI counted 3,826 signatories; of those, 609 asset owners represent USD 121.3 trillion assets under management. To support and encourage collective shareholder engagement, at the end of 2006, the PRI launched the Clearinghouse, a collaborative online shareholder engagement platform. Second, a multiplicity of standards and regulations emerged. Some were related to non-financial reporting disclosure, such as the Global Reporting Initiative in 1999, the Sustainability Accounting Standards Board in 2011, and the European Union Non-Financial Reporting Directive (2014/95/EU). Others targeted more specific investors, such as the 2005 UK Pension Disclosure Act that mandates all private sector pension funds include voting rights and environmental and social issues in their investment criteria; the French Article 173-VI of the Energy Transition Act of 2015 that requires institutional investors and asset managers to report on their approach to ESG issues; the 2018 European Commission action plan on sustainable finance; and the 2019 Sustainable Finance Disclosure Regulation. Third, in the 2000s, numerous ESG rating agencies were created and went through a strong consolidation trend in the mid-2010s (Avetisyan & Hockerts, 2017; Wong, Brackley, & Petroy, 2019). For example, RiskMetrics acquired KLD and Innovest, which subsequently was acquired by MSCI; ISS took over Oekom in 2017; VigeoEiris was absorbed by Moody's in 2019; and in 2020, Standard & Poor's acquired Robeco-SAM and Morningstar bought Sustainalytics. Overall, these elements contributed to the increasing visibility and legitimacy of social shareholder activism and led to the increasing interest of institutional investors, such as pension funds, insurance companies, and union groups. Passive investors (such as the big three of Vanguard, BlackRock, and State Street) and financially driven activists (such as Trian Fund Management, Blue Harbour, Red Mountain Capital, and Value Act) became increasingly concerned about ESG issues such as climate risk but also about board diversity, employee retention, environmental policies, supply chain ethics, and data security and privacy. Consequently, the social and environmental logic that first drove social shareholder activism came to increasingly intersect with the market and financial logic, and socially motivated shareholder activists started to work hand in hand with financially driven shareholders. In the 2010s, non-profit organizations such as Friends of the Earth, Amnesty International, the World Wildlife Fund (WWF), Oxfam, and Greenpeace started to use the tools of shareholder activism to engage with companies directly. Specialized organizations such as Ceres were founded with the specific aim of using shareholder activism to further social good and encourage collaborative actions. For example, in 2009, ShareAction, a UK non-profit founded in 2005, worked with Greenpeace, WWF, and UNISON to draft and file two resolutions at BP and Shell demanding risk assessments of their tar sands projects. The initial campaign was followed by a number of institutional investors that joined in 2015 to file a second set of resolutions on related environmental issues. Other campaigns, such as the fossil fuel divestment campaign by 350.org and Climate Action 100+, have brought together diverse investors focused on the issue of climate change.

4. Methodology

Given the historical differences and continual development of shareholder activism and in light of the recent high-profile cases of shareholder activism, such as Engine No. 1/Exxon, GameStop, Danone, and BlackRock's statement, we took an explorative approach to investigate our research questions, which are the following: What are the latest trends in shareholder activism? How will these evolve going forward? What implications could these have for investee companies, shareholder activists, and the wider society? We took a qualitative approach using semi-structured interviews with professionals and key players in the field of shareholder activism. Our questions prompted responses about interviewees' roles and activities in terms of shareholder activism and engagement and how they are evolving; the issues they see moving center stage; how their practices, tactics, and tools are being adapted to address the issues; and their outlook on future trends.

We conducted 11 interviews (coded Int1 to Int11) between September and November 2021. Table 2 shows a list of all interviewees. The three authors, all with previous research and practical expertise in financial and ESG investment and shareholder activism, identified long-standing experts in shareholder activism in the US, the UK, and France. Next, more recent high-profile cases appearing in the news and social media were identified, and related actors were contacted for interviews. The authors then took a snowball approach and asked interviewees to identify other key and emerging actors in the field. The interviews lasted between 30 and 60 min, with an average duration of 55 min. Interviews were conducted online with either two or three of the authors in attendance who followed a semi-structured interview protocol. The interviews were recorded with the permission of the interviewees, and the authors noted emerging themes and discussed them immediately after each interview.

The interview recordings were transcribed and read by all the authors to identify the pertinent quotes relating to new issues, new actors, and new

Table 2. Summary of interviews.

Organization type	**Function**	**Length (minutes)**
Investment Manager, France	Head of Corporate Governance & ESG	44
ICCR, US	Board member	60
PRI, UK	Specialist, Stewardship	66
ShareAction, UK	Senior Manager, Health	60
ShareAction, UK	Senior Campaign Manager, Climate	30
ESG Asset Management, France	CEO	60
Global Investment Advisors, US	Chairman and President, Former President of the New York Stock Exchange	60
ISS, France	Global Head of Stewardship	60+
		60
Law firm, Securities Litigation, France	Lawyer	60
Tumelo, UK	Co-Founder, Head of Stewardship	60

strategies and tactics in shareholder activism and the additional themes noted after each interview. Follow-up emails were sent to the interviewees to ask for further clarification where necessary. The themes were refined through iterative discussions between the three authors to ensure key trends and implications were identified.

5. New Trends in Shareholder Activism

In this section, we present the new trends that emerged from our analysis. We identified four main categories of trends in shareholder activism around which we have organized the section and which are shown in Figure 2.

5.1. *The beneficiary revolution*

The first important new trend in shareholder activism is a change on the demand side, what we call the beneficiary revolution. The ultimate owners or beneficiaries want to know where and how their money is being invested. Expressing the beneficiaries' desire to take a more active role, financial professionals and the everyday person on the street have been increasingly demanding participation in shareholder activism. If tools

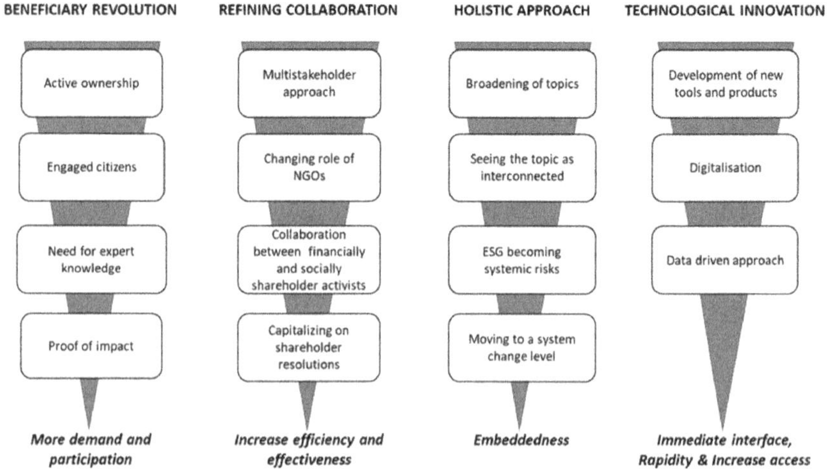

Figure 2. New trends in shareholder activism.

have contributed to making this possible, then expert knowledge remains critical because the issues are complex, the range of topics is broad, and the amount of data is vast.

Both soft law, such as the PRI and the various stewardship codes around the world, and hard law, particularly in Europe with the introduction of the Sustainable Finance Disclosure Regulation in 2021, have contributed to the acceleration of shareholder activism. However, it is not only about regulation; as revealed by the experts we talked with, there has been "a real revolution" (Int9) in asset owners' demands for active management and transparency regarding the engagement activities of asset managers. It is no longer enough to make general statements about engagement or to be a PRI signatory; asset owners want to know precisely what is being done and where, whether, and how it is having an impact on investee companies. Our interviewees highlighted the need and push for *active ownership* and even more the notion of stewardship, that it is the responsibility of investors to act as "stewards" of the companies they hold shares in. The latter entails "holding the board to account for the fulfilment of its responsibilities" (Financial Reporting Council, 2012, p. 1).

This beneficiary revolution may be partly due to the pressure being put on investors by NGOs that are making the link between asset owners and issues by targeting shareholders specifically. In the UK where private pensions have been mandatory since 2012, this has created a huge "untapped potential" (Int4) *where everyone is a shareholder* (*engaged citizen*) and awareness of the rights that conveys is becoming more widespread. Overall, the experts observe a "greater awareness in society about the role that investors play and the responsibility that they have in addressing a lot of the issues we work on" (Int2). ShareAction has managed to bring together interested citizens or "individuals in the street" (Int4) and involve them in engagement through writing letters, asking questions at AGMs, and becoming more active in filing resolutions.

It is in this spirit that Tumelo was founded in 2018 by Cambridge graduates. Reaching out to the "everyday person on the street" (Int3), they have created a user-friendly web platform that allows investors to obtain succinct and easy-to-read information about the companies in their fund portfolios. In addition, the platform conveys their proxy voting preferences to the people who manage their funds. Their vision is further evidence of a growing trend of shareholders recognizing and asserting their rights with ever stronger demands for transparency and active asset management. As our interviewee highlighted: "If you think about it, there is no world that exists in the future where people don't know where their money is invested and they don't have access to influence those companies through their shareholder rights; that's just not a future that exists" (Int3). With the goal of giving a billion people access to their shareholder rights and planned international expansion, Tumelo confirms this trend and along the same lines imagines activism by individuals on collaborative platforms who join their shares and take action on a range of issues.

Although a new force in shareholder activism, this movement of increasingly engaged citizen shareholders will not diminish *the role and importance of experts and fund managers* who will still act as delegates for many beneficial owners. One reason for this is the need for knowledge, expertise, and data on a range of issues in a society where investors do not have time to do "thorough research" (Int4) but also where issues such as climate change are requiring ever more technical knowledge. This in turn provides an opportunity for data providers and intermediaries, such as the services offered by ISS, that can engage on specific issues, target very specific companies, build the narrative around the engagement, and measure the impact of the engagement.

The question of impact is increasingly important. One of our interviewees stated, "that's what we'd like to see, reporting on stewardship that has led to real world change rather than just activity metrics" (Int11). Tumelo's platform provides easy visualization of voting results so that each user can track their preferences alongside the final outcome of the vote. The development of more detailed case studies planned by the company also brings transparency and a richer picture of the engagement and its outcomes. However, attributing the outcome of an engagement to any specific actor or action remains challenging. One interviewee stated, "I can say this is the success of my engagement, except that in reality there could have been 50 other shareholders who have been asking the same thing for the last three years" (Int9). This makes it difficult for asset managers to distinguish their contribution and establish a competitive advantage vis-à-vis competitors.

5.2. *Refining collaboration*

The second trend that emerged from our results is the reinforcement and refinement of collaboration. Not only are financial and social shareholder activists tending to collaborate on specific issues — what we call the "convergence" turn — but activists are also working with other stakeholders, particularly NGOs. This trend contributes to enhancing the efficiency and effectiveness of shareholder activism by pooling their resources, knowledge, and strengths.

Our interviewees pointed at a move toward a *multi-stakeholder approach* to shareholder activism and a *changing role for NGOs*. While this is not entirely new, as evidenced by the collaborative work that has been taking place for many years, for example, at ICCR and over the past decade through the PRI and others, we identify a shift toward convergence in the way different stakeholders work together.

As one of our interviewees noted, "Engagement is no longer something that investors do but today all categories of stakeholders are doing engagement and we often see a better alignment between these stakeholders" (Int6). This may involve labor unions but especially NGOs contacting investors to highlight controversies and help with more proactive action. One interviewee (Int11) told us that after the collapse of the dams owned by the mining company Vale in Brazil in 2019, the Church of England and the Council on Ethics fund created a new standard in the tailings dam industry. "NGOs will become important players because they have a 'different perception' and 'values'. Moreover, they are 'less aggressive' and 'they are heard by more people'" (Int10). Another interviewee (Int 9) highlighted that NGOs "have become more sophisticated and they understand that having investors on their side adds extra voices that will permit the same message to pass through different channels and it's often like that that we change things." NGOs also have a role in opening the conversation on an issue more widely. One interviewee stated, "Regulators don't tend to come in on topics where there isn't a lot of positive action happening or good practice, so I do think that NGOs in general and we for example in the investor space, have got opportunities in starting to create some of those good practice examples to encourage regulators to then come in and propagate that change" (Int4). Interestingly, NGOs and social activists had a central role in the early stages of social shareholder activism but became less visible in the 2000s. It seems that they are coming back onto the shareholder activism stage but with a more legitimate and expert role. Beyond unions and NGOs, we see the return of a lost practice, that of talking with stakeholders where some asset managers are going as far as to contact the suppliers of certain companies. Conversely, some stakeholders do not hesitate to contact the head of stewardship of certain institutional investors.

In light of our earlier sections discussing the history of both financial and social shareholder activism, we also identify a trend toward the *convergence of these two traditionally separate streams of activism*. "What we try to do is look for the intersection between the financial risk and the positive public impact" (Int4). As a result, new alliances are being formed between financial and social activists that incorporate "traditional" performance and strategy concerns with an ESG angle. "The discussion on climate and investment has been normalized and everyone feels quite comfortable to be part of that" (Int4).

This convergence has enabled financial and social shareholders to *capitalize on shareholder resolutions*. On specific issues, such as not only climate change but also biodiversity and other grand challenges, large shareholder activists from the two streams have been willing to join resolutions. While earlier collaborations typically brought together small and medium investors, 2021 has seen some of the largest asset managers and hedge funds participating in the resolution process for the first time (Int2). Thus, clustered shareholder activism, already observed in previous periods (Artiga González & Calluzzo, 2019), is intensifying.

As one of our interviewees told us, shareholder resolutions have proved themselves to be a "powerful tool" after resolution successes in 2021 at HSBC on fossil fuels and Tesco on health issues (Int2). Even without such successes (ESG issues have typically received a low percentage of votes), a recognition of the value of raising issues and questions with companies to create awareness and open debate more widely in society is deemed highly effective. Our experts noted that resolutions are still underutilized, and the PRI aim to address this with their Active Ownership 2.0 initiative launched in 2019 that reinforces shareholder resolutions as a mechanism with notable potential for impact offering support and facilitating access to this tool.

Further refinement of collaboration between a range of different stakeholders to increase efficiency and effectiveness is to be expected. In addition, a convergence between typically divided social and financial shareholder activists in terms of the filing of resolutions is becoming more evident.

5.3. *A holistic approach*

A third emerging trend is a change in approach. Shareholder activism is moving toward a holistic approach both in terms of issues and as a lever for change. Financial and social shareholder activism are increasingly recognizing that they are embedded in the same global systems, even if the two streams keep their own identity and motivation.

All interviewees agreed that climate has become the number one pressing issue with concrete and specific demands, and an ever-growing pool of investors agree "it's a systemic risk which is important for all investors and all businesses and today it's emergency number one for humanity" (Int6). Another environmental issue that is becoming a priority is biodiversity. However, social issues are not far behind, especially in the last year or two with the COVID crisis shining a light on human capital management and well-being. In addition, they include the diversity issue driven by the Black Lives Matter movement in the US, as well as a growing focus on the protection of human rights in the supply chain. ShareAction pointed out food and health as a very recent growing issue and one that has a lot of traction with the general public. Its resolution filed with Tesco asking for healthier food to be offered in its stores highlights this as an upcoming area of focus.

In the last several years, a *broadening of topics* has become evident. One interviewee stated "Investors are just starting to understand how every issue relates to one another" (Int11). Investors are also starting to *connect the issues*, to see them as interdependent, like parts of the same system. This trend is likely a result of growing familiarity with the SDGs that investors seem concerned about. The link between environmental and social issues also seems to be better understood. For example, as one interviewee stated, "When you talk about deforestation you're talking about biodiversity and climate change and human rights because you're talking about land rights and indigenous rights" (Int11).

While ESG may have been peripheral to mainstream investors, it is no longer surprising to find Chief Investment Officers specialized in ESG issues integrating them at a more strategic level. Many social and environmental issues have become *systemic risks*. For large investors, "The problem when we do index investing is that our portfolio is a copy of the economy and while the economy pollutes, the portfolio pollutes" (Int9). A new generation of index ESG activist funds has emerged (Barzuza, Curtis, & Webber, 2020), and we can expect to see new ESG indexes emerging. However, as one interviewee stated, "It's expensive and it will take time before all the clients decide to sell S&P500 and buy S&P500 ESG knowing that it is not guaranteed to have a better performance" (Int9). A continuing convergence between financial and social activist interests is inevitable as issues such as climate change present widespread systemic risk. Another interviewee stated, "The bad news is that this will never be enough, it has to be the investors, the companies and the governments and regulators who all work together" (Int6). This comment highlights another future trend, that of an evolution toward public policy and sovereign engagement. Both are driven by the systemic risk to universal owners generated by complex social and environmental issues. With such diverse portfolios, it is more efficient for large investors to seek to influence regulation rather than to speak to companies one by one. This type of engagement includes responding to public consultations and demanding a seat at the table on regulatory issues to push for tougher restrictions on emissions, both of which are happening more frequently. Another approach, sovereign engagement, sees investors working to influence the countries whose debt they hold. For example, open letters were released in 2020 and 2021 by a group of investors to put pressure on the Brazilian government to scrap proposed laws strengthening the rights of squatters on public land which was argued would lead to increased deforestation.

This development reveals that shareholder activism is moving to another level — *system change*. Activists do not only target companies and sectors but also governments. The PRI is prioritizing this push for more policy engagement, which they believe falls within the broad stewardship agenda. According to one interviewee, "For these systemic issues, you need those policy interventions and you need that regulatory environment to enable good behavior and to prevent bad behaviors" (Int11). Consistency between messaging and actions is increasingly under scrutiny, in parallel with broader demands for transparency throughout the investment industry. Another interviewee states that "There's no point engaging with companies and getting them to align to the UN guiding principles if then they lobby their government to reduce regulation around human rights" (Int11). This lack of consistency is also observed in the public sector. As one interviewee states, "If you looked carefully at the investment of a lot of the public funds, you would see there is no alignment between the aim of the public body and what their investments are tied in" (Int4).

A systemic and outcome-oriented future is clearly envisaged by the experts we interviewed. A shift toward a wider systems perspective is expected that takes into account the complexity and interconnectedness of challenges and that acknowledges the need for action across sectors and at multiple levels.

5.4. *Technological innovation*

The fourth trend is technological innovation. *New tools and products have emerged* in recent years, and more are in the pipeline. Innovations are motivated by a highly data-driven approach to finance. They not only enable new types of investors to engage in shareholder activism but also provide immediate interfaces to users.

Although there are many technological innovations, we highlight the role of ETFs, a new generation of funds with lower costs that utilize high-frequency trading. Although the first ETFs were created in early 1993, it is only very recently that they have grown significantly in number (7,602 ETFs at the end of 2020, an increase of 42% between 2017 and 2020) (Sourd & Safaee, 2021). ETFs have several specific features. Unlike other funds, they can be traded continuously, that is, they can be bought or sold throughout the day. While all ETFs aim to replicate the performance of an index, there are several categories. We are most interested in index ETFs that incorporate more sophisticated activist investment strategies.

The Engine No. 1 Transform 500 ETF combines two investment strategies; it is both an index fund following the S&P 500 index and an activist fund that describes itself as an impact investing group designed to create long-term value using a data-driven approach to assign a tangible value to environmental, social, or governance actions. As ESG issues become increasingly important, index funds want to mitigate the risk of investing in unsustainable companies. To this end, Engine No. 1 selects a company that violates sustainability practices, such as EXXON, from its investment portfolio of several companies in the same index, criticizes it, and instigates ESG improvements through a vote at either the AGM or an EGM. This vote has consequences for the portfolio itself, as the decline in the stock price of the criticized company results in a decline in the performance of the index. However, this decline can be mitigated if the voting campaign encourages other companies in the portfolio to internalize negative externalities (e.g., by reducing carbon emissions or undertaking climate risk-related reforms). This new product shifts shareholder activism more toward "systematic risk" management (Int10).

Digital tools are also playing an increasing role in shareholder activism. They allow online communities to interact more quickly with a larger number of shareholders. Reddit, a popular site where every topic takes the form of a forum, allows stock traders to share their news and biggest wins and biggest losses on a daily basis. Having heard about hedge fund short selling at Gamestop, Reddit's individual stock traders wanted to see if they could play Robin Hood with their small means. And finally, they succeeded.

On-line participation at AGMs, mainly driven by COVID, has also been positive according to the experts we interviewed, as it has allowed more shareholders to attend. Some concerns remain about "how issues are brought to the AGM; how those issues are handled or represented by the company; whether they are selected; whether they are summarized in a way that makes them easier to respond to; as well as any technical issues related to companies accessing the AGM" (Int11). However, these initial issues will likely be resolved with experience, making a regular hybrid option for AGMs almost inevitable.

Tumelo also uses an interface to address this growing demand for information and direct voting from investment platform users, namely, "knowing where your money is" (Int 3). One interviewee (Int10) states that information relayed in this way — but also by whistleblowers and NGOs — has an impact on companies such as Danone, as these electronic media convey "sensationalism that will be picked up and relayed." In this sense, "activism becomes more emotional," which can be problematic.

A need for a data-driven approach: How to communicate the impact of the vote becomes an important issue to be taken into account according to one interviewee (Int3). "That's why we're going back to storytelling, the narrative we have to push about our case studies. We need to communicate to people what the impact is." The challenge also lies in the processing of the information. In particular, "Who is going to read the 6,500 pages?" (Int10). What is going to be read by a user of investment platforms who spends only a few seconds on his or her screen? (Int3), and is it already too late when we assess "the risk from carbon data that is 18–24 months old"? (Int10). "To assess risk, you have to be up to date" (Int10). As a result, data have become an important issue in the exercise of shareholder activism and require more sophisticated approaches in order to immediately analyze its impact.

6. Discussion and Conclusion

Along with these new trends in shareholder activism, our discussions with experts also led us to identify a number of challenges that we foresee on the horizon.

6.1. *Diversity of demand*

Such a wide range of complex topics and the growing technicality of climate questions demanding in-depth knowledge of the subject mean there is a lot of work to do to cover all the relevant information, data, and knowledge. Expertise is needed, and this may be held by a wide variety of different stakeholders. As well as dedicated investment services such as ISS and PRI, NGOs, academics, religious organizations, and scientists are among those stakeholders who have become experts on specific topics and who can provide technical or precise subject knowledge in engagements or in the public discourse. One challenge is to identify sources of relevant and reliable information among the plethora of data now available. These sources may be more traditional suppliers of information or asset owners, and managers may be required to seek out and work with more unusual partners. Individual shareholders are likely to have time and cost restraints potentially limiting their access to expertise while simultaneously claiming their rights to make demands on their investee companies. Furthermore, as pointed out in our interviews, despite some convergence at the institutional level toward a more holistic or systemic approach, it is not obvious that individual shareholders are all asking the same thing "You'd really think on the platform you'd see such a clear cut on environment votes right where it's like 90%, 99% vote in favor of the environment. It's not true" (Int3).

6.2. *Democratization*

The trend that we observe and that is shared by a number of experts we interviewed is the trend toward an opening up or democratizing of shareholder activism by creating awareness and accessibility for individuals to exercise their shareholder rights and involving everyday citizens in collaboration with larger investors. However, as in all other aspects of our democracies, this comes with challenges. Given the difficulty of picking informed data sources and the complexity and technicality of some issues, there may be a significant knowledge gap between the demands placed on companies and the true nature or impact of the issue of concern. Voting preferences may be based on emotion, identity, or politics, leading to populist rather than informed engagement. Our interviewees fully support the engagement of all shareholders: "I think if people can vote in a general election, then they can vote on the companies that they own through their shares" (Int3). However, some concerns were expressed: "A lot of analysis goes into making these decisions and consumers might not be aware of the business implications of that" (Int11). "It's interesting to think about the downstream consequences of [democratization]... you get a lot more shareholder proposals put forward and you get people paying a lot more attention to these things" (Int3). One recent example, the case of GameStop in 2021 that we discussed earlier, may offer a glimpse of the future that may lead to unintended consequences. A final consideration in terms of the democratization of shareholder activism would be some reflection on whether it includes the diverse and conflicting perspectives that are represented more widely in society.

6.3. *Temporality*

The shift toward transparency of the engagement process and company activities as well as more digital interfaces to access this information brings the challenge of temporality. Important in engagement up to now has been the building of relationships between shareholder activists and companies over time to establish trust and to work toward long-term, challenging goals. A new generation born into the age of social media alternatively seeks instant gratification. "The temporality thing is a real problem though, especially in terms of engaging users and communicating to them the impact. Everyone is so used to the 'like' button on Facebook or Instagram and instant gratification and that's giving them the dopamine hit that they need. We are talking about multi-year change here and that is the challenge: keeping people engaged with this and keeping people voting" (Int3). Organizational and institutional change can take time, and it is not clear how this difference in temporalities will play out. This becomes more acute when considering the multi-stakeholder nature of collaborations and will undoubtedly be one of the key challenges for shareholder activism going forward.

6.4. *Increasing polarization between leaders and laggards*

As more mainstream, large investors make a significant move toward ESG and new indexes are developed, those companies engaging with these issues are likely to shift into a virtuous circle, enlarging the scope and variety of SDG-related issues they address. However, there is more limited reflection on what happens to those "dirty" companies that fall off the ESG radar (Int1). Without shareholders to promote ESG issues and ask the company to work on them, there is no knowledge or transparency of what is happening and no one to stimulate change. Ultimately, the pressure on these companies is taken off, leaving dirty companies to become even dirtier. Legislation or litigation will likely become the only means of addressing the ESG performance of such companies (Int1), reinforcing the role of government and the public sector. A key question for shareholder activism going forward is how to ensure that new investment products and engagement tactics can improve performance at a more systemic level and not leave laggards behind.

7. Conclusion

Our account of shareholder activism from its origins to its new horizons aims to bring together the wide array of different issues, actors, and tactics that have evolved since its early beginnings to the present day. While we have aimed to be as inclusive as possible, there are undoubtedly some omissions. What is clear is that shareholder activism is becoming increasingly visible to a more diverse group of stakeholders than ever before. The extensive international experience and expertise of our interviewees provide diverse and valuable insights into the future trends for shareholder activism and raise important questions and considerations not only for those in the investment sector but also more widely for the management, economic, political, and social sectors/disciplines.

These issues concern the dual role of shareholders — maximizing shareholder value and caring about the impact of companies on society and their stakeholders. Can these things really be aligned? Do they lead to an even stronger financialization of our system/society? Can we trust shareholders to act to re-embed corporations within society?

References

Admati, A. R. and Pfleiderer, P. (2009). The "Wall Street Walk" and shareholder activism: Exit as a form of voice. *The Review of Financial Studies*, 22(7): 2645–2685.

Albouy, M. and Schatt, A. (2009). Activisme et proxy fight. *Revue Française de Gestion*, 198–199: 297–315.

Artiga González, T. and Calluzzo, P. (2019). Clustered shareholder activism. *Corporate Governance: An International Review*, 27(3): 210–225.

Avetisyan, E. and Hockerts, K. (2017). The consolidation of the ESG rating industry as an enactment of institutional retrogression. *Business Strategy & the Environment*, 26(3): 316–330.

Barzuza, M., Curtis, Q., and Webber, D. H. (2020). Shareholder value(s): Index fund ESG activism and the new millennial corporate governance. *Southern California Law Review*, 93: 1243–1321.

Bebchuk, L. and Hirst, S. (2019). Index fund and the future of corporate governance: Theory, evidence, and policy. *Columbia Law Review*, 119(8): 2029–2145.

Becht, M., Franks, J., Grant, J., and Wagner, H. F. (2017). Returns to hedge fund activism: An international study. *The Review of Financial Studies*, 30(9): 2933–2971.

Berle, A. and Means, G. (1932). *The Modern Corporation & Private Property*. New York: McMillan.

Brav, A., Jiang, W., Li, T., and Pinnington, J. (2021). Picking friends before picking (proxy) fights: How mutual fund voting shapes proxy contests. In E. C. G. I. (ECGI) (Ed.), *Finance Working Paper*.

Brav, A., Jiang, W., Partnoy, F., and Thomas, R. (2008). Hedge fund activism, corporate governance, and firm performance. *The Journal of Finance*, 63(4): 1729–1775.

Carrothers, A. (2017). Friends or foes? Activist hedge funds and other institutional investors. *Economics and Business Review*, 3(17): 38–72.

Cheffins, B. R. and Amour, J. (2011). The past, present and future of shareholder activism by hedge funds. *Journal of Corporation Law*, 37: 51–102.

Chung, H. and Talaulicar, T. (2010). Forms and effects of shareholder activism. *Corporate Governance: An International Review*, 18(4): 253–257.

Crutchley, C. E., Hudson, C. D., and Jensen, M. R. H. (1998). Shareholder wealth effects of CalPERS' activism. *Financial Services Review*, 7(1): 1–10.

Dubois, E., McGinty, S., and Uchida, K. (2019). What Roles Proxy Advisors Play: Evidence from International Comparison. Available at SSRN: https://ssrn.com/abstract=2666078 or http://dx.doi.org/10.2139/ssrn.2666078.

Dumas, C. and Louche, C. (2016). Collective beliefs on responsible investment. *Business & Society*, 55(3): 427–457.

Financial Reporting Council. 2012. The UK stewardship code. London: FRC.

Fisch, J. E. (2021). Mutual fund stewardship and the empty voting problem. In E. C. G. Institute (Ed.), *Law Working Paper*. Available at SSRN: https://ssrn.com/abstract=3939112.

Gantchev, N. (2013). The costs of shareholder activism: Evidence from a sequential decision model. *Journal of Financial Economics*, 107(3): 610–631.

Gillan, S. L. and Starks, L. T. (2000). Corporate governance proposals and shareholder activism: The role of institutional investors. *Journal of Financial Economics*, 57(2): 275–305.

Gillan, S. L. and Starks, L. T. (2009). The evolution of shareholder activism in the United States. In H. C. Donald, & L. G. Stuart (Eds.), U.S. Corporate Governance: 202–240: Columbia University Press.

Gilson, R. J. and Gordon, J. N. (2019). The rise of agency capitalism and the role of shareholder activists in making it work. *Journal of Applied Corporate Finance*, 31(1): 8–22.

Girard, C. and Gates, S. (2014). Global drivers of and local resistance to French shareholder activism. *Journal of Applied Corporate Finance*, 26(1): 26–32.

Goodman, J., Louche, C., Cranenburgh, K., and Arenas, D. (2014). Social shareholder engagement: The dynamics of voice and exit. *Journal of Business Ethics*, 125(2): 193–210.

Goranova, M. and Ryan, L. V. (2014). Shareholder activism. *Journal of Management*, 40(5): 1230–1268.

Guercio, D. D. and Hawkins, J. (1999). The motivation and impact of pension fund activism. *Journal of Financial Economics*, 52(3): 293–340.

Hirschman, A. O. (1970). *Exit, Voice and Loyalty: Responses to Decline in Firms, Organizations, and States*. Cambridge, MA: Harvard University Press.

Huimin, C. and Talaulicar, T. (2010). Forms and effects of shareholder activism. *Corporate Governance: An International Review*, 18: 253–257.

Hunt, C., Weber, O., and Dordi, T. (2017). A comparative analysis of the anti-Apartheid and fossil fuel divestment campaigns. *Journal of Sustainable Finance & Investment*, 7(1): 64–81.

Insightia. (2021). *The Activist Investing Annual Review. The Eighth Annual Review of Trends in Shareholder Activism.*

John, N. (2000). The campaign against British bank involvement in Apartheid South Africa. *African Affairs*, 99(396): 415–433.

King, L. and Gish, E. (2015). Marketizing social change: Social shareholder activism and responsible investing. *Sociological Perspectives*, 58(4): 711–730.

Kurtz, L. (2008). Socially responsible investment and shareholder activism. In A. Crane, D. Matten, J. Moon, and D. S. Siegel (Eds.), *The Oxford Handbook of Corporate Social Responsibility*. Oxford: Oxford University Press.

Lazard's Shareholder Advisory Group. (2019). 2018 Review of Shareholder Activism. https://www.lazard.com/perspective/lazards-annual-review-of-shareholder-activism-2018/.

Lee, M.-D. P. and Lounsbury, M. (2011). Domesticating radical rant and rage: An exploration of the consequences of environmental shareholder resolutions on corporate environmental performance. *Business & Society*, 50(1): 155–188.

Louche, C. and Lydenberg, S. (2006). Socially responsible investment: difference between Europe and United States. Vlerick Leuven Gent Management School Working Papers.

Marens, R. (2002). Inventing corporate governance: The mid-century emergence of shareholder activism. *Journal of Business & Management*, Fall: 8(4): 365–389.

McNulty, T. and Nordberg, D. (2016). Ownership, activism and engagement: Institutional investors as active owners. *Corporate Governance: An International Review*, 24(3): 346–358.

Milgrom, P. and Roberts, J. (1997). Economie, organisation et management: De Boeck Université, éds. Presses Universitaires de Grenoble.

Mitchell, R. K., Agle, B. R., and Wood, D. J. (1997). Toward a theory of stakeholder identification and salience: Defining the principle of who and what really counts. *Academy of Management Review*, 22: 853–886.

Monks, R. A. G. and Minow, N. (2011). *Corporate Governance* (5th ed.). Chichester, West Sussex, U.K., Wiley.

Roberts, J., Sanderson, P., Barker, R., and Hendry, J. (2006). In the mirror of the market: The disciplinary effects of company/fund manager meetings. *Accounting, Organizations and Society*, 31(3): 277–294.

Schwartz, D. E. (1971). Proxy power and social goals — How Campaign GM succeeded. *St. John's Law Review*, 45(4): 764–771.

Smith, M. P. (1996). Shareholder activism by institutional investors: Evidence from CalPERS. *The Journal of Finance*, 51(1): 227–252.

Le Sourd, V. and Shahyar, S. (2021). The European ETF market: Growth, trends, and impact on underlying instruments. *The Journal of Portfolio Management*, 47(7): 95–111.

Strickland, D., Wiles, K. W., and Zenner, M. (1996). A requiem for the USA is small shareholder monitoring effective? *Journal of Financial Economics*, 40(2): 319–338.

Welker, M. and Wood, D. (2011). Shareholder activism and alienation. *Current Anthropology*, 52(S3): S57–S69.

Wong, C., Brackley, A., and Petroy, E. (2019). *Rate the Raters 2019: Expert Views on ESG Ratings*. London, UK: Sustainability.

Yan, S., Ferraro, F., and Almandoz, J. (2018). The rise of socially responsible investment funds: The paradoxical role of the financial logic. *Administrative Science Quarterly*, 64(2): 466–501.

© 2023 World Scientific Publishing Company
https://doi.org/10.1142/9789811260483_0008

Chapter 8

Ethics of the Sharing Economy: The Example of Reward- and Equity-Based Crowdfunding

Sandrine Frémeaux and Carine Girard-Guerraud

Audencia Business School, Nantes, France

Abstract

The sharing economy may be an opportunity to respond to real societal needs through the mutualization of resources and to encourage new communities through the democratization of power. Mutualization and democratization do not guarantee the ethical nature of this movement. Our research question is under what conditions the sharing economy can present the ethical dimensions highlighted by sharing-related literature. To answer that question, we explore the theoretical and empirical context of crowdfunding (CF) and focus on the comparative analysis of five reward- and equity-based CF platforms. This study emphasizes the conditions needed for ethical CF and, more generally, for an ethical sharing economy: the possibility to give gratuitously; the pursuit of a societal purpose; cooperation within and between groups of actors; long-term stability of spaces and times dedicated to cooperation; virtual and possibly physical arenas of cooperation; and people dedicated to cooperation.

Keywords: Crowdfunding; ethics; mutualization; democratization; sharing economy

1. Introduction

The sharing economy reflects a paradigm shift that leads to an economy based more on use than on ownership. The major difficulty confronting us when attempting to define the sharing economy is the ethical dimension. Indeed, the emergence of the sharing economy "reveals a transition from a declining social contract wherein the State was predominantly responsible for the common good toward an emerging social contract characterized by a co-responsibility of multiple agents in this respect" (De Bettignies & Lépineux, 2009, p. 159). The question is whether a sharing economy is a way for economic actors to "exercise a collaborative responsibility" (Wettstein, 2012) and to support and promote the common good. While some scholars call into question the ethical impact of this new economic movement (Battilana & Dorado, 2010; Parguel, Lunardo, & Benoit-Moreau, 2016), considering it as a sort of neo-liberal nightmare (Moore & Robinson, 2015), others emphasize the societal, social, and environmental usefulness of the sharing economy (Schor & Wengronowitz, 2017).

In the first perspective, the sharing economy would include uberization, also known as the gig economy, which is a source of the degradation of working conditions (Meelen & Frenken, 2015), and does not reflect the community dynamics that normally characterize a sharing economy (Botsman, 2014a). In the second perspective, these consumption, production, funding, and educational patterns permit a response to societal needs and the creation of new communities. Scholars such as Belk (2010, 2014), Battilana and Dorado (2010), Botsman (2014a, 2014b), and Parguel *et al.* (2016) have identified two main characteristics of the sharing economy: the mutualization and optimization of resources and the democratization of relations and power.

However, despite these two characteristics, it is by no means certain that the sharing economy is an opportunity to act ethically. Indeed, the researchers who have addressed the issue of sharing by drawing on the gift theory (Godbout & Caillé, 2000), the commons theory (Ostrom, 2000), and the common good theory (Sison & Fontrodona, 2012) have argued that the ethical dimension of sharing is unclear because sharing is not a good in itself but requires the presence of certain conditions. Therefore, the question is under what conditions could the sharing economy constitute an ethical economic movement.

To answer this question, we focus both theoretically and empirically on crowdfunding (CF) platforms the objective of which is to put project initiators and potential funders into contact with each other (Tomczak & Brem, 2013; André, Bureau, & Gautier, 2017). CF can be defined as "an open call through the internet for the provision of financial resources either in form of donation or in exchange for some form of reward and/or voting rights in order to support initiatives for specific purposes" (Belleflamme, Lambert, & Schwienbacher, 2014). CF platforms appear to meet the two aforementioned criteria of the sharing economy. On one hand, CF platforms facilitate a mutualization of human and physical resources because they connect people in pursuit of the same goals. On the other hand, CF platforms encourage democratization, enabling entrepreneurs to obtain access to both capital and the support of a whole community of investors who validate their businesses.

The remainder of the article is organized as follows. Section 2 introduces the concept of the sharing economy and focuses on its ethical characteristics. Section 3 presents a literature review on sharing-related theories, including the gift theory, the commons theory, and the common good theory. Section 4 explores the theoretical and empirical context of CF and concentrates on a comparative analysis of five reward- and equity-based CF platforms. Section 5 is a discussion of the conditions needed for ethical CF and for an ethical sharing economy. Section 6 consists of the conclusion.

2. Ethical Characteristics of the Sharing Economy

Interpreted restrictively, the sharing economy is reduced to an access economy (Botsman & Rogers, 2010; Botsman, 2014a, 2014b) whereby individuals grant each other temporary access to under-utilized physical assets ("idle capacity"), possibly in exchange for money (Frenken & Schor, 2017). Lamberton and Rose (2012) and Sundararajan (2016) consider the sharing economy as a class of economic arrangements in which asset owners and users mutualize access to the products or services associated with those assets. This definition seems to overlook the ethical advantages of the sharing economy in terms of reducing negative environmental impact, accelerating sustainable consumption, improving the quality of service and production, creating stronger communities, and increasing participatory democracy. It also places too much emphasis on new technologies the use of which does not necessarily constitute a characteristic of the sharing economy. For example, shared physical locations, such as Repair Café or Fab Lab, that are available free of charge to all and that facilitate the use of some production resources along with collective learning are undoubtedly based on the dynamics of sharing and are, therefore, part of the sharing economy.

Another vision of the sharing economy highlights its positive impact, both environmental and social, and has generated debate in recent literature. Environmentally, the sharing economy that is assumed to reduce the demand for new goods or the construction of new facilities is less resource-intensive (Schor & Wengronowitz, 2017). According to Frenken and Schor (2017), there is as yet no empirical evidence for these claims, apart from car sharing where substantial reductions in CO_2 emissions are achieved. Those who participate in a sharing economy for ecological reasons would not necessarily adopt the most virtuous forms of behavior. Parguel *et al.* (2016) reveal the phenomenon of overconsumption on a platform for buying and selling used goods between private individuals. The possibility to buy used goods would provide a justification for overconsumption; buyers, recyclers, or borrowers would use these platforms to gain access to goods that are not substitutes for but are added to existing assets. Socially, the sharing economy is assumed to provide people with access to goods they cannot usually have access to. However, sharing platforms may also strengthen the individualization of work, weaken the social protection of entrepreneurs (Slee, 2016), undermine social cohesion, and increase discrimination and exclusionary forms of behavior in the choice of partners or collaborators (Frenken & Schor, 2017).

This literature review puts forward two potentially ethical characteristics of the sharing economy, as follows:

- Societal usefulness based on the mutualization of resources: The mutualization of resources contributes to a sustainable economic system by unlocking the value of unused or underutilized assets, by fostering their shared use, or by reducing the need to produce new goods (Benkler, 2004; Battilana & Dorado, 2010; Parguel *et al.*, 2016). The mutualization of resources also allows individuals to help people in need and to contribute to societal usefulness.
- Democratization of power based on horizontal structures: The sharing economy is built on democratization of power that creates a sense of belonging, a collective accountability, and a mutual benefit throughout the community (Williamson & De Meyer, 2012; Belk, 2014).

Therefore, we define the sharing economy as a socioeconomic system built around the sharing of resources and based on the ethical search for societal purpose and democratization, enabling existing or emergent communities to flourish.

3. Literature Review on Sharing-Related Theories in the Context of the Sharing Economy

3.1. *The gift theory*

In his analysis of the functioning of archaic societies, Mauss (1924) emphasizes that the gift leads to reciprocity that manifests itself through the countergift while acknowledging that the gift includes both an interested and a disinterested dimension, which Bourdieu calls the double truth of the gift (2001). Durkheim (1893) uses the term "homo duplex" to describe this tension between a moral ideal of "disinterestedness, attachment to something other than ourselves" and a "necessarily selfish" utilitarian motive. Mauss (1924) proposes an anthropology of the "total man". This broad and unrestricted anthropology allows the combination of the two human facets, the homo donator and the homo reciprocus, without reducing the human being to an individual whose only joy would be to give for free or to a solely calculating individual motivated by greed. As a homo donator and a homo reciprocus, the human being needs to share by experiencing both gratuitousness and exchange.

3.1.1. *Societal usefulness of gratuitousness*

The sharing economy may rely on this anthropological vision whereby the human being deeply needs to experience gratuitousness (André *et al.*, 2017). What characterizes gratuitousness is the lack of a right or a guarantee to profit in any way (Godbout & Caillé, 2000). A gift does not exclude the possibility of a genuine countergift or of a later narcissistic benefit, but gratification or satisfaction is not the primary purpose of gratuitousness. The primary purpose of gratuitousness is to respond to the recipients' needs (Frémeaux & Michelson, 2011). Therefore, individuals may be interdependent and interconnected not only because goods and services circulate among them but also because they can experience gratuitousness through their participation in a project that responds to societal needs.

3.1.2. *Gratuitousness as a factor of cooperation*

The sharing economy may give the opportunity to experience both gratuitousness and generalized reciprocity. Gift theorists have observed that gratuitousness is a factor of exchange and of generalized reciprocity (A gives to B, B gives to C) (Godbout & Caillé, 2000; Bruni, 2008, 2012). Similarly, virtual or non-virtual communities are stimulated by gifts that do not necessarily return to the initial givers but generate gift dynamics (Belk, 2010; Fitzmaurice *et al.*, 2016; Frenken & Schor, 2017). Gratuitousness can result in a generalized reciprocity of information, advice, and services on platforms or even in face-to-face meetings.

3.1.3. *Virtue development resulting from gift dynamics*

Just as the gratuitous gift can encourage the spreading of virtues (Godbout & Caillé, 2000; Bruni, 2008, 2012), the sharing economy might be an opportunity to develop virtues. Benkler and Nissenbaum (2006) admit that the sharing economy can be rooted in a "gift culture" generating the pleasure or satisfaction of giving for the sake of generosity, kindness, and benevolence. Consequently, these scholars consider the sharing economy as a factor in human progress; the sharing economy "serves not only as the source of knowledge and information but as a platform for virtuous practices and the development of virtue in its participants" (Benkler & Nissenbaum, 2006, p. 419).

3.2. *The commons theory*

Elinor Ostrom was a political scientist at Indiana University who received the Nobel Prize for her research on the importance of the commons around the world. Proposed in 1990, Ostrom's self-regulation model was supplemented by subsequent research (Ostrom, 2000) and has been documented by numerous case studies (Hess & Ostrom, 2007). It justifies decentralized governance for rival commons (such as limited natural common-pool resources). Ostrom's work has been used to question self-organizing governance for non-rival common goods, such as knowledge and software (Benkler & Nissenbaum, 2006; Bollier & Helfrich, 2014; Akrivou & Sison, 2016; Albareda & Sison, 2020).

3.2.1. *Local cooperation*

The commons theory is based on the importance of dialog at the operational level; community members have rapid and easy access to a local arena to solve their conflicts at a low cost (Hess and Ostrom, 2007). The governance systems within the sharing economy are based on the idea that local cooperation is more effective than control exercised by a centralized authority, as it involves the most competent and motivated members of the community (Benkler and Nissenbaum, 2006).

3.2.2. *Cooperation between levels*

The key strategy of self-organized and self-governed individuals when facing a disagreement at an operational level is to move back and forth between the different levels. In certain platforms of the sharing economy, when an agreement cannot be obtained at the local level, mediation procedures allow third parties who are foreign to the conflict to intervene. These specific mediation arenas are added to the local arenas and examine the disagreements on ways of implementing the project (Benkler & Nissenbaum, 2006).

3.3. *The common good theory*

Based on the Aristotelian–Thomistic tradition, the concept of common good is defined as a set of conditions, i.e., economic, social, moral, and spiritual, that favor personal fulfillment. For instance, Messner defines the common good as "that order of society in which every member enjoys the possibility of realizing his true self by participating in the effects of the cooperation of all" (Messner, 1965, p. 124). The common good principle is characterized by a simultaneous pursuit of a community good and a personal good (Sison & Fontrodona, 2012; Frémeaux, 2020; Frémeaux, Puyou, & Michelson, 2020).

While there is no reference to the common good theory in the literature on the sharing economy, there seems to be a widespread "common good" claim by a number of platforms (Fitzmaurice *et al.*, 2016), which may be connected to the main characteristics of the common good principle (Sison & Fontrondona, 2012; Albareda & Sison, 2020; Frémeaux, 2020): subsidiarity, teleological hierarchy, and the pursuit of human development.

3.3.1. *Subsidiarity, teleological hierarchy, and the pursuit of human development*

The common good principle relies on both subsidiarity and teleological hierarchy (Melé, 2009; Sison & Fontrodona, 2012; Frémeaux & Michelson, 2017; Frémeaux, 2020). The concept of subsidiarity means that each community level should have flexibility and autonomy in the exercise of its responsibilities. This implies that the different community levels can be interweaved in the common perspective of human development. The notion of teleological hierarchy means that the different disciplines are interlinked by a hierarchy, whereby the lower levels, material and economic, are at the service of the higher levels, ethical and spiritual. This teleological hierarchy principle aims to ensure that all the levels are committed to the same purpose, which is human development (Sison & Fontrodona, 2012; Tedmanson *et al.*, 2015). This reduces the risk of focusing on the higher levels and neglecting the economic dimension on the assumption that this dimension constitutes the lower level. It also avoids the risk of ignoring the social and environmental objectives on the pretext that the economic objectives have not been reached. Concerns about economic performance do not supplant the central question of how a community good can contribute to human development. In the context of the sharing economy, this means that the pursuit of an economic interest can be part of the quest for a higher purpose, i.e., social, ethical, or environmental, that ensures human development. Likewise, the participants do not individually support projects, but they participate together in the realization of projects. They abandon being known as the main contributors and accept as a fundamental and priority objective their support for a collective cause.

4. The Example of Crowdfunding

4.1. *Theoretical analysis of crowdfunding platforms*

The purpose of our study is to determine the conditions for a responsible sharing economy (Table 1) by using the specific case of CF. Although a relatively recent research subject, CF has already given rise to numerous exploratory studies that Bruton, Khavul, Siegel, and Wright (2014) have structured around five research orientations: CF regulations and the importance of the institutional context; supply of capital, more

Table 1. Comparative analysis of sharing economy theories and sharing-related theories. 1.

Literature on sharing-related theories	Societal usefulness based on the mutualization of resources	Democratization of power based on horizontal structures
	(Benkler, 2004; Benkler & Nissenbaum, 2006; Battilana & Dorado, 2010; Belk, 2010, 2014; Battilana & Dorado, 2010; Botsman, 2014a, 2014b; Parguel *et al.*, 2016; André *et al.*, 2017)	(Benkler & Nissenbaum, 2006; Belk, 2010, 2014; Battilana & Dorado, 2010; Williamson & De Meyer, 2012; Botsman, 2014a, 2014b; Parguel *et al.*, 2016; Fitzmaurice *et al.*, 2016; Frenken & Schor, 2017)
Theory of gift (Mauss, 1924, 1950; Godbout & Caillé, 2000; Bruni, 2008, 2012)	Societal usefulness of gratuitousness Virtue development resulting from gift dynamics	Gratuitousness as a factor of cooperation
Theory of commons (Ostrom, 1990, 2000; Hess & Ostrom, 2007)	Rival commons	Local cooperation Cooperation between levels
Theory of common good (Melé, 2009; Sison & Fontrodona, 2012)	Teleological hierarchy Pursuit of human development	Subsidiarity

specifically the role played by online platforms in providing alternative and traditionally funded sources; demand for capital; ownership and new corporate governance issues; and outcomes. Recent studies on CF have focused on the positive financial impact of CF platforms. Participations have a high combined impact (Lehner, 2013; Agrawal, Catalini, & Goldfard, 2013, 2016; Mollick, 2014), allowing project initiators to benefit from the bandwagon effect (Match & Weatherston, 2014) and to acquire further external funding (Bellavatis *et al.*, 2017).

France occupies a leading position in Europe (European Alternative Finance Industry Report, 2016) notably due to the high number of CF platforms (Dushnitsky *et al.*, 2016) and due to the country's flexible and attractive CF regulations. It was one of the first countries (by virtue of Ordinance no. 2014-559 of May 30, 2014) to grant legal status to equity CF platforms so as to alert crowd investors to the risks of illiquidity and dilution of their capital. Since Ordinance no. 2016-520 of April 28, 2016, platforms with the status of Participative Investment Advisor conferred by the French Markets Authority can issue any type of share to a value of 2.5 million Euros (previously 1 million Euros for shares). In the United States, the Jumpstart Our Business Startup (JOBS) Act has recently encouraged the development of crowd equity by relaxing the regulatory constraints, particularly that of Chapter 3 that hitherto prohibited CF involving unqualified investors. By 2025, the World Bank forecasts that CF will account for over USD 300 billion in cumulative transactions worldwide (Meyskens & Bird, 2015).

One first ethical issue raised by CF relates to the type of business model used by the platforms. Previous studies have developed classifications of platform types according to sources of funding (Schwienbacher & Larralde, 2012; Bruton *et al.*, 2014) by distinguishing donation-based CF (donation without reward), reward-based CF (donation with reward), and investment-based CF, including lending and equity (purchase of shares). Some platforms have adopted a mixed model (Cholakova & Clarysse, 2015) with a combination of different sources of funding. As noted by Short, Ketchen, McKenny, Alisson, and Ireland (2017), approximately a quarter of existing studies have focused on the potential of CF to inform and influence lending decisions.

Another ethical issue is CF investors' motivation, which is related to the type and stage of the project to be funded. Gerber and Hui (2016) classify crowd investors according to their motivations and distinguish between those who seek financial or non-financial rewards and those who wish to help others, be part of a community, or support a cause. On one hand, a financial or non-financial countergift may be the only objective of the contributors. For example, in the Netherlands, Cholakova and Clarysse (2015) examined 155 surveys completed by investors at Sympid, the country's largest equity CF platform, and found that crowd investors are only motivated by financial and utilitarian concerns. In looking at the French WiSEED platform for equity CF, Hervé, manthé, Sannajust, and Schwienbacher (2017) used a behavioral finance approach that helps explain motivations and potential biases in making investments. The authors found that an overwhelming 93% of investors in projects are male, as males tend to have a lower level of risk aversion than women. On the other hand, with certain platforms, most of the crowd investors do not look at the business plan but rather focus on the ideas embodied by the firm and consequently its legitimacy (Lehner, 2013). The crowd, therefore, acts as a real vector of confidence (Gerber & Hui, 2016) and only supports a project if they believe their contribution will make a societal impact (Mollick, 2014; Kuppuswamy & Bayus, 2017).

Yet another ethical issue is the degree of cooperation in the pre-investment phase. Calling for crowd participation in any form opens up possibilities of benefitting from crowd wisdom, crowd creation, crowd voting, and CF. Through a constant dialog with the platform's community, a company can pre-test its products, design its goods and/or services, mobilize individual expertise and skills, and use social networks to create a "buzz". To this end, the project initiators should improve signal quality to reduce information asymmetries between project initiators and crowd investors (Ahlers *et al.*, 2015). Based on experimental research, Drover, Wood, and Zacharakis (2017b) underline certification effects linked to the CF platform itself. This certification gives a positive signal to partners (e.g., business angels), encouraging them to participate in the later stages of investment (Drover *et al.*, 2017a). According to Tomboc (2013), there is nevertheless a problem of adverse selection due to the fact that the average investor on a CF platform does not have the capacity to evaluate the project. Cooperation can be activated to reduce this information asymmetry in the pre-investment phase, but this often implies a high minimum contribution (Hornuf & Schwienbacher, 2014) and co-investment (Ley & Weaven, 2011; Löher, 2017).

The last ethical issue is the encouragement of cooperation in the post-investment phase. Reducing the moral hazard risk and potential conflicts of interest remains a major corporate governance challenge for platforms after capital has been raised. Drover *et al.* (2017b) indicate that the power shifts to project initiators in the post-investment phase. Indeed, crowd investors are managed in an investment vehicle called a holding (Tomczak & Brem, 2013). Within this holding, their collective coalition is weak due to the absence of veto rights coupled with a minority share in capital (Schwienbacher & Larralde, 2012).

This literature review highlights four ethical issues raised by CF: the business model based on donation, reward, or investment (including lending and equity); the ideas embodied by the project initiator; cooperation in the pre-investment phase; and cooperation in the post-investment phase.

4.2. *Empirical analysis of crowdfunding platforms*

Our empirical analysis of CF took place in France because it is one of the European leaders with the highest number of CF platforms, second only to the United Kingdom (Dushnistky *et al.*, 2016). According to the CF barometer in France (KPMG-FPF, 2017), 153.6 million Euros were collected by the end of the first half of 2017, which represents an increase of 48% over the year before. In total, 79.1 million Euros were collected by lending-based platforms; 35.4 million Euros were collected by reward-based platforms; 32.2 million Euros were collected by equity-based platforms; and 6.9 million Euros were collected by donation-based platforms. These figures reveal that the equity- and reward-based models raise an almost equivalent amount and constitute the most important business models (after the lending-based one).

Therefore, to be able to make a comparative analysis, we chose to focus on reward- and equity-based platforms and selected five: Tudigo, LITA.co, WiSEED, KissKissBankBank, and Ulule. To reflect the heterogeneity of these two models, we made three sampling choices: selecting a platform with a mixed model (Tudigo); choosing the leader in equity-based CF (WiSEED) and the leader in reward-based CF (KissKissBankBank); and selecting platforms with B Corp certification, which is conferred by a non-governmental organization called B Lab on firms committed to the common good (LITA.co and Ulule). This certification is based on five criteria: environment, workers, customers, community, and governance. A minimum of 80 out of 200 items must be validated in the B impact assessment to be eligible for the certification. Ulule, the French reward-based platform, is certified because it supports cultural, educative, solidarity, environmental, and citizenship projects (among them is the founding of an app for hospitalized children). LITA.co is the second-largest equity-based French CF platform with B Corp certification. Its purpose is to "make sense of savings" through its "Live Impact Trust Act". LITA.co specializes in growth, environmental transition, social housing, inclusion, health, and society.

Unlike Ulule, LITA.co, Tudigo, and KissKissBankBank have the status of participative investment advisor (Conseiller en Investissement Participatif or CIP) granted by the French Markets Authority, which authorizes platforms to issue equity and loans up to a value of 2.5 million Euros. WiSEED is the only equity CF platform to have investment services provider (Prestataire de Services d'Investissement or PSI) status granted by the French Supervisory Authority, which allows it to issue shares up to a value of 5 million Euros.

The two reward CF platforms, KissKissBankBank and Ulule, are owned by banks that accept co-financing one nominated project each month within the limit of 50% of the amount collected by the crowdfunders for La Banque Postale and KissKissBankBank and 7,500 Euros for BNPParibas and Ulule. The three equity CF platforms have several partners, including banks, business angel networks, advisory firms, incubators, and chambers of commerce.

To provide further insight into societal usefulness and the democratization of power, we conducted an in-depth analysis of the institutional website of each platform. To supplement this information, we translated and analyzed existing French empirical research, including Onnée and Renault (2014) focusing on Ulule and KissKissBankBank (analysis of two specific projects based on information provided by the platform and semi-directive interviews with project initiators), Bessière and Stéphany (2015) focusing on WiSEED (in-depth study of the platform based on semi-directive interviews with its directors and business managers), and Girard and Deffains-Crapsky (2016) focusing on Tudigo and WiSEED (analysis of websites, expert opinions on the sites, and semi-directive interviews with managers). Bessière and Stéphany (2017) devoted a part of their book *Le crowdfunding — Fondements et pratiques* to an in-depth analysis of the projects supported by KissKissBankBank.

The comparative analysis of CF platforms reveals a diversity of rules and practices related to the business models used by the platforms, the ideas embodied by the project initiators, and the modalities of cooperation implemented during the different phases of investment. The analysis of the business models (equity- or reward-based CF) and of the ideas embodied by the project initiators (economic, ethical, social, and environmental impacts) reveals the different dynamics of mutualization (Table 2). The focus on the modalities of cooperation in the pre- and post-investment phases reflects the various forms of democratization (Table 3). Cooperation arenas implemented by CF platforms are outlined in Figure 1.

A deeper analysis of the platforms results in the following general observations:

- The dynamic of gratuitousness can exist in all types of CF platforms.

We use the general term of investors to refer to both backers in the reward-based system and crowd investors in the equity-based system because in both models they invest money to support projects that may contribute to a societal purpose. The gratuitous gifts identified in this study are not gifts without return, according to the aforementioned literature on gifts where return is not a primary goal. In the hypothesis of reward-based CF, i.e., gifts with rewards, gratuitousness may be a

Table 2. Dynamics of mutualization in equity- or reward-based crowdfunding platforms.

Crowdfunding platforms	Reward- or equity-based models	Ideas embodied by the project initiators
Tudigo CIP status	Mixed model based on reward and equity	Specialized: sustainable projects with positive impact in local areas (i.e., economic, social, and/or environmental impact)
LITA.co (ex 1001Pact) CIP status B-Corp certification	Equity-based	Specialized: growth, environmental transition, social housing, inclusion, health, and society
WiSEED PSI status	Equity-based	Generalist: start-ups, housing, social innovation, renewable energy, and agroforestry
KissKissBankBank CIP status	Reward-based	Specialized: creativity and innovation. Dedicated to directors, journalists, musicians, designers, artists, photographers, humanists, explorers, navigators, athletes, and farmers.
Ulule B-Corp certification	Reward-based	Generalist: culture, learning, solidarity, environment, and citizenship

significant component of the business model. Indeed, rewards (that can take the form of a thank you note or a customized product) can hardly be analyzed as the primary or sole objective of the gifts. Investors share a common hope that these gifts will benefit others in a generalized reciprocity.

In the case of equity-based CF, profit-sharing and the exercise of voting power at annual general meetings are the expected countergifts. Investors take the risk of facing a lack of profits or even a financial loss. However, this financial risk-taking would not be considered as gratuitous gifts in the gift literature because the financial returns can be the primary goal of these gifts.

There are, however, aspects of gratuitousness in both business models; the time, the opinions, the advice, the networking with experts, and

Table 3. Dynamics of democratization and cooperation in equity- or reward-based crowdfunding platforms.

Platforms	Cooperation in the pre-investment phase	Cooperation in the post-investment phase
Tudigo CIP status	• Business plan co-constructed by project initiators, the platform, and partners and available to investors • Public information on the platform website for each project • Questions and ideas communicated by the crowd to the platform through help@ bulbintown.com • Possibility for the crowd to ask direct questions to the project initiators • No indication of physical meetings during specific events on the website • Social networks and blogs • One community manager in charge of the campaign	• Access to quarterly and annual reporting sent in by the project initiators • Possible direct dialog with the project initiators • Vote at the annual general meetings (AGMs) • One person in charge of investor relations
LITA.co (ex 1001Pact) CIP status B-Corp certification	• Selection committee with criteria based on social and environmental impact, corporate social responsibility and growth perspectives • Business plan co-constructed by project initiators, the platform, and partners and available to investors • Public information on the platform website for each project • Access to indicators related to societal impact • Direct dialog with the project initiators • E-vote • Social networks and blogs • No indication of physical meetings during specific events on the website	• Access for investors to financial and extra-financial reporting • Possibility for investors to bring their expertise • Vote at the AGMs • Access to information on all funded projects
WiSEED PSI status	• Selection committee • Scoring tool to alert investors to risk levels • E-vote as a selection activity • Business plan co-constructed by project initiators, the platform, and partners and available to investors	• Access to financial reporting made available by the head of investment. • Involvement of mentors on the

(*Continued*)

Table 3. (*Continued*)

	• Public information on the platform website for each project • Virtual and physical meetings (platform's team and potential crowd investors) • Forum between crowd investors and project initiators • Involvement of partners through contacts (social and personal networks) • Social networks and blogs • Physical meetings during specific events (on average, five per month)	board or strategic committee • Space dedicated to the management of the investment portfolio • Through this, possibility to have a direct dialog between investors and project initiators • One person in charge of investor relations
KissKiss BankBank CIP status	• Comments on the project webpage • Selection process involving other partners (institutions, associations, media, and business schools) • Involvement of partners through contacts (social and personal networks)	• "Follow the project" on the website on an optional basis
Ulule B-Corp certification	• Forum between crowd investors and project initiators (Ulule community) • Events • Three internet cooperation tools for a successful campaign (buffer, tweetdeck, and feedly) • Two community managers in charge of the campaign	

the involvement of investors are undoubtedly the result of a dynamic of gratuitousness. Focusing on reward-based CF, Onnée and Renault (2014) observe that project initiators receive both relational and emotional gifts thanks to the communication provided and the confidence granted by the investors. "Investors promote the project through their social networks and acquaintances. (…) While the project initiators come initially to collect money, they leave loaded with a more emotional baggage: a tenfold-boosted self-confidence and a feeling of shared optimism" (p. 129).

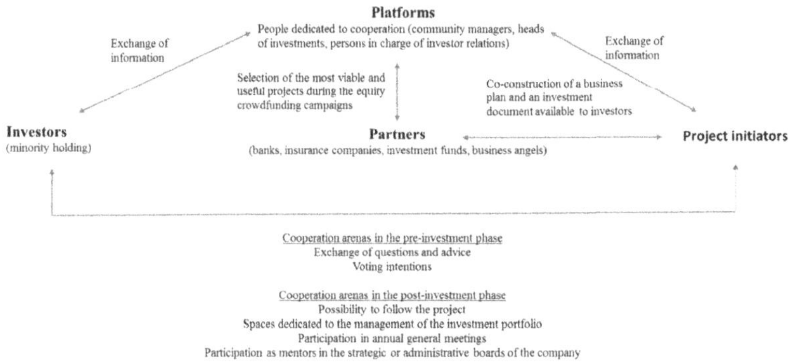

Figure 1. Possible cooperation arenas implemented by crowdfunding platforms.

Exploring equity-based CF, Girard and Deffains-Crapsky (2016) describe e-voting as a collective gift. "E-voting helps to build a stable and motivated collective opinion on the success of the project" (p. 12). Some investors involved in the pre-investment phase as mentors can attend the strategic or administrative board meetings of the company in the post-investment phase. This involvement is another example of possible gratuitousness in both business models, as these mentors will not receive any attendance fees during their term of office. More generally, Bessière and Stéphany (2015) evoke the altruistic motivation of the investors in equity- and reward-based CF given the "willingness to participate and get involved in a societal project" (p. 35).

- The pursuit of a societal purpose can exist in all types of CF platforms.

Specialized platforms can visibly pursue a societal purpose by monitoring the positive social or environmental impact of the projects, but generalist platforms can also support projects that respond to a more broadly defined societal need. For example, the generalist platform Tudigo has developed a plan for the recovery of the firm Jeannette, producer of "madeleine" cakes, founded in 1812. Following a court-ordered liquidation, this firm was unable to obtain loans from banks, but it has become self-sufficient thanks to gift-based (100k Euros) and equity-based (300k Euros) crowd participation. Therefore, the platform has contributed to economic and social development at various levels: filling the equity gap of the firm; drawing on crowd participation to convince bankers of the viability of the new project; saving 18 direct jobs; and having a positive impact on the economic environment by enabling the firm to occupy an undeniable place among the main actors of the region.

Bessière and Stéphany (2015) show that the community perspective does not exclude the pursuit of an individual interest but is stimulated by the search for a higher ethical objective:

> The crowd can be seen from a community perspective, as a group of individuals who share common goals and values. Belonging to a community comes from two fundamental motivations: interest and passion. For the community driven by passion, the feeling of sharing a vision, bringing new ideas, and thus participating in the development of the projects presented by the platform determines its aspiration to invest in the projects (p. 10).

These authors carry out a typology of projects financed by platforms, distinguishing between "entrepreneurial projects and heritage, publishing, film, music, and journalistic projects" (p. 72). "A generalist platform such as KissKissBankBank wants to support projects which are not only innovative and creative but also have a specific purpose (p. 77)."

- The democratization of power is based on the existence of cooperation arenas within and between groups of actors.

The democratization of power is encouraged by transparency (formal or informal sharing of information) and the possibility for the crowd to ask questions and provide advice. This implies the introduction of local cooperation arenas (particularly between investors) and cooperation arenas between the main stakeholders (between investors and platforms, between platforms and project initiators, between platforms and partners, and between investors and project initiators).

Whatever the business model used by the CF platform, the success of fundraising activities is related to the possibility for the investors to comment on the project drafts on the website; share information and experience directly with project initiators; and provide expertise, vision, and address books.

> Interactive information throughout the financing process, mainly due to direct contacts between crowders and project leaders, with exchanges visible on the platform, in real time, in which any investor can participate.

> This is a new form of direct communication between a very large group of investors and the project leaders (Bessière & Stéphany, 2015, p. 9).

> Control mechanisms are complemented by more open systems to integrate the resources, knowledge, and expertise of the crowd (Girard & Deffains-Crapsky, 2016, p. 12).

Our comparative analysis also shows that each platform is characterized by specific cooperation arenas between groups. For example, the platform Ulule creates specific arenas in which it can provide advice to project initiators in terms of communication on social networks, such as Twitter, Facebook, and LinkedIn. The platform also recommends the use of Internet cooperation tools, including Buffer, which facilitates the programming of the posts, the sharing of news, and the identification of the best moments to post; TweetDeck, which allows the choice and selection of information; and Feedly, which gathers the articles in the fields that are of interest to the project initiators.

Likewise, the equity-based platforms propose cooperation arenas that reduce information asymmetry and provide advice to investors. To that end, they co-construct with project initiators and partners (banks, insurance companies, investment funds, and business angels) an investment document and a business model that are made available to investors. These crowd equity platforms also organize local cooperation arenas between partners or between partners and members of the platforms during the equity CF campaigns in order to select the most viable and useful projects. For example, as a partner of the platform LITA.co that draws on indicators related to social impact, Aviva Impact Investing provides information and invests the same amount as the crowd. Therefore, direct relationships between investors and project initiators and between partners and project initiators are frequently encouraged, while the platforms do not appear to stimulate cooperation between investors and partners who, however, share the same objective of obtaining sufficient and relevant information to enable them to make complementary or combined choices.

- The democratization of power is based on the long-term stability of spaces and times dedicated to cooperation.

The opportunity for investors to provide advice and opinions is frequently provided during the pre-investment phase, but it becomes rarer or even non-existent in the post-investment phase. While KissKissBankBank proposes to the investors on an optional basis the possibility of "following the project", there is no such indication on the Ulule website. The three equity-based CF platforms give the possibility for investors and project initiators to continue the information exchange on the financial and strategic aspects and on the rules related to the exit of investors. However, the minority participation of the holding bringing the crowd investors together weakens their collective expression in general meetings. Regarding the post-investment phase, Girard and Deffains-Crapsky (2016) even state that "The goal is to have sleeping partners by not giving the crowd any power (p. 9)." The investors only benefit from a space dedicated to the management of their investment portfolio and to the connection with project initiators. However, LITA.co gives investors the opportunity to express themselves regarding the social and societal purpose of the project during meetings.

- The democratization of power is based on virtual and physical cooperation arenas.

Physical cooperation appears to be incompatible with the dynamics of CF because of the frequent geographical remoteness of the different actors. Nevertheless, mentors are chosen from among investors during the pre-investment phase and can be physically present in cooperation arenas, such as strategic committees and boards of directors. For example, WiSEED favors physical meetings between mentors and project initiators on the subject of the strategic and economic choices of the firms.

- The democratization of power is based on the recruitment of people dedicated to cooperation.

Certain CF platforms have recruited people dedicated to cooperation: community managers in charge of cooperation in the pre-investment phase, heads of investment, and people in charge of investor relations who oversee cooperation in the post-investment phase. The platforms that recruit people dedicated to cooperation have more easily succeeded in maintaining support for projects and direct relationships with investors in the post-investment phase.

> The effectiveness of the system depends on the platform's human and technical resources to ensure effective monitoring of participation. It also involves a strong interaction between investors and the platform's

project manager in charge of supporting the start-up (Bessière & Stéphany, 2015, p. 14).

5. Discussion

This study follows on from the work of André *et al.* (2017) that analyzes reciprocal giving in reward-based CF and confirms that this model is characterized by a spirit of cooperation based on gift and reciprocity. Building on a comparative analysis of the platforms, we would add that this dynamic of cooperation is itself rooted in areas of freedom enabling investors to give money and advice freely without having expectations other than rewards. This illustrates that gratuitousness is likely to trigger reciprocity and cooperation (Godbout & Caillé, 2000) and thus shows that gratuitousness plays a central role in reward-based CF (and not exclusively in donation-based CF). We also observe that the dynamic of cooperation is weakly developed in the post-investment phase, while in the process of reward-based CF, certain investors may want to continue supporting project initiators without any expectation of return because they may consider their intervention as virtuous (Bruni, 2008, 2012) or meaningful (Sison & Fontrodona, 2012).

Likewise, this study reveals that equity-based CF can also aim to support projects of societal utility and can draw on frequent and sustainable cooperation arenas (Hess & Ostrom, 2007). The risk highlighted in this research is that the spirit of monitoring inherent to financial participation prevails over the spirit of cooperation, leading investors to request additional information rather than sharing the information and the expertise they may have.

In order to avoid these risks, to stimulate the pursuit of societal purpose, and to encourage both democratization and cooperation, we suggest six possible ethical recommendations regarding the role of CF platforms, both reward- and equity-based.

(1) CF platforms can recognize and favor spaces dedicated to gratuitousness where investors can give without return being either certain or a primary objective. The freedom to choose how to make non-financial donations (advice and information) may help investors make sense of their investments.

(2) Whether specialized or generalist, CF platforms can select and highlight the societal usefulness of entrepreneurial projects. Societal usefulness is widely understood, including the economic dimension, the ethical dimension (culture, education, citizenship, health, and society), the environmental dimension (renewable energy and reduction of energy consumption), and the social dimension (solidarity, social housing, and inclusion). The investors can give meaning to both the societal usefulness of the project and their support of people who cannot afford to start their own businesses without their help.
(3) CF platforms can provide spaces and times (organized or spontaneous) of cooperation within and between groups of actors (crowd investors, project initiators, platforms, and partners).
(4) CF platforms can promote cooperation in the long term. They can ensure that spaces and times dedicated to cooperation continue after the pre-investment phase and that project initiators can seek the opinion of the crowd during the post-investment phase. However, our examples show that few platforms still do this.
(5) CF platforms can simultaneously organize virtual and physical cooperation arenas. While recent research has shown that the average distance between the investor and the performer–entrepreneur is approximately 4,830 km (Agrawal *et al.*, 2013) and that geographical remoteness is a distinguishing feature of the democratization of start-up funding thanks to CF (Mollick, 2014; Mollick & Robb, 2016), some platforms are characterized by a high level of geographical concentration, allowing physical cooperation and interpersonal relationships.
(6) CF platforms can recruit people dedicated to cooperation, such as community managers (in the pre-investment phase) or heads of investments (in the post-investment phase).

Depending on the use of new technologies (platforms or physical locations) and the activity sector, the different forms of the sharing economy do not provide the same areas of freedom, do not pursue the same societal objectives, and do not implement the same cooperation arenas, but the same issues arise in each of them. Therefore, these results complement sharing-related theories, i.e., the gift theory, the commons theory, and the common good theory, and sharing economy theories by underscoring criteria for ethics common to all forms of the sharing economy.

First, the sharing economy is characterized by the phenomenon of mutualization that enables more individuals to have access to resources. Most communities of the sharing economy are formed with the objective of answering clearly identified societal needs by easing the access to resources considered useful. This study emphasizes that the ethical conditions for the mutualization inherent to the sharing economy would be two-fold — spaces where stakeholders can give gratuitously without return being a certain or primary objective and the identification of a societal purpose broadly defined on the basis of economic, ethical, social, and environmental criteria.

Second, the sharing economy is also characterized by a democratization of power based on cooperation arenas. In order to avoid an increase in conflicts, democratization should be accompanied by the respect of ethical conditions: the introduction of cooperation arenas within and between groups of actors; the long-term stability of spaces and times dedicated to cooperation; the implementation of virtual and possibly physical cooperation arenas; and the recruitment of people dedicated to cooperation.

This study reveals the limits of an empirical analysis of CF platforms. On one hand, the information available on the websites does not allow a full understanding of the functioning of the platforms. A deeper analysis of the rules and practices within the platforms would involve entering each of them as a crowd investor and experimenting with the relationships between stakeholders. On the other hand, CF platforms are not governed by formal and homogeneous rules. This observation can lead future studies to question the relevance in the CF sector of further regulation designed to clarify the arrangements for cooperation within and between groups of actors. The risk is that these cooperation spaces constitute monitoring arenas. For example, the audit activity called due diligence carried out by the platform, which has the function of reducing the risk of information asymmetry, is analyzed as a monitoring mechanism (Agrawal *et al.*, 2013, 2016; Hornuf & Schwienbacher, 2014; Ley & Weaven, 2011; Wilson & Testoni, 2014) and not as a cooperation mechanism. Cooperation cannot result from rules that would require the project initiators to increase the time dedicated to reporting. Cooperation is necessarily the result of areas of freedom enabling investors to experience spontaneous and collective support.

Future empirical studies could also verify whether our ethical criteria apply to every form of the sharing economy. While the different funding, production, consumption, and education patterns in the sharing economy are based on mutualization and democratization, they encourage to a greater or lesser extent gratuitousness, societal purpose, autonomy, and cooperation. Interviews with stakeholders could enrich our results by revealing how mutualization and democratization are perceived by the different groups of actors. An ethnographic approach that includes a long-term observation of several types of sharing economy platforms would provide a richer understanding of the ongoing dynamics of sharing.

6. Conclusion

Our study has drawn on an integrated analysis of sharing-related theories along with a comparative analysis of CF platforms in order to identify the conditions required for a responsible sharing economy. We have shown that the two main dynamics of the sharing economy, mutualization and democratization, should meet a set of conditions: (1) the establishment of spaces where stakeholders can give gratuitously without return being a certain or primary objective; (2) the identification of a societal purpose broadly defined on the basis of economic, ethical, social, and environmental criteria; (3) the introduction of cooperation arenas within and between groups of actors; (4) the long-term stability of spaces and times dedicated to cooperation; (5) the implementation of virtual and possibly physical cooperation arenas; and (6) the recruitment of people dedicated to cooperation. These conditions should encourage the freedom of action of the different stakeholders, the pursuit of a higher purpose, and a genuine and sustainable form of cooperation. Under these conditions, the sharing economy may be an area enabling individuals to benefit from the dynamics of sharing and to adopt a supporter's ethical stance that transcends the mere status of consumer, user, or investor.

References

Agrawal, A., Catalini G., and Goldfard, A. (2013). Some simple economics of crowdfunding. *Innovation Policy and the Economy*, 14(1): 63–97.

Agrawal, A., Catalini, G., and Goldfard, A. (2016). Are syndicates the killer app of equity crowdfunding? *California Management Review*, 58(2): 111–124.

Ahlers, G. K., Cumming, D., Guenther, C., and Schweizer, D. (2015). Signaling in equity crowdfunding. *Entrepreneurship: Theory & Practice*, 39(4): 299–320.

Akrivou, K. and Sison, A. J. G. (eds.). (2016). *The Challenges of Capitalism for Virtue Ethics and the Common Good: Interdisciplinary Perspectives*. Edward Elgar Publishing.

Albareda, L. and Sison, A. J. G. (2020). Commons organizing: Embedding common good and institutions for collective action. Insights from ethics and economics. *Journal of Business Ethics*, 166(4): 727–743.

Allison, T. H., Davis, B. C., Short, J. C., and Webb, J. W. (2015). Crowdfunding in prosocial microlending environment: Examining the role of intrinsic versus extrinsic cues. *Entrepreneurship: Theory & Practice*, 39(1): 53–73.

André, K., Bureau, S., Gautier, A., and Rubel, O. (2017). Beyond the opposition between altruism and self-interest: Reciprocal giving in reward-based crowdfunding. *Journal of Business Ethics,* 146: 313–332.

Battilana, J. and Dorado, S. (2010). Building sustainable hybrid organizations: The case of commercial microfinance organizations. *Academy of Management Journal*, 53(6): 1419–1440.

Belk, R. (2010). Sharing. *Journal of Consumer Research*, 36(5): 715–734.

Belk, R. (2014). You are what you can access: Sharing and collaborative consumption online. *Journal of Business Research*, 67(8): 1595–1600.

Bellavatis, C., Filatotchev, I., Kamurino, D. S., and Vanacker, T. (2017). Entrepreneurial finance: New frontiers of research and practice. *Venture Capital*, 19(1–2): 1–16.

Belleflamme, P. Lambert, T., and Schwienbacher, A. (2014). Crowdfunding: Tapping the right crowd. *Journal of Business Venturing*, 29(5): 585–609.

Benkler, Y. (2004). Sharing nicely: On shareable goods and the emergence of sharing as a modality of economic production. *Yale Law Journal*, 114(2): 273–358.

Benkler, Y., and Nissenbaum, H. (2006). Commons-based peer production and virtue. *Journal of Political Philosophy*, 14(4): 394–419.

Bessière, V. and Stéphany, E. (2015). Financement et gouvernance des start-ups en equitycrowdfunding. *Finance Contrôle Stratégie*, 18(4): 1–26.

Bessière, V. and Stéphany, E. (2017). *Le crowdfunding*. De Boeck.

Bollier, D., and Helfrich, S. (eds.) (2014). The Wealth of the Commons: A World Beyond Market and State. Amherst: Levellers Press.

Botsman, R. and Rogers, R. (2010). *What's Mine Is Yours. How Collaborative Consumption Is Changing the Way We Live*. London: Collins.

Botsman, R. (2014a). *The Sharing Economy Lacks a Shared Definition.* Co.Exist. http://www.fastcoexist.com/3022028/the-sharing-economy-lacks-a-shared-definition.

Botsman, R. (2014b). Sharing's not just for start-ups: What Marriott, GE, and other traditional companies are learning about the collaborative economy. *Harvard Business Review*, 92(9): 23–25.

Bourdieu, P. (2001). Pascalian Mediations. Cambridge: Polity Press.

Bruni, L. (2008). *Reciprocity, Altruism and Civil Society: In Praise of Heterogeneity*. London/New York: Routledge.

Bruni, L. (2012). *The Wound and the Blessing. Economics, Relationships, and Happiness*. New York: New City Press.

Bruton, G., Khavul, S., Siegel, D., and Wright, M. (2014). New financial alternatives in seeding entrepreneurship: Microfinance, crowdfunding, and peer-to-peer innovations. *Entrepreneurship: Theory & Practice*, 39(1): 9–26.

Cholakova, M. and Clarysse, B. (2015). Does the possibility to make equity investments in crowdfunding projects crowd out reward-based investments? *Entrepreneurship: Theory & Practice*, 39(1): 145–172.

De Bettignies, H.-C. and Lépineux, F. (2009). Can multinational corporations afford to ignore the global common good? *Business and Society Review*, 114(2): 153–182.

Durkheim, E. (1893/1960). *The Division of Labor in Society*. (G. Simpson, Trans.) New York: The Free Press.

Dushnitsky, G., Guerini, M., Piva, E., and Rossi-Lamastra, C. (2016). Crowdfunding in Europe. Determinants of platform creation across countries. *California Management Review*, 58(2): 44–71.

Drover, W., Busenitz, L., Matusik, S., Townsend, D., Anglin, A., and Dushnitsky, G. (2017a). A review and road map of entrepreneurial equity financing research: Venture capital, corporate venture capital, angel investment, crowdfunding, and accelerators. *Journal of Management*, 43(6): 1820–1853.

Drover, W., Wood, M. S., and Zacharakis, A. (2017b). Attributes of angel and crowdfunded investments as determinants of VC screening. *Entrepreneurship: Theory & Practice*, 41(3): 323–347.

European Alternative Finance Industry Report (2016). *The 2nd European Alternative Finance Industry Report*. http://eurocrowd.org/wp-content/blogs.dir/sites/85/2016/09/Sustaining-Momentum-Embargoed.pdf.

Fitzmaurice, C., Ladegaard, I., Attwood-Charles, W., Carfagna, L., Cansoy, M., Shor, J., and Wengronowitz, R. (2016). *Domesticating the Market: Moral Exchange and the Sharing Economy*. Unpublished paper, Boston College.

Frémeaux, S. (2020). A common good perspective on diversity. *Business Ethics Quarterly*, 30(2): 200–228.

Frémeaux S. and Michelson, G. (2011). No strings attached: Welcoming the existential gift in business. *Journal of Business Ethics*, 99(1): 63–75.

Frémeaux, S. and Michelson, G. (2017). The common good of the firm and humanistic management: Conscious capitalism and economy of communion. *Journal of Business Ethics*. DOI: 10.1007/s10551-016-3118-6.

Frémeaux, S., Puyou, F. R., and Michelson, G. (2020). Beyond accountants as technocrats: A common good perspective. *Critical Perspectives on Accounting*, 67–68 (March): 1–14.

Frenken K. and Schor, J. (2017). Putting the sharing economy into perspective. *Environmental Innovation and Societal Transitions*, 23: 3–10.
Gedda, D., Nilsson, B., Sathen, Z., and Solberg Soilen, K. (2016). Crowdfunding: Finding the optimal platform for funders and entrepreneurs. *Technology Innovation Management Review*, 6(3): 31–40.
Gerber, L. and Hui, J. (2016). Crowdfunding: How and why people participate. In Méric, J., Maque, I., and Brabet J. (eds.), *International Perspectives on Crowdfunding: Positive, Normative and Critical Theory* (pp. 37–64). Bingley: Emerald.
Girard, C. and Deffains-Crapsky, C. (2016). Les mécanismes de gouvernance disciplinaires et cognitifs en equity crowdfunding: Le cas de la France. *Finance Contrôle Stratégie*, 19(3): 1–15.
Godbout, J. and Caillé, A. (2000). *The World of the Gift*. McGill-Queen's Press.
Hess, C. and Ostrom, E. (2007). Understanding Knowledge as a Commons. From Theory to Practice. Cambridge: MIT Press.
Hervé, F., Manthé, E., Sannajust, A., and Schwienbacher, A. (2017). Investor motivations in investment-based crowdfunding. DOI: 10.2139/ssrn.2746398.
Hornuf, L. and Schwienbacher, A. (2014). Crowdinvesting–Angel Investing for the masses? In Landtröm, H. and Masson, C. (eds.), Handbook of Research on Business Angels (pp. 381–398). Cheltenham: Edward Elgar.
KPMG-FPF. (2017). *Le baromètre du crowdfunding en France – Premier semestre 2017*. https://assets.kpmg.com/content/dam/kpmg/fr/.
Kuppuswamy, V. and Bayus, B. L. (2017). Does my contribution to your crowdfunding project matter? *Journal of Business Venturing*, 32: 72–89.
Lamberton, C. P. and Rose, R. L. (2012). When is ours better than mine? A framework for understanding and altering participation in commercial sharing systems. *Journal of Marketing*, 76(4): 109–125.
Lehner, O. M. (2013). Crowdfunding social ventures: A model and research agenda. *Venture Capital*, 15(4): 289–311.
Ley, A., and Weaven, S. (2011). Exploring agency dynamics of crowdfunding in start-up capital financing. *Academy of Entrepreneurial Journal*, 17(1): 85–110.
Löher, J. (2017). The interaction of equity crowdfunding platforms and ventures: An analysis of the preselection process. *Venture Capital*, 19(1–2): 51–74.
Match, S. A., and Weatherston, J. (2014). The benefits of online crowdfunding for fund-seeking business ventures. *Strategic Change*, 23(1/2): 1–14.
Matzler, K., Veider, V., and Kathan, W. (2015). Adapting to the sharing economy. *MIT Sloan Management Review*, 56(2): 71–77.
Mauss, M. (1924/1967). *The Gift, Forms and Functions of Exchange in Archaic Societies*. New York: Norton Library.
Mauss, M. (1950/1990). *The Gift*. (W.D. Hallis, trans.). London: Routledge.

Meelen, T. and Frenken, K. (2015). *Stop Saying Uber is Part of the Sharing Economy*. https://www.fastcompany.com/3040863/stop-saying-uber-is-part-of-the-sharing-economy.

Melé, D. (2009). Integrating personalism into virtue-based business ethics: The personalist and the common good principles. *Journal of Business Ethics*, 88(1): 227–244.

Messner, J. (1965). *Social Ethics: Natural Law in the Modern World*. Herder.

Meyskens, M. and Bird, L. (2015). Crowdfunding and value creation. *Entrepreneurship Research Journal*, 5(2): 155–166.

Mollick, E. (2014). The dynamics of crowdfunding: An exploratory study. *Journal of Business Venturing*, 29(1): 1–16.

Mollick, E. and Robb, A. (2016). Democratizing innovation and capital access: The role of crowdfunding. *California Management Review*, 58(2): 72–87.

Moore, P. and Robinson, A. (2015). The quantified self: What counts in the neoliberal workplace. *New Media & Society*, 18(11). DOI:1461444815604328.

Onnée, S. and Renault, S. (2014). Crowdfunding: Vers une compréhension du rôle joué par la foule. *Management & Avenir*, 8(74): 117–133.

Ostrom, E. (1990). *Governing the Commons: The Evolution of Institutions for Collective Action*. Cambridge University Press.

Ostrom, E. (2000). Collective action and the evolution of social norms. *Journal of Economic perspectives*, 14(3): 137–158.

Parguel, B., Lunardo, R., and Benoit-Moreau, F. (2016). Sustainability of collaborative consumption in question: When second-hand peer-to-peer platforms stimulate green consumers' impulse buying and overconsumption. *Marketing and Public Policy Conference Proceedings*, 26: 54–55.

Schwienbacher, A. and Larralde, B. (2012). Crowdfunding of small entrepreneurial venture. In Cumming D. (eds.), *The Oxford Handbook of Entrepreneurial Finance*. Oxford University Press.

Schor, J. and Wengronowitz, R. (2017). The new sharing economy: Enacting the eco-habitus. In Brown, H., Cohen, M., and Vergragt, P. (eds.), *Sustainable Consumption and Social Change*. London: Routledge.

Short, J. C., Ketchen Jr, D. J., McKenny, A. F., Alisson, T. H., and Ireland, R. D. (2017). Research on crowdfunding: Reviewing the (very recent) past and celebrating the present. *Entrepreneurship: Theory & Practice*, 41(2): 149–160.

Sison, A. J. and Fontrodona, J. (2012). The common good of the firm in the Aristotelian-Thomistic tradition. *Business Ethics Quarterly*, 22(2): 211–246.

Slee, T. (2016). *What's Yours Is Mine*. Goodreads.

Sundararajan, A. (2016). *The Sharing Economy: The End of Employment and the Rise of Crowd-Based Capitalism*. MIT Press.

Tedmanson, D., Essers, C., Dey, P., and Verduyn, K. (2015). An uncommon wealth. Transforming the commons with purpose, for people and not for profit! *Journal of Management Inquiry*, 24(4): 439–444.

Tomboc, G. F. (2013). The lemons problem in crowdfunding. *The John Marshall Journal of Information Technology & Privacy Law*, 30(2): 252–280.

Tomczak, A. and Brem, A. (2013). A conceptualized investment model of crowd-funding. *Venture Capital: An International Journal of Entrepreneurial Finance*, 15(4): 335–359.

Wettstein, F. (2012). Corporate responsibility in the collective age: Toward a conception of collaborative responsibility. *Business and Society Review*, 117(2): 155–184.

Wilson, K. E. and Testoni, M. (2014). Improving the role of equity crowdfunding in Europe's capital markets. *Bruegel Policy Contribution*, 2014(9): 1–14.

Williamson, P. J. and De Meyer, A. (2012). Ecosystem advantage: How to successfully harness the power of partners. *California Management Review*, 55(1): 24–46.

© 2023 World Scientific Publishing Company
https://doi.org/10.1142/9789811260483_0009

Chapter 9

Measuring, Accounting, and Reporting Impact

Delphine Gibassier

Audencia, Nantes, France

Abstract

Impact can be qualified as a "hembig" concept, that is, an important concept that is intellectually problematic and vague. As it has gained considerable traction in practice, both in finance and accounting, we explore the interrelationships between the measure of impact and its effects on the allocation of capitals in practice. After reviewing its conceptual meaning and current standards, frameworks, and practices, we propose a multi-dimensional framework to analyze impact accounts. We conclude by acknowledging the limits of impact measurement devices and key takeaways from practice.

Keywords: Impact; hembig concept; impact accounts; system value; detachment

1. Introduction

We live in the "Generation Impact" (Richards & Nicholls, 2021) and the "Impact Revolution" (Cohen, 2020). The concept of "impact" is everywhere (Yang, O'Leary & Tregidga, 2021), and the impact agenda has taken over the political agenda and even pervaded religious discourses.

Indeed, recently, "As part of the UK's G7 2021 presidency, the UK government has unveiled plans for an independent impact taskforce (ITF) to come up with solutions for a sustainable and inclusive recovery from the COVID-19 crisis and promote impact-driven economies and societies in the long term" (Impact Investing Institute, 2021). This followed the first taskforce established in 2014, by the same United Kingdom, to work "with other G8 nations to grow the social investment market and increase investment, allowing the best social innovations to spread and help tackle our shared social and economic challenges" (Social Impact Investment Taskforce, 2014). The Pope himself also placed impact investing on governments' agendas when he urged, in June 2014, "for governments throughout the world [to] commit themselves to developing an international framework capable of promoting a market of high impact investments and thus to combating an economy which excludes and discards" (cited by Florman, Klingler-Vidra, & Facada, 2016). According to Cohen (2020, p. 89), "there is hardly a company boardroom in the world where the subject of impact is not being actively discussed."

Therefore, "impact" is a concept that can be qualified as hegemonic, ambiguous, and big (Alvesson & Blom, 2022). Alvesson and Sandberg (2020, p. 3) define the term hembig concept as a "scientific concept characterized by its broad scope and ambiguous meanings, which at the same time and somewhat paradoxically, through its dominance crowds out other less fashionable concepts or prevents the development of a more precise terminology." Hembig concepts, while important and broadly applicable (Alvesson & Blom, 2022), are also intellectually problematic and vague (Yang *et al.*, 2021).

In 2007, the term "impact investing" was coined to replace "social investment" at a meeting hosted by the Rockefeller Foundation (Cohen, 2020). According to Cohen (2020, p. 11), "impact is the measure of an action's benefit to people and the planet. It goes beyond minimizing harmful outcomes to actively creating good ones by creating positive impact." Through impact investing, Cohen (2020, p. 12) proposes to "shift to a system that encourages making as much money as possible but in a way that is consistent with achieving the highest impact and with the lowest level of risk." The measurement mindset is that of "blended value" (Nicholls, Nicholls, & Paton, 2015b) or "shared value" (Porter & Kramer, 2011). He further describes the current trend as the "impact revolution," to be "as world-changing as the industrial revolution" (p. 14).

Impact accounting can be defined as "creating accounts of the consequences of a decision on selected socio-ecological systems" (Thomson, 2021, p. 236). According to Thomson (2021, p. 237), developing meaningful impact accounts lies "at the core of sustainability accounting and accountability research" and "is key to untangling many connected environmental governance, accounting, and accountability problems." Without robust impact accounts, "the transformative potential of sustainable governance is diminished" (Thomson, 2021, p. 237).

What links impact investing and accounting is that "it seems intuitively obvious that any social investor engaging in the social finance market would show a concern for proof that her investment is creating the value that it claimed it would" (Nicholls *et al.*, 2015, p. 253), which means, "impact investing" would rely on "impact accounting" as their navigation system (Cohen, 2020). Impact measurement would avoid "impact washing" — as impact claims could be considered as little as "marketing ploys" (Cohen, 2020, p. 30).

Consequently, as this hembig concept has become pervasive both in finance (impact investing and impact bonds) and accounting (impact accounting, impact for the SDGs, and impact valuation), it is first important to consider its historical meaning, characteristics, and epistemic linkages. Second, we will describe its current accounting standards and applications in practice. Third, we will analyze the multi-dimensions of this concept in research and practice. Finally, we will conclude by looking at the limits of current impact accounting practice, takeaways for practice, and the future of "impact accounting" research.

2. What Is Impact?

The notion of impact is complex and multi-faceted. The word comes from the latin "impactus" which means "dash against," with a "marked effect or influence" (Oxford Dictionary). According to an analysis of several existing definitions of impact (see Appendix 1), we can say that it is an assemblage of different elements including the following (Figure 1):

The effects described in impact definitions can be as follows:

- environmental and social effects, or for the economy
- positive or negative
- intended or unintended

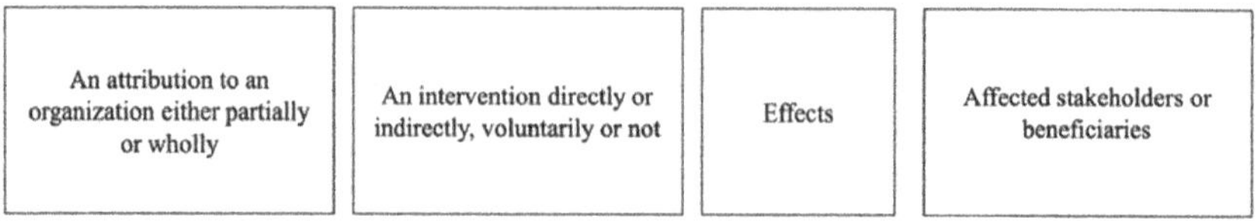

Figure 1. The different dimensions of impact.

- short term or long term
- direct or indirect
- primary or secondary

Definitions also underline that impact is more than just "direct effects": "It also concerns changes occurring in systems beyond direct effects, beyond direct outcomes, it aims to assess the ultimate impacts on individuals and society" (Hervieux and Voltan, 2019, citing Epstein & Yuthas, 2014). Harji and Nicholls (2020) add that the effects (or changes) have to be material, and "beyond what would have been expected to occur."

Next to the term "impact," another term is more and more associated with it, and that term is "value." According to Nicholls and Richards (2021, p. 3), "impact relates to those things that are not included in market prices." Therefore, if "they can be identified and valued, they have the potential to be included in the prices that drive our decisions" (Nicholls & Richards, 2021, p. 3).

The term "impact," however, is multi-faceted also because it is used in different epistemic arenas, with their own socio-political-scientific debates and characteristics. Notably, it is present in environmental accounts, development, non-profit, and social entrepreneurship, as well as finance and in accounting (see Sections 2 and 3). It is, therefore, important to recognize how its definitions and uses in different arenas can shape our understanding and use of potential impact accounts.

2.1. *Impacts in environmental accounts*

"Impact" has been used in life cycle assessment for 50 years. It is a step where the flows are assigned a coefficient that reflects the impact of each input or output with respect to the impact considered (Grisel & Osset,

2004). This step translates flows in potential impacts, using the knowledge accumulated by biologists and ecologists (Grisel & Osset, 2004). The actual input/output has no consequences on the environment; it is what it becomes in that environment, sometimes with long cause and effect chains, that has impacts on the equilibrium of the actual site (Grisel & Osset, 2004). The impact categories represent environmental issues of concern to which the life cycle assessment results may be assigned.[1] Often, current impact accounts directly jump to impact on human health, while rendering silent the impact categories for the environment itself.

Environmental impact assessments are "a process to help ensure environment and social consequences are integrated into and given due attention in the consenting or financing of development" (Carroll, Fothergill, Murphy & Turpin, 2020, p. 1). In environmental impact assessments, a predicted change in concentrations causes an impact (for example, on air quality), and then the "effect" on human health is judged to be either "significant" or "not significant" (Carroll *et al.*, 2020). The results of the assessment are used to decide to grant permission for new projects by local or national authorities, in combination with other dimensions such as stakeholder perspectives, cultural aspects, or competing proposals.

One can note that in the environmental arena, impacts are mostly considered potential negative long-term effects.

2.2. *Social impact in the development, non-profit, and social entrepreneurship arenas*

"Impact" is the development arena is used to measure the effects of a non-governmental organization (NGO) program or a group of NGOs' actions, a given policy option or intervention (see, for example, Ebrahim, 2013). It has been introduced to be able to define where to allocate funds and to be able to reward projects that could really measure their impact. According to Yang *et al.* (2021, p. 320), social impact measurement practices are implemented "to appease formal, narrow, and funder-driven hierarchical accountability requirements rather than attempts to fully realize and analyze the social impact a particular organization is working towards."

[1]An example of impact categories for the wind energy industry can be found here: https://www.wind-energy-the-facts.org/impact-categories.html.

In the development field, the change is supposed to be inherently "positive" — despite definitions being inclusive of negative and positive, intended, and unintended (Yang *et al.*, 2021), as the intervention is there to "alter the state of the world" (International Initiative for Impact Evaluation, 2012), to affect a beneficiary population, or to "change people's life" (United Nations Development Group, 2011).

Impact often refers to "higher-level effects of a program that occur in the medium or long(er) term" (US Agency for International Development, 2009) and are defined as "fundamental and durable" (Global Environment Facility, 2009). In this regard, it is recognized that "long-term cumulative effects over time" (Joint United Nations PRogramme on HIV/Aids, 2009) are rarely attributable to a single program or organization but to an accumulation of programs and interventions.

According to the World Bank (as cited by White (2009) in Hearn & Buffardy, 2016), impact is, therefore, measured in comparing the status without intervention (Y_0) and with intervention (Y_1) (impact = Y_1-Y_0), while taking into consideration "the context of its environment, as it interacts with the multiple factors affecting development change" (Australian Department of Foreign Affairs & Trade Office of Development Effectiveness, 2012).

According to Hertel *et al.* (2020), the role of entrepreneurs in society is to "move models to change things in real life." Changing the status quo produced affects an audience, which in turn will generate a return on investment. They continue by saying "thinking about impact creates a tremendous opportunity to approach the world strategically — which is often the most difficult part of an entrepreneur's routine."

The movement followed in the footsteps of public policy evaluations to integrate social aspects that are deemed invisible in traditional impact studies (Leclerc, 2020). The movement of "impact" measurement in social entrepreneurship has grown under the impetus of funders. Like for the developing worlds and NGOs, funders want to "rationalize" their budgets and to understand if they are funding entrepreneurs with a social impact or not.

2.3. *Impact investing*

Impact measurement transferred from the non-profit and social entrepreneurship arenas to the world of investment through funders of specific social programs or start-ups. Similar to what we just described in Section 2.2, by referring to the notion of "impact," investment management professionals want to show that they make a change through their market transactions.

Likewise to the development arena, change is defined as what "investors cause above what would happen anyhow" (Heeb, 2020), and only so, would it result in "real change" (Heeb, 2020) or a "lasting change" (Impak, 2020) to the circumstances of people or the planet. It is, therefore, important to compare the situation to what the situation would have been without the investment. The Rockefeller Foundation further specifies that "net impact" is what occurred "above and beyond what would have happened" without the intervention (Durand, Rodgers & Lee, 2019).

Contrary to development programs, interventions, or social entrepreneurship, investor impact is indirect and enabling, through investment allowing a company to affect people and the planet (Heeb, 2020). The impact of investment can be described as "the non-financial consequences of investing" something that is, however, often not measured (University of Cambridge Institute for Sustainability Leadership (CISL), 2019).

While impacts include positive and negative impacts (see Section 2), negative impacts have, in the case of finance, gradually been silenced. Indeed, "if the impacts of a portfolio are intentionally positive, one might describe the process as impact investing" (CISL, 2019). UNEP-FI Principles for Positive Impact Finance (2017) nuances the potential positive contributions by stating that it can only be delivered "once any potential negative impacts to any of the pillars have been duly identified and mitigated" and so does the definition of impact investing written by the Finance for Tomorrow (2021). However, this trend of silencing negative impacts to pursue a definition of "impact" that would only be positive is well embedded in the discourse around the "impact revolution": businesses "are now beginning to realize that they must deliver positive impact if they want to survive" (Cohen, 2020, p. 89). To re-emphasize the shift to impact investing, Wilson (2021) acknowledges that ESG approaches have for objective to mitigate risks, while current investments will seek "measurable positive impact that results in increased well-being of stakeholders" (p. 15).

In addition, a change caused by investors' market transactions is now often aligned with, or put in the context of, a broader environmental, societal, or financial system goal, such as, for example, the Paris Agreement, or the Sustainable Development Goals (Wilson, 2021; Burckart, Lydenberg & Ziegler, 2018).

To conclude, and according to Finance for Tomorrow (2021, p. 4), "Impact finance is an investment or financing strategy that aims to accelerate the fair and sustainable transformation and sustainable transformation of the real economy by providing proof of its beneficial effects." It relies on intentionality, additionality, and impact measurement.

3. Impact in Accounting and Reporting Methodologies, Standards, and Frameworks

Impacts accounts can be used to measure actual impacts or as predictive instruments to help in decision-making processes. Therefore, they allow evaluation, monitoring, and management of the effects of activities and actions (Hervieux & Voltan, 2019). We will review current standards, frameworks, and practices in impact accounting, and critically examine how they elaborate their accounting assemblage (Thomson, 2021). Social impact is "a multi-level, multi-dimensional concept, the measurement of which is challenging" (Nicholls *et al.*, 2015, p. 254).

3.1. *The first two "impact" standards*

3.1.1. *The B Lab "Impact Assessment"*

The B Lab Impact Assessment (BIA) is a questionnaire used by B Lab corporations not only to assess whether they are in line with the certification (you would need to obtain over 80 points out of 200 to be certified) but also to assess progress, as it is a free online tool. It was first released in 2007.

Impact metrics that they use are similar, according to their website, to those used by the Global Reporting Initiative or the IRIS database (Global Impact Investing Network). However, they differentiate themselves from "reporting" initiative by "evaluat[ing] whether the company has either increased or decreased its emissions relative to the company's revenues or relative to the practices of other businesses."[2]

---

[2]B Lab website: https://bimpactassessment.net/how-it-works/frequently-asked-questions/top-10?_ga=2.75203792.350797689.1643277346-378352494.1643277346#how-does-this-relate-to-other-impact-measurement-systems, accessed on January 2022.

Like many "impact" approaches, a focus on the "positive" is taken: "practices that intentionally address a social or environmental issue are measured, not practices that simply comply with existing laws or norms."[3] However, their impact definition differs from what we have seen in Section 2. Indeed, there is no additionality, no focus on long-term impacts beyond outputs or outcomes. We did not find any reference to the theory of change, for example. Output and outcomes represent 71% of the questions in the BIA. According to a 2017 comparison of the BIA with the Impact Management Project,[4] there is a need for the BIA to work on "contribution" (additionality), risks, and material effects on stakeholders featured in the assessment.

3.1.2. *IRIS from Global Impact Investing Network*

According to the BIA website, "the Impact Reporting and Investment Standards (IRIS) provide a common reporting language to describe social and environmental performance and ensure uniform measurement and articulation of impact across companies."[5] The Global Impact Investing Network, B Lab, Acumen Fund, and the Rockefeller Foundation helped launch IRIS, with support from Hitachi, Deloitte, and PriceWaterhouseCoopers, in the early 2008s. By 2014, more than 5,000 organizations were using IRIS (Nicholls *et al.*, 2015).

According to the Global Impact Investing Network (GIIN) website, IRIS+ is the generally accepted impact accounting system that leading impact investors use to measure, manage, and optimize their impact.[6] "The IRIS+ system is designed to minimize confusion for how to set objectives, describe and understand impact, assess success, and clearly communicate impact performance with other impact investing stakeholders."

---

[3]B Lab website: https://bimpactassessment.net/how-it-works/frequently-asked-questions/the-basics?_ga=2.120301770.350797689.1643277346-378352494.1643277346#what-makes-the-assessment-different-than-other-systems, accessed on January 2022.

[4] Impact Management Project website: https://impactmanagementproject.com/signposting/signposting-to-shared-fundamentals-b-impact-assessment/, accessed on January 2022.

[5]B Lab website: https://bimpactassessment.net/how-it-works/frequently-asked-questions/the-standards, accessed on January 2022.

[6]GIIN website: https://iris.thegiin.org/standards/, accessed on January 2022.

IRIS+ is not completely aligned with the recent Impact Management Project five dimensions (see the section on the Impact Management Project (IMP)) but, however, plans to align in the future (Table 1).

Similar to the B Lab Impact Assessment, IRIS+ does not refer to additionality (metrics do not align with "contribution" (GIIN, 2020)) or to the theory of change. IRIS+ also admits that "historically, IRIS metrics have largely been proxy outcome metrics. IRIS+ has begun to incorporate

Table 1. Dimensions alignment IRIS+ and IMP.

IMP dimensions	IRIS+ dimensions
What outcomes the enterprise is contributing to and how important the outcomes are to?	Outcome level in period, outcome threshold, SDG, importance of outcome to stakeholders
Who experiences the effect and how underserved are they in relation to the outcome?	Stakeholder type, geographical boundary, baseline level of outcome, stakeholder characteristics
How much of the effect occurs in the time period?	Scale: number of people experiencing the outcome (social outcomes only) Depth: degree of change experienced by the stakeholder Duration: time period for which the stakeholder experiences the outcome
How does the effect compare and contribute to what would likely occur anyway?	Depth: An enterprise's contribution to the depth of an outcome by factoring in the estimated degree of change that would have otherwise happened. Duration: An enterprise's contribution to the duration of an outcome by factoring in the estimated duration that the outcome would have otherwise endured.
Which risk factors are significant and how likely is it that the outcome is different from the expected one?	The type of impact risk, typically described using one of 10 risk factors: evidence risk, external risk, execution risk, stakeholder participation risk, drop-off risk, unexpected impact risk, efficiency risk, contribution risk, alignment risk, and endurance risk.

Source: "IRIS+, the five dimensions of impact," GIIN (2020).

outcome metrics" (GIIN, 2020). There are some limitations to their accounting of period of change as well (GIIN, 2020).

Both frameworks are closer to the list of metrics in reporting frameworks than to the current definition of impact measurement. However, both the BIA and Social Value International have made comparisons with the recent impact management norms (see the section on the Impact Management Project) and plan to close the gap between their current practice and the newly prescribed dimensions of impact.

3.2. *The two Global Impact Frameworks*

3.2.1. *The Impact Management Project (IMP)*

The IMP started in 2016, hosted by an independent non-profit set up by the UK-based Bridges Fund Management, exclusively for the purpose of building the market for sustainable business and investment. It was tasked with building "global consensus on how we talk about, measure, and manage our ESG risks and positive impacts." The main result of their work is the "impact management norms" (Table 2).

3.2.2. *Social Value International Principles*

Social Value accounting is an approach to understanding and managing the value of the social, economic, and environmental outcomes created by an activity or an organization (Social Value International and B Lab, 2016) (Table 3). It is principle-based (like the IMP) and reflects "the changes experienced by people" (Social Value International, 2021, p. 3).

The two international frameworks are closely aligned as they both cover "who" (stakeholders) understand change ("what" and "contribution"). However, Social Value Principles insist on materiality of impacts, attributability of impacts, transparency, and verification. On the other side, the impact management norms insist on the risks to impact results and measurement.

3.3. *Impact accounts in practice*

3.3.1. *Social return on investment*

Hall and Millo (2016) define social return on investment (SROI) as "an accounting methodology that aims to capture and quantify the value

Table 2. Impact Management Norms, Impact Management Project.[a]

Impact dimension	**Impact data category**
What	Outcome level in period
	Outcome threshold*
	Importance of outcome to stakeholder
	SDG or other global goals
Who	Stakeholder
	Geographical boundary
	Outcome level at baseline
	Stakeholder characteristics
How much	Scale
	Depth
	Duration
Contribution	Depth counterfactual
	Duration counterfactual
Risk	Risk type
	Risk level

Note: *"the level of outcome that the stakeholder considers to be a positive outcome. Anything below this level is considered a negative outcome. The outcome threshold can be a nationally or an internationally agreed standard".

[a] Impact Management Project website: https://impactmanagementproject.com/impact-management/impact-management-norms/ accessed on January 2022.

created by social purpose organizations, and employs techniques of monetization and the expression of value as a ratio of benefits for investments" (p. 1). In 1996, the Roberts Enterprise Development Fund (REDF) published a retrospective SROI analysis of two social purpose enterprises, and later, SROI was developed by the New Economics Foundation in the UK (Hall & Millo, 2016). According to the REDF SROI methodology handbook (2001), there are six steps in the SROI calculation: calculate enterprise value, calculate social purpose value, calculate blended value, calculate enterprise index of return, calculate social purpose index of return, and calculate blended index of return. The REDF SROI framework (2001) seeks to "identify direct, demonstrable cost savings and revenues contributions that are associated with individuals' employment in a social purpose enterprise" (p. 3). SROI

Table 3. Social Value Principles.

Involve stakeholders — understand change by involving stakeholders
Understand change — positive and negative as the source of wider value
Value what matters — to help decide which are important, to allow discussion about mutually exclusive options, and to assess efficiency
Only include what is material — as we can't manage all outcomes and so need a framework to decide which
Do not overclaim — since the material outcomes may require involvement of other organizations and need to be attributable to the activities under analysis. And since our activities may only cause displacement of existing outcomes
Be transparent — so we can assess the level of rigor applied, and how the questions were answered and by who
Verify the result — since judgments are inevitably involved, we need them to be reviewed before the information will be credible and so useful

Source: Social Value International (2021), https://www.socialvalueint.org/standards-and-guidance, accessed on January 2022.

can be used in combination with social impact findings to advocate for financial support of social enterprises. For example, Figure 2 shows that enterprise ABC has a social index of return of USD 47.14. This means that for each dollar invested in the enterprise, there are public cost savings and increased tax revenues of USD 47.14.

The SROI tool employs monetization, relies on the impact mindset of "blended value," and oversimplifies causality per the logic model.

3.3.2. *The IIRC Value Creation Model*

The six capitals are represented in the integrated reporting framework through an "octopus" figure that names them as inputs to the business model and as outputs and potential outcomes, as Figure 3 describes. In this case, outputs (products, services, and waste) decrease, increase, or transform the stock of capitals through positive or negative outcomes.[7] Despite

[7]Definition of outcomes: The internal and external consequences (positive and negative) for the capitals as a result of an organization's business activities and outputs (The IIRC, 2021).

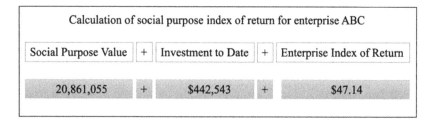

Calculation of social purpose index of return for enterprise ABC				
Social Purpose Value	+	Investment to Date	+	Enterprise Index of Return
20,861,055	+	$442,543	+	$47.14

Figure 2. Social index of return (Source: REDF SROI framework, 2001).

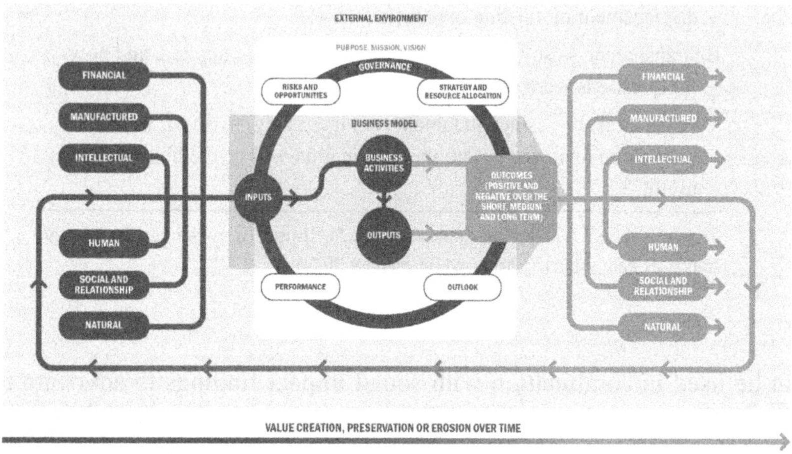

Figure 3. The Value Creation Model of the IR Framework 2021.

Source: The IIRC Website (The Value Reporting Foundation website: https://www.integratedreporting.org/what-the-tool-for-better-reporting/get-to-grips-with-the-six-capitals/ accessed on January 2022.).

using the theory of change, the IR framework never mentions "impact" and the "octopus" figures designed by companies rarely quantify beyond outputs. Stakeholders (who?) are often not cited in those proposed figures in integrated reports, and the attributability and additionality are, for example, never discussed. Often, outputs or outcomes are monetized.

3.3.3. *The E P&L*

The E(nvironmental) P&L is a methodology elaborated within the company Kering (through a test run in the Puma division in 2011), with close

	EMISSIONS AND RESOURCE USE	ENVIRONMENTAL CHANGE	CHANGE IN WELLBEING
AIR POLLUTION	Emissions of pollutants ($PM_{2.5}$, PM_{10}, NOx, SOx, VOCs, NH_3) in kg	Increase in concentration of pollution	Respiratory disease, agricultural losses, reduced visability
GREENHOUSE GAS EMISIONS	Emissions of greenhouse gases (CO_2, N_2O, CH_4, CFC's etc) in kg	Climate change	Health impacts, economic losses, change in natural environment
LAND USE	Area of tropical forest, temperate forest, inland wetland etc in hectares	Reduced ecosystem services	Health impacts, economic losses, reduced recreational and cultural benefits
WASTE	Hazardous and non-hazardous waste in kg	Climate change, disamenity and contamination	Reduced enjoyment of local environment, decontamination costs
WATER CONSUMPTION	Water consumption in m^3	Increasing water scarcity	Malnutrition and disease
WATER POLLUTION	Release of specific heavy metals, nutrients, toxic compounds in kg	Reduced water quality	Health impacts, eutrophication, economic losses

Figure 4. Impacts valuation in the E P&L.

Source: E P&L methodology (2013, p. 13).

roots with "full cost accounting" and the pricing of negative externalities. In the case of the E P&L, the impact is anthropocentric and defined through "change in well-being" (see Figure 4). The change in well-being is expressed in monetary terms. In this case, the stakeholder is broadly "society," but attributionality or additionality is also not discussed. There are also no references to thresholds, defining what is acceptable or not. Instead, the E P&L accounts only for negative impacts and considers all impacts to be problematic, aiming toward a hypothetical "zero impact." Sustainability Assessment Models (e.g., True Value from KPMG) take the same approach to impact measurement, which is monetization of consequences on well-being or human health, and no references to allocations and thresholds, planetary boundaries, and social foundations.

3.3.4. *Social impact valuation*

Impact accounts are present in multiple formats in practice today. Both full cost accounts (such as the E P&L) and Sustainability Assessment Models (such as True Value, used in practice by Holcim and Cementos Argos) have a connection to "impact" through monetization. More broadly, capital accounting, which looks at "dependencies and impacts," when used for internal decision-making, refers to the same group of accounts. For example, Nestlé (with Valuing Nature) published a case study of impact accounting for living wage in 2017. They assessed the relationship between working conditions (here the income, measured by the living wage), as a social determinant of health, and employee health, measured via the life quality and expectancy (measured in DALYs: disability adjusted life years). Results show contrasted results with a higher social impact for intermediate incomes, while higher incomes demonstrate no positive impact.

3.3.5. *The Impak Score*

The French–Canadian start-up company Impak developed the "Impak Score" in the last few years. Its primary goal, through its impact assessment and scoring solution, is to channel capital toward businesses with a positive social or environmental impact.[8]

The Impak Score™ has been developed using the IMP norms and in connection with the Sustainable Development Goals. As per many of the impact methods or standards, the Impak Score claims to rectify what current Environmental, Social, and Governance (ESG) standards do not measure, that is, the positive consequences of businesses: "This type of analysis only takes into account how they mitigate the negative impacts of their activity, thus accepting that economic growth is a negative net contributor to the social and environmental progress. Impact assessments look at investments from a holistic point of view, where positive outcomes are taken into account in addition to the mitigation of the negative ones. And this is the heart of the question: shouldn't companies be judged on the good they do AND how well they clean up the damage they cause rather than just on the latter?" (Impak, 2020, p. 4). While they pick only five positive impacts versus 10 negative impacts to analyze, their final score overweighs positive impacts (500 points out of 1,000 versus 300 for negative impacts and 200 for governance). While Impak does reduce positive impacts of organizations by 20% if they happen to show a single negative impact in the "may cause harm"

[8]Impak website: https://www.impakfinance.com/story-of-impak/, accessed on January 2022.

category, it does not completely avoid the pitfall of netting negative and positive impacts.[9]

According to their impact rating methodology document, intentionality and the theory of change are key backbones of their work. The theory of change allows validating the logic behind the creation of impact, and intentionality is measured through the weighing of each positive impact using the percentage of activities it represents for the company (Impak, 2020).

3.4. *Convergence of financial accounting and impact accounting*

More and more organizations, standard-setters, and research groups have become interested in how impacts could be included within financial accounts. The goal would be to adjust financial accounts to reflect natural and social capital impacts as well as economic ones. Two recent reports have extensively presented those tentative accounts and experimentations: the "Improving nature's visibility in financial accounting" report from the Capitals Coalition (2020) and the "What connections are there between financial and non-financial accounting?" report from Antheaume and Gibassier (2020).

For example, the Impact Weighted Accounts Initiative is based at Harvard and was initiated by the Global Steering Group for Impact Investment (GSG) and the Impact Management Project (IMP). Its aim is to enable better decision-making by including (monetized) environmental and social impacts within financial accounts. To do so, it will create "line items on a financial statement, such as an income statement or a balance sheet, which are added to supplement the statement of financial health and performance by reflecting a company's positive and negative impacts on employees, customers, the environment, and the broader society" (Serafeim *et al.*, 2019). According to Cohen (2020, p. 107), impact weighted accounts "make it possible for impact to take its rightful place alongside profit by enabling us to arrive at a company's net impact or, putting it in other words, its social and environmental bottom line."

Unfortunately, those integrated impact accounts do not refer to thresholds and allocations (e.g., planetary boundaries), and, therefore,

[9]If an organization has a negative impact in the category 'does cause harm', the Impak Score does decrease positive impacts by 100%.

performance is only defined in a monetized comparative manner with peers. IWAI redefines sustainable development performance through a monetized efficiency performance measure of absolute physical measures, therefore obfuscating the possibility to draw meaningful conclusions for allocating funds to best-in-class organizations, while environmental and social performance has been defined in the past through comparison to baselines in the same company (incremental performance) and efficiency measures to compare with peers through a common denominator such as revenue (comparative performance). However, the only possible way to measure environmental and social performance is to compare with carrying capacities of earth's budgets (for the environment) or to compare with social foundations (Raworth, 2017), often defined by international treaties and organizations.

While IWAI claims to be based on the IMP norms, their work, based on publicly decontextualized available database-derived data, does not allow for consideration of stakeholders, context, and complexity of causality chains.

4. A Multi-dimensional Framework to Analyze Impact Accounts

Based on our analysis of current definitions of "impact," as well as current standards and practices in impact accounts, we propose a multi-dimensional framework to analyze impact accounts: the actors, the calculative device, and the socio-ecological system in which the assemblage occurs.

4.1. *Actors: Human calculators, beneficiaries, and the organization*

Accountants are the human calculators (Thomson, 2021, p. 239) that construct the calculative space, and, therefore, it is important to recognize the constitute agency of those involved in "choosing how measurements are made and used" (Thomson, 2021, p. 239). They choose measures, data, calculative devices, contextual information, and how results are going to be used in decision-making processes. These endeavors of creating impact accounts engage a level of risks and uncertainty in the calculation processes and results that need to be acknowledged. Impacts are often long term and systemic, and it has been recognized that long-term thinking is humanly difficult (Krznaric, 2020; Bansal & DesJardine, 2014).

Impact accounts are often organizational accounts that allow funders to address fund allocations through attributing responsibility for (positive) impacts. However, attributing particular elements of a long-term impact is a challenge (Yang *et al.*, 2021). Systemic change is often the result of a global effort, something that is embodied in the Sustainable Development Goal 17, "partnerships." For example, saving species can take up to 50 years, and collaboration between NGOs, communities, and local government is paramount to success.

Impact also helps make decisions in relation to different options with different impacts. Those different impacts could be valued differently by different people, in particular, those affected by impact (Nicholls & Richards, 2021). However, those who are affected have no contractual relationship with the organization that "impacts" them and, therefore, it is difficult to hold that organization to account.

4.2. *Calculative devices*

Impact accounts are devices of the quantification of "change." The concept that is most often used in impact accounts in the theory of change (or logic model). The Rockefeller Foundation defines the theory using the concepts of "outputs," "outcomes," and "impacts" of social activities by referring to "the impact value chain" concept (Table 4).

Rockefeller Foundation further specifies that "net impact" is what occurred "above and beyond what would have happened" without the intervention (Durand, Rodgers, & Lee, 2019). To be able to calculate impact, a counterfactual is needed. The question that is being asked is as follows: what would have happened in the absence of the program or intervention? (White 2010). In development, counterfactuals include randomized controls trials, but other techniques include revealed and expressed preference models or cost-benefits analyses (Nicholls *et al.*, 2015).

It is also important to understand the measurement mindset behind the measurement tools proposed, as well as the legitimacy of the impact measurement proposed. According to Cohen (2020), impact's mindset is to drive "shared value," shifting from "minimizing the harm business has on society" to "focusing on maximizing the competitive value of solving social problems" (p. 92, citing Porter & Kramer, 2011). Nicholls *et al.*

Table 4. The different concepts of the impact value chain.

Inputs	They include both the resources that are available (financial and other resources) and constraints that an organization faces
Activities (or processes)	They include all that an organization does with the inputs and the steps to be taken to achieve the desired impact
Outputs	The direct results of the organization's activities
Outcomes	The intermediate effects on the target population that are necessary to achieve the desired impact. They may include the systematic and fundamental progress on meeting social objectives
Impacts	They are the ultimate goals of a social purpose organization

Source: IPADE (2017).

(2015, p. 256) emphasize that impact investing is about "the complex set of relationships between social and financial value creation" and that it is important not "to treat these two streams of value as separate and unrelated." In addition, Finance for Tomorrow (2021, p. 4) confirms that impact investing is "on the joint search for ecological and social performance, but also a higher financial profitability with a minimum of capital preservation, in order to honor fiduciary responsibilities." This measurement mindset puts the emphasis on the interaction between profit and sustainable development. This excludes the financing of projects with no profitable value for the organization, even if it might have to be pursued for societal or environmental reasons.

However, today, the Future Fit Benchmark as well as the think tank R3.0 have brought back to the forefront the idea that the economy is embedded within society and society within the environment (Passet, 1979). They name this new approach "system value," defined as "Business in no way hinders — and ideally contributes to — society's progress toward future-fitness" (Future Fit Benchmark[10]) or "System value can only be created when the outcomes of a business model maintain capital stocks and flows within the thresholds of their carrying capacities" (Baue, 2020). To allow for this mindset to be embedded into impact accounts, a possibility would be to define performance through the doughnut, which includes both the planetary boundaries and social foundations (Raworth, 2017).

[10]Future Fit Benchmark website: https://futurefitbusiness.org/what-you-need-to-know/, accessed on January 2022.

4.3. *The messiness of our world: Systemic embeddedness*

Our analysis of definitions of impacts led us to understand that "impact" is itself hard to capture. It can be positive or negative, intended or unintended, short or long term, direct or indirect, primary or secondary. It is often more complex than the theory of change allows to describe (Nicholls *et al.*, 2015).

Impact accounts with only one category of impact, such as the one provided by Nestlé on living wage, "are unlikely to provide useful insights into the multi-dimensional challenges associated with sustainable transformation or adaptation" (Thomson, 2021, p. 244). Therefore, it is advised to allow for multi-dimensional accounts of sustainable development (such as the Impak Score or the E P&L).

Impacts also happen in a context, and "it is critical to recognize that there is a contradiction between the detachment needed for valuation and the holistic nature of socioecological systems" (Thomson, 2021, p. 241). Any kind of impact accounting will involve choices in measurement indicators that will automatically involve a form of reduction in complexity of the actual system to be measured. In that sense, it is important to recognize what the impact renders visible and what is potentially rendered invisible to the decision-maker and the stakeholders of the impact account, not only quantitatively but also by silencing qualitative accounts of the situation (Ruff, 2021).

5. The Future of Impact Accounting and Reporting

Accounting is not neutral and is an instrument of power and responsibility (Yang *et al.*, 2021). It constructs, rather than merely reflects, the world around us (Hines, 1988; Yang *et al.*, 2021). In practice, accounting has the capacity to impact behavior and decision-making (Vesty, Telgenkamp, & Roscoe, 2015), promote trust, and coordinate and legitimize relationships and practices (Yang *et al.*, 2021). Therefore, it is important to reflect on the limits of the current impact accounting practice, as well as define future avenues for critical research in this area.

5.1. *Limits of current impact accounting practice*

Following our multi-dimensional framework, we would like to raise limits and concerns in relation to the impact accounts assemblages that we see in practice. Impact accounts can be very disempowering and silencing. Moreover, calculative devices can obfuscate and erase key elements of impacts. Finally, by means of "detachment" (Thomson, 2021), impact accounts decontextualize elements that are, in fact, part of a socio-ecological system.

5.1.1. *Disempowering and silencing*

In impact investing, "the person who receives the financial return is generally different from the person who receives the social return" (Nicholls *et al.*, 2015, p. 256). Therefore, it creates an accountability gap which is uncomfortable. Impact accounts silence beneficiaries and misrepresent their feeling and impressions of what "impact" is for them (Ruff, 2021).

Within the construction of impact accounts, "the less representative and the later participants are involved, the more likely the measure will contain bias or privilege the powerful" (Thomson, 2021, p. 244). Yang *et al.* (2021) concur that social impact often only demonstrates the intention of power stakeholders, e.g., charity funders. However, a participatory approach to impact measurement "can itself create an additional 'process' social value for the external stakeholders" (Nicholls, *et al.*, 2015, p. 264).

5.1.2. *Obfuscating by simplifying and translating*

The logic model, or theory of change, has been widely criticized for "being oversimplistic it is assumption that each of its five stages leads to the next" (Nicholls *et al.*, 2015, p. 258). Some researchers have, therefore, called for a stronger engagement with system thinking (Williams *et al.*, 2017). According to Hervieux and Voltan (2019, p. 265), "social impact assessment must encapsulate the lens of systems change and the interrelated, complex nature of social problems."

Nicholls *et al.* (2015) question the simplification of impact accounts by questioning if they should only measure direct impacts or all impacts, including accidental effects, often negative. They also argue for considering the complexity of the construction of the calculation through the choice of unit of analysis, when context and contingency are important, but also argue that a range of populations could be affected beyond the intended beneficiaries, potentially creating an overall negative impact.

Impact valuation has colonized impact measurements and become pervasive. For example, the E P&L transforms all outcomes into financialized values on human well-being and health. However, this translation of environmental or social impacts in monetary terms is not without consequences. For example, plants and animals are transformed into financial commodities (Hines, 1991), putting some distance between us (humans) on the world around us. Only environmental service producing natural capital is rendered visible, while the value of nature's materiality itself goes unrepresented (Sullivan & Hannis, 2017).

5.1.3. *Ignoring and erasing*

A vast majority of impact accounts ignore planetary boundaries and the doughnut with social foundations[11] (Raworth, 2017). They do not attend "to ecological and social thresholds[12] (or the carrying capacities of capitals)" (Baue, 2021, p. 73). By doing so, they ignore the possibility to measure environmental and social performance according to earth and society's budgets and foundations, and continue to measure either incrementally, or through efficiency benchmarks.

Impact accounts have the tendency to erase negative impacts from calculations. Most impact accounting is about "positive" impacts (only positive or netting) (Yang, O'Leary & Tregidga, 2021, p. 322). Nicholls *et al.* (2015, p. 256) agree that, while impact could be both positive and negative, "there is a general, normative assumption that social impact always benefits key stakeholders."

When negative impacts are considered, impact accounts often allow for netting between capitals and across negative and positive impacts (Nicholls *et al.*, 2015) (e.g., Impak Score). "They assume impacts on the various capitals are fungible, and, therefore, impacts on one capital can substitute for impacts on another capital, which clearly does not reflect reality" (Baue,

---

[11] To the exception of the Integrated Impact Statement from Olam (https://www.olamgroup.com/sustainability/innovation-technology/finance-for-sustainability.html). Two models of multi-capital accounts also take into account the doughnut: the Multicapital Scorecard (https://www.multicapitalscorecard.com/multicapital-scorecard/) and LIFTS Accounting Model (https://multi-capital-performance.audencia.com/en/research-and-studies/lifts-accounting-modelc/).

[12] Impact Management Platform website: https://impactmanagementplatform.org/thresholds-and-allocations/.

2021, p. 73). However, transparency of each capital's impacts is key. Indeed, it would enable an "assessment of cross-capital impact dynamics revealing if progress toward sustainability of one capital spurs progress or regress toward sustainability of others" (Baue, 2021, p. 73).

5.1.4. *Decontextualizing and selecting*

Impact accounts involve choices, such as "how and what things are detached from other systems" (Thomson, 2021, p. 239). Questions around the choices of boundaries in time and space around the notion of impact accounts can be raised (Yang *et al.*, 2021). When you include certain categories of impacts and exclude others, you frame the sensemaking of the reader and decision-maker (Ruff, 2021). What is detached or excluded shapes the calculative possibilities of the device, reduces complexity (Thomson, 2021). It is inherently contrary to "the holistic nature of socio-ecological systems" (Thomson, 2021, p. 241). Consequently, social impact accounts end up being "what can be easily measured and selectively reported to demonstrate a higher level of impact to gain organizational legitimacy" (Yang *et al.*, 2021, p. 325).

5.2. *Takeaways for practice*

For "human calculators" (Thomson, 2021, p. 239), it is important to be highly aware of biases in the measures they produce, and that they should systematically identify omissions and misrepresentations (Ruff, 2021). Choosing or designing or even implementing an impact account is not a neutral process, but it reflects key power relations and "is, in effect, an act of control" (Nicholls *et al.*, 2015). Notably, accountants can make the wrong choices, perform detachment, and manipulate or transform data (Thomson, 2021).

Impact accounts are not neutral as they "alter our understanding of the past and knowledge of future consequences and aim to draw this new knowledge into organizational decision-making and governance" Thomson (2021, p. 239). For example, Gibbon and Dey (2011) highlight the shortcomings of SROI as a tool for social impact measurement: its subjectivity because of the quality and availability of data, how calculations can be manipulated depending on the "human calculator" (Thomson, 2021, p. 239), and problematic comparability which is rendered impossible because of the causality, correlation problems, and timeframe used. The risk of "simplifying" systemic issues such as climate change or poverty can lead to incomplete accounts and wrong decision-making.

Impact washing is a concern in the impact measurement arena (Global Impact Investing Network, 2020), and transparency of practices could mitigate that risk. Thomson (2021, p. 244) calls for the use of "calculative transformation protocols and algorithms that are more dialogic, transparent, inclusive, multi-dimensional, multi-disciplinary, culturally sensitive, and aligned to sustainability sciences" as problematic impact accounts "can falsely label a solution as sustainable" (Thomson, 2021, p. 240). Indeed, we have seen that impact accounts could be "selecting" and "decontextualizing."

Impact accounts "must make visible and thinkable the sustainable governance of economic, ecological, and social life, in particular, rendering visible and governable the risks of unsustainable consequences across systems and generations" (Thomson, 2021, p. 240). Therefore, it is important to re-empower beneficiaries and stakeholders in designing impact accounts, re-contextualize, and embed calculations into the doughnut (Raworth, 2017) to connect impact to a vision of strong sustainability.

Finally, Ruff (2021) calls to keep a plurality of impact measures to better serve the sector, in opposition to the galloping run toward standardization that actors in practice are pursuing currently (Value Balancing Alliance, IWAI, Business For Inclusive Growth (B4IG)). She insists on the complementary of approaches, and the need to train users of impact accounts to critically assess the tools they use and the results they produce, their omissions, and misrepresentations.

5.3. *Future research*

It is important to pursue critical research on the hembig concept "impact" in accounting but also in its relationship and connections with the field of impact investing. Indeed, the backbone of impact investing is the ability to measure impact. Therefore, researchers in accounting have the responsibility to investigate the construction of impact accounts in practice beyond social impact in the non-profit and social entrepreneurship arenas (Ruff, 2021; Gibbon & Dey, 2011; Costa & Pesci, 2013), to unearth and expose the limits of current practices and potentially provide guidance as to how to develop accounts that could be "more dialogic, transparent, inclusive, multi-dimensional, multi-disciplinary, culturally sensitive, and aligned to sustainability sciences" (Thomson, 2021, p. 244). Moreover, it is critical to investigate how to reconnect beneficiaries and communities to co-produce impact accounts, and the effects of disempowering and silencing on the individuals impacted (Yang *et al.*, 2021).

References

3ie (2012). *Impact Evaluation Glossary.*

Alvesson, M. and Blom, M. (2022). The hegemonic ambiguity of big concepts in organization studies. *Human Relations*, 75(1): 58–86.

Alvesson, M. and Sandberg, J. (2020). The problematising review: a counterpoint to elsbach and van knippenberg's argument for integrative reviews. *Journal of Management Studies*, 57(6): 1290–1304.

Antheaume, N. and Gibassier, D. (2020). *What Connections are There Between Financial and Non-financial Accounting?* Multicapital Integrated Performance Research Centre. https://multi-capital-performance.audencia.com/en/research-and-studies/research/.

AusAID Office of Development Effectiveness (2012). Impact Evaluation: A Discussion Paper for AusAID Practitioners.

Bansal, P. and DesJardine, M. R. (2014). Business sustainability: It is about time. *Strategic Organization*, 12(1): 70–78.

Baue, B. (2020). *From Monocapitalism to Multicapitalism: 21st Century System Value Creation.* R3.0 White Paper No. 1.

Baue, B. (2021). Chapter 7 "From impact management to system value creation", In Richards, A. and Nicholls, J. (eds.), *Generation Impact. International Perspectives on Impact Accounting.* Bingley: Emerald Publishing Limited, pp. 73–86.

Burckart W., Lydenberg S. and et Ziegler J. (2018). *Measuring Effectiveness: Roadmap to Assessing System-Level and SDG Investing*. TIIP The Investment Integration Project. IRRC Institute.

Capitals Coalition (2020). *Improving Nature's Visibility in Financial Accounting.* https://capitalscoalition.org/publication/improving-natures-visibility-in-financial-accounting/.

Carroll, B., Fothergill, J., Murphy, J. and Turpin, T. (2020). *Environmental Impact Assessment Handbook. A Practical Guide for Planners, Developers and Communities.* Third Edition. ICE Publishing.

Costa, E. and Pesci, C. (2016). Social impact measurement: Why do stakeholders matter? *Sustainability Accounting, Management and Policy Journal*, 7(1): 99–124.

Cohen, R. (2020). *Impact. Reshaping Capitalism to Drive Real Change.* Ebury Publishing.

Dun Rappaport, C. and McCreless, M. (2020). *Impact Ratings: Quantified not Monetized. A Summary of Discussions with the IMP's Practitioner Community*. Impact Management Project.

Durand, R., Rodgers, Z. and Lee, S. (2019). *Social Impact Assessment Strategy Report*. HEC. https://www.hec.edu/fr/faculte-et-recherche/centres/institut-society-organizations-so/reflechir/social-impact-assessment-strategy-report.

Ebrahim, A. (2013). *Let's Be Realistic About Measuring Impact*. Harvard Business Review Blogs. http://blogs.hbr.org/hbsfaculty/2013/03/lets-be-realistic-about-measur.html.

Epstein, M. J. and Yuthas, K. (2014). *Measuring and Improving Social Impacts: A Guide for Nonprofits, Companies, and Impact Investors*. BK Business.

European Commission. *Glossary*. http://bit.ly/2060g24.

Finance for Tomorrow (2021). *Définition de la finance à impact*. https://finance-fortomorrow.com/actualites/finance-a-impact-publication-des-premiers-travaux-du-groupe-de-place/.

Florman, M., Klingler-Vidra, R. and Facada, M. J. (2016). *A Critical Evaluation of Social Impact Assessment Methodologies and a Call to Measure Economic and Social Impact Holistically Through the External Rate of Return Platform*. London School of Economics, UK. http://eprints.lse.ac.uk/65393/1/Assessing%20social%20impact%20assessment%20methods% 20report%20-%20final.pdf.

Gibbon, J. and Dey, C. (2011). Developments in social impact measurement in the third sector: Scaling up or dumbing down? *Social and Environmental Accountability Journal*, 31(1): 63–72.

Global Impact Investing Network (GIIN) (2020). *IRIS+, The Five Dimensions of Impact*. https://iris.thegiin.org/document/iris-and-the-five-dimensions/.

Global Environment Facility (2009). *The ROtI Handbook: Towards Enhancing The Impacts of Environmental Projects*.

Global Impact Investing Network (2020). *The State of Impact Measurement and Management Practice*. https://thegiin.org/research/publication/imm-survey-second-edition.

Grisel, L. and Osset, P. (2004). *L'analyse du cycle de vie d'un produit ou d'un service. Applications et mise en pratique*. Afnor Editions.

Hall, M. and Millo, Y. (2018). Choosing an accounting method to explain public policy: Social return on investment and UK non-profit sector policy. *European Accounting Review*, 27(2): 339–361.

Harji, K. and Nicholls, A. (2020). *The Imperative for Impact Measurement*. https://www.sbs.ox.ac.uk/oxford-answers/imperative-impact-measurement.

Heeb, F. (2020). *Sustainable Investing Is Booming — But Where Is the Impact?* https://www.milkenreview.org/articles/sustainable-investing-is-booming-but-where-is-the-impact.

Hearn, S. and Buffardi, A. L. (2016). *What Is Impact?* The Methods Lab. Overseas Development Institute.

Hertel, C., Bacq, S. and Lumpkin, G. T. (2020). Chapter "Social performance and social impact in the context of social enterprises — A holistic perspective". *Handbook of Social Innovation and Social Enterprises*, https://www.researchgate.net/publication/343126135_Social_Performance_and_Social_Impact_in_the_Context_of_Social_Enterprises-A_Holistic_Perspective.

Hervieux, C. and Voltan, A. (2019). Toward a systems approach to social impact assessment. *Social Enterprise Journal*, 15(2): 264–286.

Hines, R. (1988). Financial accounting: In communicating reality, we construct reality. *Accounting, Organizations and Society*, 13(3): 251–261.

Hines, R. (1991). On valuing nature. *Accounting, Auditing & Accountability Journal*, 4(3).

The IIRC (2021). *The <IR> Framework*. https://www.integratedreporting.org/resource/international-ir-framework/.

Impact Investing Institute (2021). *Press Release: UK backs Impact Taskforce under its G7 presidency led by the Impact Investing Institute and the Global Steering Group for Impact Investment*. https://www.impactinvest.org.uk/press-release-uk-backs-impact-taskforce-under-its-g7-presidency-led-by-the-impact-investing-institute-and-the-global-steering-group-for-impact-investment/?utm_source=value+balancing+alliance&utm_campaign=2d3ff5990c-EMAIL_CAMPAIGN_2021_07_30&utm_medium=email&utm_term=0_4405851b96-2d3ff5990c-373727981.

Impak (2020). *Impak Finance Impact Rating Methodology*.

International Fund for Agricultural Development. *Glossary of M&E Concepts and Terms*.

IPADE (Epstein, M.) (2017). *IPADE Business School. Social Impact*.

Joint United Nations Programme on HIV/AIDS. *Glossary: Monitoring and Evaluation Terms. Working draft*. http://bit.ly/1ZTLy8M.

Kering (2013). *Kering Environmental Profit & Loss (E P&L). Methodology and 2013 Group Results*.

Krznaric, R. (2020). *The Good Ancestor: How to Think Long Term in a Short-Term World*. WH Allen.

Leclerc, E. (2020). *La mesure d'impact est un marché complexe et encore mouvant*.https://www.carenews.com/fr/news/elise-leclerc-essec-la-mesure-d-impact-est-un-marche-complexe-et-encore-mouvant.

Nicholls, J. and Richards, A. (2021). Introduction. In Richards, A. and Nicholls, J., (eds.), *Generation Impact. International Perspectives on Impact Accounting*. Bingley: Emerald Publishing Limited, pp. 3–10.

Nicholls, A., Nicholls, J. and Paton, R. (2015) Chapter 9 "Measuring social impact". In Nicholls, A., Paton, R., and Emerson, J. (eds.), *Social Finance*. Oxford: Oxford University Press, pp 253–281.

OECD (2002). *Glossary of Key Terms in Evaluation and Results Based Management*. http://bit.ly/1KG9WUk.

Passet, R. (1979). *L'économique et le vivant*. Payot, re-edited 1996 Economica, Paris.

Porter, M. E. and Kramer, M. R (2011). Creating Shared Value. How to reinvent capitalism — and unleash a wave of innovation and growth. *Harvard Business Review* .January-February.

Raworth, K. (2017). *Doughnut Economics: Seven Ways to Think Like a 21st-Century Economist*. Random House Business.

REDF (2001). SROI Methodology. Analyzing the Value of Social Purpose Enterprise Within a Social Return Investment Framework. https://redfworkshop.org/learn/sroi-methodology-2001/.

Richards, A. and Nicholls, J. (2021). *Generation Impact. International Perspectives on Impact Accounting.* Emerald Publishing Limited.

Ruff, K. (2021). How impact measurement devices act: The performativity of theory of change, SROI and dashboards. *Qualitative Research in Accounting & Management*, 18(3): 332–360.

Serafeim, G., Zochowski, T. R. and Downing, J. (2019). *Impact-Weighted Financial Accounts: The Missing Piece for an Impact Economy*. White Paper, Harvard Business School, Boston, MA. https://www.hbs.edu/faculty/Pages/item.aspx?num=59129.

Social Impact Investment Taskforce (2014). *Impact Investment: The Invisible Heart of Markets*. https://gsgii.org/reports/impact-investment-the-invisible-heart-of-markets/.

Social Value International and B Lab (2016). Measuring Outcomes Using the Social Value Principles.

Social Value International (2021). *The Principles of Social Value*. https://www.socialvalueint.org/principles.

Sullivan, S. and Hannis, M. (2017). "Mathematics maybe, but not money": On balance sheets, numbers and nature in ecological accounting. *Accounting, Auditing & Accountability Journal*, 30(7): 1459–1480.

Thomson, I. (2021) Chapter 17 "Designing environmental impact-valuation assemblages for sustainable decision-making", In Bebbington, J., Larrinaga, C., O'Dwyer, B., and Thomson, I. (eds.), *Routledge Handbook of Environmental Accounting.* Oxon and New York: Routledge, pp. 236–250.

UNEP-FI (2017). *Principles for Positive Impact Finance*. https://www.unepfi.org/positive-impact/principles-for-positive-impact-finance/.

United Nations Development Group (2011). *Results-Based Management Handbook.*

University of Cambridge Institute for Sustainability Leadership (CISL). (2019). *In Search of Impact: Measuring the Full Value of Capital*. Update: The Sustainable Investment Framework. Cambridge, UK: Cambridge Institute for

Sustainability Leadership. https://www.cisl.cam.ac.uk/resources/sustainable-finance-publications/in-search-impact-measuring-full-value-capital-update.

USAID (2009). *Glossary of Evaluation Terms.*

Vesty, G. M., Telgenkamp, A. and Roscoe, P. J. (2015). Creating numbers: Carbon and capital investment. *Accounting, Auditing & Accountability Journal*, 28(3): 302–324.

Vionnet, S. and Pollard, D. (2017). *Social Impact Valuation. A Social Impact Model of Employment and Nestlé Case Study.* Valuing Nature and Nestlé.

White, H. (2009). Theory-based impact evaluation: Principles and Practice. International Initiative for Impact Evaluation. Working Paper 3. New Delhi: 3ie.

White, H. (2010). A contribution to current debates in impact evaluation. *Evaluation*, 16(2): 153–164.

Williams, A., Kennedy, S., Philipp, F. and Whiteman, G. (2017). Systems thinking: A review of sustainability management research. *Journal of Cleaner Production*, 148: 866–881.

Wilson, K. E. (2021). Chapter 1 "The imperative for impact: The global context". In Richards, A. and Nicholls, J. (eds.), *Generation Impact. International Perspectives on Impact Accounting.* Bingley: Emerald Publishing Limited, pp. 11–22.

World Health Organisation. *The Results Chain.* http://bit.ly/1VsVAN4.

Yang, C., O'Leary, S. and Tregidga, H. (2021). Social impact in accounting: Is it at risk of becoming a hembig concept and does this matter? *Qualitative Research in Accounting & Management*, 18(3): 313–331.

Appendix

Appendix 1: List of impact definitions

Nicholls *et al.* (2015, p. 256)	Significant changes in the well-being of key populations, whether intended or unintended, brought about by the allocation of social investment capital, going beyond what would otherwise have been expected to occur.
Cohen (2020, p. 11)	Impact is the measure of an action's benefit to people and the planet. It goes beyond minimizing harmful outcomes to actively creating good ones by creating positive impact.
Dun Rappaport and McCreless, Impact Management Project, 2020	By impact, we mean a change in outcome2 for people, the environment, or the economy, caused by an organization either partially or wholly. An impact can be positive or negative, intended or unintended.
Organization for Economic Co-operation and Development — Development Assistance Committee (OECD-DAC, 2002)	Positive and negative, primary and secondary long-term effects produced by a development intervention, directly or indirectly, intended or unintended.
World Bank (as cited by White, 2009)	The difference in the indicator of interest (Y) with the intervention (Y1) and without the intervention (Y0). That is, impact = Y1 − Y0.
International Initiative for Impact Evaluation (3ie, 2012)	How an intervention alters the state of the world. Impact evaluations typically focus on the effect of the intervention on the outcome for the beneficiary population.
Australian Department of Foreign Affairs & Trade Office of Development Effectiveness (DFAT ODE, 2012)	Impacts are positive or negative changes produced by a development intervention–directly or indirectly, intended or unintended–in the context of its environment, as it interacts with the multiple factors affecting development change.
US Agency for International Development (USAID, 2009)	A result [sic] or effect that is caused by or attributable to a project or program. Impact is often used to refer to higher-level effects of a program that occur in the medium or long term, and can be intended or unintended and positive or negative.

(*Continued*)

Appendix 1: (*Continued*)

European Commission	In an impact assessment process, the term impact describes all the changes which are expected to happen due to the implementation and application of a given policy option/intervention. Such impacts may occur over different timescales, affect different actors and be relevant at different scales (local, regional, national, and the EU). In an evaluation context, impact refers to the changes associated with a particular intervention which occur over the longer term.
United Nations Development Group (UNDG, 2011)	Impact implies changes in people's lives. This might include changes in knowledge, skill, behavior, health, or living conditions for children, adults, families, or communities. Such changes are positive or negative long-term effects on identifiable population groups produced by a development intervention, directly or indirectly, intended or unintended. These effects can be economic, socio-cultural, institutional, environmental, technological, or of other types. Positive impacts should have some relationship to the Millennium Development Goals (MDGs), internationally-agreed development goals, national development goals (as well as human rights as enshrined in constitutions), and national commitments to international conventions and treaties.
Global Environment Facility (GEF, 2009)	A fundamental and durable change in the condition of people and their environment brought about by the project.
International Fund for Agricultural Development (IFAD)	The changes in the lives of rural people, as perceived by them and their partners at the time of evaluation, plus sustainability-enhancing change in their environment to which the project has contributed. Changes can be positive or negative, intended or unintended. In the log frame terminology, these "perceived changes in the lives of the people" may correspond either to the purpose level or to the goal level of project intervention.

Appendix 1: (*Continued*)

World Health Organization (WHO)	Improved health outcomes achieved. The overall impact of the Organization sits at the highest level of the results chain, with eight impact goals. Outcomes can combine in different ways to contribute toward one or more impacts.
Joint United Nations PRogram on HIV/AIDS (UNAIDS)	The long-term, cumulative effect of programs/interventions over time on what they ultimately aim to change, such as a change in HIV infection, AIDS-related morbidity, and mortality. Note: Impacts at a population level are rarely attributable to a single program/intervention, but a specific program/intervention may, together with other programs/interventions, contribute to impacts on a population.

Source: Modified from Hearn & Buffardi (2016).

© 2023 World Scientific Publishing Company
https://doi.org/10.1142/9789811260483_bmatter

Index

Printed in the United States
by Baker & Taylor Publisher Services